Social Work Practice and People of Color
A Process-Stage Approach

Social Work Practice and People of Color
A Process-Stage Approach

Doman Lum
California State University, Sacramento

 Brooks/Cole Publishing Company
Monterey, California

Brooks/Cole Publishing Company
A Division of Wadsworth, Inc.

Printed in the United States of America
10 9 8 7 6 5 4 3 2

Library of Congress Cataloging-in-Publication Data

Lum, Doman, [date]
  Social work practice and people of color.

  Includes bibliographies and index.
  1. Social work with minorities—United States.
2. Minorities—United States. I. Title.
HV3176.L9 1986   362.8'4   85-17047
ISBN 0-534-05586-9

Sponsoring Editor: Claire Verduin
Editorial Assistant: Linda Wright
Production Editor: Phyllis Larimore
Production Associate: Dorothy Bell
Manuscript Editor: Meredy Amyx
Permissions Editor: Mary Kay Hancharick
Interior and Cover Design: Sharon L. Kinghan
Art Coordinator: Judith Macdonald
Interior Illustration: John Foster
Typesetting: Instant Type, Monterey, California
Printing and Binding: Fairfield Graphics, Fairfield, Pennsylvania

To the teachers who have influenced my academic and professional development:

Merrill F. Heiser,
who developed and encouraged my love of English literature and writing.

Howard J. Clinebell, Jr.,
who served as a role model of a classroom teacher par excellence, a friend to students, and a diligent and insightful scholar/writer.

Norman L. Farberow,
who guided me as a clinical intern and assisted me with difficult cases and was instrumental in my development of crisis intervention theory.

Arthur Blum,
who impressed me as a teacher who commanded a vast knowledge of social welfare planning and policy analysis, articulated with humor and insight.

Gregory M. St. L. O'Brien,
who gave me a model for aspiration to administration in higher education with a driving, hardworking, and highly personal lifestyle.

and
to ethnic minority social work educators and practitioners, with the hope that they will contribute to the field of ethnic minority social work practice.

Foreword

With the publication of Doman Lum's *Social Work Practice and People of Color: A Process-Stage Approach,* the literature on social work practice with ethnic minority communities has reached a new level of development. That literature, to date, has generally been of two characters. One body of literature, historically early, represents works that focus on socioeconomic problems of ethnic minority communities that are interpreted as consequences of varying states of dysfunction, deviance, or pathology. This literature may be characterized as reflecting a "blaming the victim" mentality in which ethnic minority communities are held up as responsible for causing their own problems. A second body of literature, historically later, focuses upon the uniqueness of particular ethnic minority communities and dwells upon the distinctive cultural values, attitudes, and behaviors that are said to differentiate each ethnic community from others. This literature may be characterized as reflecting a strong bias in favor of cultural pluralism and, insofar as this perspective promotes tolerance and acceptance of difference, it may be seen as representing an advance over the earlier "blaming the victim" approach.

However, in neither case does the previous literature offer much of substantive value to the social work practitioner who is directly engaged in daily practice with ethnic minority individuals, families, groups, and communities. The previous literature has provided knowledge that can be applied to practice situations only on an ad hoc, case-by-case basis. The critical deficiency of such knowledge is that it cannot be generalized or applied to a class of cases and does not afford a systematic basis for knowledge building and knowledge transfer.

Doman Lum's new work meets the deficiency of the previous literature by providing, for the first time, a clearly defined mode of social work practice that is applicable to all ethnic minority communities. He does this by focusing on universal characteristics or problem situations, value beliefs, and practice approaches that are applicable across the board to all ethnic minority groups, rather than to emphasize what is culturally distinct for each group. Lum provides us with a general conceptual framework for social work practice with all ethnic minority communities. His notion of social work practice as comprising five distinct process stages—contact, problem identification, assessment, intervention, and termination—gives social work practitioners a familiar and pragmatic guideline for their daily encounters. His use of a single family case study, which links up the five process stages in a logical sequence and creates an integrated, holistic example, is an effective heuristic device. Throughout his work, Lum has skillfully drawn upon supporting current literature and relevant research to amplify his own formulations.

   Social Work Practice and People of Color: A Process-Stage Approach is a signal contribution to the literature. It fulfills a long-unmet need for a reference that combines social science theory with practice wisdom to answer perplexing questions for practitioners engaged in social work practice with ethnic minority communities.

Kenji Murase, D.S.W.
Professor of Social Work Education
San Francisco State University

Preface

This book was written to augment the literature in the field of ethnic minority social work practice, which has been treated marginally by major social work practice books for many years. Part of the reason for the underattention to this field has been that social work practice has focused on development of theory drawn from the behavioral and social sciences, mainly from psychiatry and psychology. Social work practice writers have failed to elaborate on cultural and ethnic factors on account of their lack of background and expertise in ethnic minority aspects of practice. This is not to excuse them from responsibility for providing adequate and differential theory and practice principles for working with people of color. Indeed, it is my contention that standard social work practice texts and leading social work practice educators have not prepared their readers and graduate students to deal adequately with ethnic minorities.

About the Field

Social Work Practice and People of Color: A Process-Stage Approach addresses the needs of ethnic minority clients and the particular skills required of social work practitioners. I use the terms *people of color* and *ethnic minority* interchangeably throughout the book. Use of the term *people of color* is gaining new currency. Its adoption was promoted at a National Association of Social Workers (NASW) conference in 1982, entitled "Color in White Society."

There are a number of distinguishing features in this book that break new ground in the field of ethnic minority social work. First, rather than accommodating ethnic minority group principles to existing social work values, knowledge theory, and practice approaches, distinctions are made between current social work practice emphases and ethnic minority characteristics. This is done partly to stimulate discussion and debate on whether social work should modify the value stances and practice positions that are taken for granted in the profession. My contention is that at some crucial points, ethnic minorities have different beliefs and behaviors from those reflected in the existing assumptions of social work practice. Accordingly, the social work profession should reexamine its theoretical orientation from the viewpoint of ethnic minorities. Second, a

framework for ethnic minority practice is constructed for general application to minority clients. I recognize that there are cultural distinctions among Black, Latino, Asian,
and Native Americans. But there are also universal principles of situational predicament,
value beliefs, and practice protocols that are applicable to minorities. Over the past 12
years, social work students have asked me whether there are principles of minority
practice that can be followed in working with minority clients. This book is an initial
attempt to define those axioms. Third, this framework for ethnic minority practice is
subdivided into practical process-stage segments. Each process stage reiterates the core
principles of the framework, offers the latest minority research, presents relevant case
study material illustrating practice issues, and provides suggestions for implementing
practice in an agency setting.

American society is composed of multiple ethnic groups interacting in a democratic
political system. The term *cultural pluralism* has been used to denote the variety of
ethnic composites with their own value assumptions, behavior patterns, and practices.
Particular beliefs, lifestyles, and cultural uniquenesses will be encountered with clients
who are ethnic minority people of color. It is incumbent on social work practice to
expand its existing value orientations and theoretical frameworks to include those that
have relevance for people of color. Existing approaches to traditional and minority
social work practice are not mutually exclusive. On the contrary, this framework for
ethnic minority social work practice process is supplementary to existing practice
structures. It elaborates the cultural and ethnic uniquenesses of people of color that must
be emphasized when working with minority clients. It infuses traditional practice
concepts such as psychosocial interaction, relationship-building, problem analysis,
assessment, intervention, and termination with ethnic minority meaning. In the final
analysis, this book is designed to delineate more clearly how existing social work values,
knowledge theory, and practice process can be supplemented or elaborated for relevancy
to minority clients.

About the Book

The book begins with the historical roots and basic concepts of minority social work. It
identifies a system of service delivery to minority clients that must be in place before
working with minority clients. It explains the importance of culture as the dominant
theme of minority social work. It contrasts professional social work and collective
minority values and compares professional and minority ethics according to the
National Association of Social Workers Code of Ethics. Social work minority knowledge theory is the basis of a framework for minority social work practice. It consists of
practice process stages, client and worker systems practice issues, and worker-client
tasks. In succeeding chapters, the process stages of contact, problem identification,
assessment, intervention, and termination form a procedural minority practice model
for social work practitioners. There are minority practice axioms, ethnic case material
and research, and client and community applications. The epilogue summarizes the
essential themes of the book and proposes new horizons for minority social work
practice.

About the Author

I must make a confession about my own background in ethnic minority social work practice. I went to undergraduate and graduate school prior to the development of ethnic minority studies on the university campus. My clinical and research experiences in cross-cultural psychotherapy in Hawaii were self-taught through contact with minority clients and case records. I had no coursework in ethnic studies or minority social work practice. In my second year of teaching at California State University, Sacramento, I was selected to coordinate the new and required core courses on poverty and minorities. Without an adequate background in either poverty or ethnic minorities, the experience was a disaster for me. However, out of the ashes of failure came a drive to learn about ethnic minority groups and minority practice principles. I began to read the literature, talk to my minority faculty colleagues, and query minority students. I again taught the core courses on poverty and minorities, this time with a measure of success. I began to reflect on ethnic minority practice themes, supervise Asian Americans writing M.S.W. theses, and write in the field of minority gerontology. In short, I taught and formulated theory and practice principles on my own.

I make this confession because I believe that too many ethnic minority social work educators and practitioners in my generation were without formal instruction and consequently taught themselves about minorities. Existing social work practice texts and senior practice professors have neglected the detailed principles of serving ethnic minority clients. However, a new day has arrived for ethnic minority social work. There is a growing body of minority social work scholars who are writing in the field. Several schools of social work, such as those at the University of Washington, Howard University, University of California at Los Angeles, Arizona State University, California State University, Sacramento, and San Diego State University, have clusters of minority faculty. The minority doctoral fellowship program of the Council on Social Work Education has assisted minority faculty with research and content abilities in social work ethnic study. As a result, the quality of ethnic minority social work courses, faculty, research, and publications should increase in the next ten years. This book is written as a means of encouraging ethnic minority social work educators, scholars, and practitioners to contribute to the field of ethnic minority social work practice.

Acknowledgments

Particular acknowledgments should be made to Claire Verduin, Phyllis Larimore, and Meredy Amyx, who were my consultants at Brooks/Cole and who helped me through the various stages of this book. I am also indebted to the following manuscript reviewers who gave excellent suggestions for revision: David Guzman, Portland State University; Paul Keys, City University of New York, Hunter College; Kenji Murase, San Francisco State University; Lonnie Snowden, University of California at Berkeley; and Barbara Solomon, University of Southern California.

Doman Lum

Contents

Chapter 9
Epilogue   209

Ethnic Minority Perspectives on Social Work Practice

The United States is composed of ethnic minorities. Generation on generation of ethnic groups and families have been assimilated into American society. Yet to varying degrees there remains a residue of ethnic and cultural language, beliefs, and customs. In large metropolitan cities and in rural sections of this country, ethnic neighborhoods and communities have continued to flourish after hundreds of years. All groups characteristically preserve their ethnic identity and culture through such communities.

Silva (1983) views people as having a common humanity but having unique differences based on inherited endowment, learned values and culture, developmental histories, specified patterns of problems, and personalized styles of coping. They are products of their culture and geographic environments, family group, local setting, regional identity, national identity and experience, and social situation. They are influenced by cultural territoriality, discrimination, institutional oppression, and normative behavior. They are members of ethnic groups with both individual and group-related identity, experiences, and social realities.

However, the *color factor* has been a barrier that has separated Black, Latino, Asian, and Native Americans from others. Anglo-Saxon and European minority groups have successfully integrated with each other and become assimilated into the mainstream of American society and power. But by and large minority people of color have been without equal access. The history of racism, discrimination, and segregation binds minority people of color together and contrasts with the experience of White Americans.

Social work is a versatile profession dealing with clients of many socioeconomic and cultural backgrounds. Social work practitioners are responsible for services ranging from mental health, corrections, and medical care to grassroots organizations and political change movements that affect the lives and problems of people and their environment. Social workers serve diverse populations and utilize multiple theories of practice, which must include the knowledge and skills of ethnic minority practice. It is particularly important that they be an integral part of the helping repertoire because ethnic minority people are at a critical turning point in the eighties. A conservative political and social mood prevails in this country. There have been budget cutbacks, federal deregulation, and a reduction of government involvement in social programs affecting poor and

1

minority people. Akin to these Washington trends are the rise of the Ku Klux Klan, dismantling of affirmative action, and racial killings, all of which reinforce a racist climate.

Ethnic minorities who have color visibility in the dominant society are vulnerable to these economic, political, and social conditions. They include recent Latino and Asian immigrants who have fled political oppression in their native countries and who have language and employment problems in the United States. They are vulnerable to social assistance cutbacks and rely on ethnic community survival mechanisms for existence. There has been a dramatic increase of minority populations, pointing to a significant change in the racial composition of this country over a ten-year period. With the clustering of minorities, it is important for the human services to respond to the psychosocial needs of people of color. Minority knowledge theory, helping skills, and cultural factors are essential ingredients in forming specific minority service delivery structures, training ethnic-sensitive workers, and executing community outreach programs.

The primary aim of this book is to advance the development of ethnic minority social work practice by setting forth a generic and integrated approach for people of color. There are four elements in this model: practice process stages, client system practice issues, worker system practice issues, and worker-client tasks. These practice themes are infused with cultural dimensions of meaning. Culture acts as a vital bridge between the ethnic community and the dominant society. It contains ethnic customs and beliefs, interdependent family networks, behavioral survival skills, and other distinguishing features. It is our hope that social workers will increase their knowledge of people of color and their ethnic minority practice skills as a result of interacting with the themes of this book.

The Field of Minority Practice

The development of social work practice theory has moved in various directions that have underemphasized ethnic and cultural issues. Theorists of social work practice formulated a generic practice model for social work client situations (Goldstein, 1973; Pincus & Minahan, 1973; Klenk & Ryan, 1974; Siporin, 1975; Meyer, 1976; Compton & Galaway, 1979; Northen, 1982). Based on a social work process model oriented to systems theory, social work forged a frame of reference for values, purposes, scientific knowledge, and technical competence. The search for a common base to unify social work practice emerged in the seventies. Theorists sought a conceptual base, a framework, that would unify individual, family, group, and community systems. A related development has been the emphasis on casework effectiveness and the blending of empirical principles into the social work practice arena. Beginning in the middle and late seventies, social work practice stressed competency and effectiveness criteria (Fischer, 1976, 1978; Reid, 1978; Jayaratne & Levy, 1979; Hepworth & Larsen, 1982). These issues preoccupied the social work practice profession to the exclusion of delineating minority theory and practice. As a result, there has been only peripheral examination of systematic ethnic minority principles in standard social work practice texts.

Growing Recognition of Minority Practice

Recently ethnic minority social work clinicians and educators have contributed to the field of social work practice. Devore and Schlesinger (1981) have written a preliminary practice text that covers general principles of ethnic-sensitive behavior, self-awareness, skills, and techniques. Green (1982) has presented an ethnic-oriented help-seeking behavior model that deals with a problem-solving approach to social work practice. He has developed the notion of cross-cultural social work and has applied ethnographic inquiry to Black, Asian and Pacific-American, Urban Indian, and Chicano Familia groups. Chunn, Dunston, and Ross-Sheriff (1983) have focused on the relationship between the content of minority practice and theory and issues in social work, psychology, psychiatry, and psychiatric nursing curricula. These are examples of practice publications that point to a growing momentum in the field of minority social work.

The state of the art in minority social work practice reflects efforts toward defining minority concepts, adopting existing social work practice theory to the minority situation, and presenting minority case study illustrations. Minority social work has reached a major developmental stage. It must articulate a clear body of minority knowledge theory, group values, and practice process and skill principles. The specific task is to develop a social work practice framework applicable to the distinct minority groups in the United States. A brief definition of ethnic minority practice is a good starting point for comprehending the nature of this field.

Definition of Minority Practice

Ethnic minority social work practice is the art and science of developing a helping relationship with an individual, family, group, and/or community whose distinctive physical/cultural characteristics and discriminatory experiences require approaches that are sensitive to ethnic and cultural environments. Social work practice relies on a person-to-person human relationship based on personality qualities of warmth, genuineness, and empathy. At the same time, it draws on relevant minority theory from the social sciences that are applicable to social work. The target groups for helping with social problems are minority individuals, families, groups, and communities. But rather than treating people of color as separate entities of concern, social workers need to see ethnic minorities as individuals in collective associations: entities in family and community cohorts. Each minority population has color, language, and behavioral characteristics that distinguish it as a unique group in a multiracial society. Racism, prejudice, and discrimination are often part of the problem complex affecting the minority client. As a result, practice approaches must address the interaction of problems which arise from these ethnic social themes.

The Purpose of Minority Social Work

Minority social work practice addresses individuals, families, and communities who have historically been oppressed on account of ethnic socioeconomic status. Its primary focus is to improve the quality of psychosocial functioning as the minority person interacts with the social situation. The term *biopsychosocial* covers the physical, cognitive-affective-behavioral, and environmental forces affecting the person. In social work practice one strives to treat the client as a biopsychosocial being. The purpose of a minority social work curriculum is to educate social work students and practitioners in specific theory and practice skills with minority clients and to facilitate social change and improvement in the lives of people of color.

Social workers should enhance and upgrade their knowledge and practice approaches to ethnic minorities. Most social workers have taken a required minority course in their university education. Fewer have been placed in minority field work agencies or have been supervised by ethnic field instructors who have practice expertise with minority clients. This text is written to present an integrated direct practice process model for ethnic minorities with the worker in mind. It is our hope to fulfill the needs and goals of the social worker as minority-oriented practitioner and the minority client as social change initiator.

Target Groups

The target groups for minority practice are people of color: Black, Latino, Asian, and Native Americans. These ethnic groups are distinguished by customs, language, history, and other differentiated characteristics. Ethnic distinctions have increasingly been emphasized as the melting pot ideology has declined and as the reality of cultural pluralism in a diverse society has become accepted. The term minority refers to a racial, religious, ethnic, or political group with less power than the controlling group in society. The consequence of their relative powerlessness is that minorities are devalued or discriminated against due to their subordinate status. Ethnic minorities are racial groups who have historically experienced prejudice and other forms of oppression due to their skin color and lifestyle in the dominant White society.

Seeing the Client in Cultural Perspective

Cultural belief systems and behavioral outlook influence the ideas, customs, and skills of people. For ethnic minorities, the cultural element reinforces positive functioning through family support systems, self-identity and self-esteem, and ethnic philosophy of living. These cultural resource strengths are coping mechanisms during stress and crisis. Likewise, one's ethnic cultural past could be a source of conflict, stigma, and embarrassment. Caught in an acculturation trap, the minority individual moves away from cultural maintenance and toward an identification with the majority society. Reacting against his or her ethnic cultural past, he or she dissociates from the language, behavior, and values of his or her cultural roots. The synthesis of the extremes—the ethnic traditionalist and the acculturated minority—is the individual who has integrated the best of both worlds. Through a sorting-out process, this person appreciates those cultural elements that express rich customs and traditions, family and ethnic community, and minority values. However, he or she realizes the minority person functions in and interacts with the real world of the majority society. Drawing on minority upbringing, this individual achieves a resolution that weaves the cultural element into daily living patterns.

The social worker, whether ethnic minority or ethnic-sensitized, should be aware of the client's state of cultural development. Northen (1982) points to a social work principle that is particularly important when working with an ethnic minority client: "The values, norms, language, customs, and traditions of a culture or subculture influence a person's opportunities for effective functioning or they become obstacles to achieving desired goals" (p. 52). Minority social work starts by determining whether ethnic, minority, and cultural elements are useful functioning forces or barriers to meaningful living. In order to make a determination, the social worker should find out about family beliefs and practices, community support systems, and other important ethnic information areas. The worker should ask the client to share meaningful minority perspectives on the problem. What particular cultural strengths are appropriate for client coping? The worker should have a minority resource who provides background on the culture and the psychosocial situation confronting the client. A minister, mental health worker, or community leader familiar with the client's community is a helpful consultant on issues related to the worker and client. With professional exploration and consultation, the social worker and client should move toward an integration of cultural resources and the psychosocial situation.

The Roots of Minority Social Work

Ancient Origins

Social welfare originated in Western civilization's view of the individual and society. During the Golden Age of Greece, Hippocrates strongly advocated the belief that problem behavior was a function of natural illness and prescribed medical treatment. Plato further believed that a person should not be punished if a criminal act was committed as a result of diminished understanding between right and wrong (Mehr, 1980). This humanistic view of people, morality, and helping merged into caring for the needs of society. Later, Western religion communicated a horizontal and vertical perspective of God and people. Judeo-Christian beliefs in the Old and New Testaments emphasized the importance of loving God and one's neighbor as well as providing for the needy. The early church was instrumental in the instituting of social welfare services through its network of parishes and monasteries. With the beginnings of the Industrial Revolution came the breakdown of the medieval feudal system, the centralization of political power in national governments, and the displacement of church power by secular government. As church funds declined, responsibility for the needs of persons displaced from feudal estates shifted to local and national government units.

Modern Trends

The Elizabethan Poor Law of 1601 was major social legislation designed to protect the affluent from these displaced and starving persons. It established three categories of the poor: the helpless, who were aged, decrepit, orphaned, lunatic, blind, lame, or diseased; the involuntarily unemployed, who were poor by situational misfortunes; and the vagrant, who were drifters, strangers, squatters, and beggars. The Poor Law created a parish welfare structure consisting of almshouses, outdoor relief, workhouses, and the indenture system. It set the precedents of national coverage and administration of public welfare, funding through voluntary contributions and a public land tax, and a work ethic for the able-bodied. During the eighteenth and nineteenth centuries, social reformers such as Philippe Pinel of France, William Tuke of England, and Benjamin Rush and Dorothea Dix of the United States sought to reform these institutional structures with the humanitarian beliefs of Hippocrates and Plato.

Modern social work in the United States arose from two models: The Charity Organization Society and The Settlement House Movement. Begun in England in 1869, the Charity Organization Society came to this country in 1877 and set up a relief system based on investigating claims, meeting individual needs, and providing minimal relief payment for the truly needy. Workers kept case records and made regular visits to recipients. In 1887, settlement houses appeared in New York, Boston, and Chicago to help European immigrants who were new arrivals in America. These community centers offered practical education, recreation, and social cohesion for those in the inner city ethnic ghettos. Hull House under Jane Addams exemplified community resources such as a free kindergarten, day nursery, playground, clubs, lectures, library, boarding house, and meeting rooms (Federico, 1980).

American Minority Social History

Social welfare agencies served mainstream society and White immigrants, while people of color struggled to exist in isolated geographic ghetto areas. They were targets of exploitation and oppression in the United States. Without the rights of citizenship, legal protection, and resource provision, each minority group suffered through its history of struggle to survive.

Group Experiences

Native Americans.   With the discovery of America and the appearance of European explorers and settlers, Native Americans were pushed steadily westward, the victims of genocide, and contained on remote reservations. Whole tribes were obliterated by disease, famine, and war. Intact families were disrupted by Bureau of Indian Affairs policies of boarding school and resettlement to urban centers. Native language, customs, and beliefs were discouraged as acculturation and Americanization took over as primary values.

Black Americans.   Black Americans came to the United States predominantly as slaves, although there were some freemen and women. Slavery resulted in the breakup of families, economic and social exploitation, and the collapse of self-esteem and individuality for Black Americans. Although they were formally freed from the institution of slavery as a result of the Civil War, Blacks continued to experience wholesale prejudice and discrimination. Separate housing patterns in undesirable parts of cities, limited employment opportunities, and segregated educational institutions characterized many parts of the United States.

Latino Americans.   The history of the United States and Spain revolved around imperialistic expansionism. After winning its independence from Spain, Mexico held the vast Southwestern territories and settlements. However, after Texas won its independence and was later admitted into the Union, Mexican landowners were disenfranchised from their estates. Later, in the Spanish-American War, Cuba and Puerto Rico were acquired by the United States. Hispanics from those territories entered the Eastern United States, while Mexicans moved to the Southwest and Western states. They came as cheap farm migrants and small shop factory workers. Economic and social exploitation was the common rule due to their temporary and illegal immigration status. Dominated by White land and factory owners, Hispanic Americans replaced Blacks, who moved to the industrial factories in the North Central and Northeastern regions.

Asian Americans.   Asians arrived in this country as farm and construction laborers at the turn of the 20th century. They did not represent a threat until there was massive unemployment and gold was discovered in California. Foreign miners tax acts and mass murders of Chinese along the West Coast resulted in the creation of protective and segregated China towns. Chinese, Pilipino, and Japanese were not allowed to own land. Immigration laws restricted the entry of Asian women and resulted in permanent bachelorhood for male laborers and a declining Asian–American population.

Group Histories

Garvin and Cox (1979) have documented the chronological history of ethnic minorities as they encountered racism in the United States. Their investigation begins with the post–Civil War period and continues to the beginning of the 20th century, a period characterized by exploitation through unjust use of the United States legal system against people of color. In Cultural Study 1-1, Garvin and Cox trace federal and state laws that were enacted to force the minority groups into conformity with the wishes of the majority society. People of color began to organize socially and politically in response to rising exploitation and the stress it created. This movement arose from within minority communities rather than from external social welfare institutions.

Cultural Study 1-1

Historical Exploitation: Minorities after the Civil War[1]

Blacks

During reconstruction there were many organizations that sought to support and sustain newly won civil rights. After the period of reconstruction there were many efforts on the part of Black people to organize themselves "to the point where they could demand those rights which had slipped away since reconstruction" (Fishel & Quarles, 1967, p. 308). The Supreme Court decision that declared the Civil Rights Act of 1875 unconstitutional was a major source of difficulty. Thus, the responsibility for protecting the rights of Black people rested largely with the states. During this period, the Populist Movement in the South was a major political force that attempted to secure Black support.

(continued)

Cultural Study 1-1 (continued)

A major concern of the Black community was to solve the problem of educational deficits, particularly in vocational and higher education. An important event was the founding of Tuskegee Institute in 1881.

It must be remembered that in the 15 years before 1900 more than 1500 Black people were lynched, and between 1900 and 1910 another 900 Black people perished in the same way.

Around 1910, many industries encouraged Black people to take positions created in the North by the termination of the large European immigrations and the expansion of war industry. This opportunity ushered in the next phase for Blacks, one in which their urban living condition also became a concern.

Chicanos

The history of protest among Chicanos began with the Treaty of Guadalupe Hidalgo, signed on February 2, 1848, which brought a formal end to the Mexican-American War. Under this treaty, Mexico lost 45 percent of its territory, including the wealth of the oil fields of Texas and the gold of California. More than 100,000 persons were added to the United States who had previously been citizens of Mexico. From this beginning, the rights of these "conquered" people were heavily infringed, with little legal redress available. Protest took the form of guerrilla activity by so-called bandits. Although armed rebellions also occurred, they were vigorously repressed by the government.

Native Americans

In the period just before the Civil War, the status of Native Americans was largely determined by the Removal Act of 1830. This act gave the president the right to remove any Native Americans who continued to survive east of the Mississippi (Howard, 1970). Some fought, as did the Seminoles of Florida and the Sac and Fox of Illinois, but most moved.

After the Civil War, that pattern continued until the passage of the Dawes Act of 1887, which authorized the president to distribute 160 acres to each Native American adult and 80 acres to each child. This act followed a series of major fights with tribes such as the Sioux in 1876, Nez Perce in 1877, Cheyenne in 1878, and Apache a few years later.

The Dawes Act was a failure in that it did not convert the Native Americans to agriculture as intended. Much of the land given was poor, and funds for its development were unavailable. As a result, between 1887 and 1932, "approximately 90 million acres out of 138 million initially held by Indians passed to white ownership" (Howard, 1970, p. 19). In view of the exploitation they suffered, the survival of many Native American tribes seems miraculous indeed.

Asian Americans

The Chinese, the first immigrants from Asia to come in large numbers, arrived on the West Coast in the 1840s. Their labor was sought after as the California economy soared with the gold rush. It was in the mining regions that serious hostility to the Chinese first developed. When the Civil War began there had been more than 50,000 Chinese in California, mostly men. By the 1870s violence was directed at Chinese, intensified by an economic depression.

Agitation continued for the rest of the decade from workers who sought anti-Chinese legislation. In 1882, Congress enacted the Chinese Exclusion Act, which was renewed in 1892 and made permanent in 1902.

About 200,000 Japanese arrived in the United States between 1890 and 1924 in an atmosphere hostile to Orientals. The early immigrants were mostly young males from rural backgrounds. Like the Chinese, they were recruited as a source of cheap labor. However, the migration of Japanese women was soon encouraged.

Perhaps California's Alien Land Bill of 1913 best exemplifies general attitudes toward the Japanese. It provided that Japanese aliens could lease agricultural lands for a maximum of three years and that lands already owned or leased could not be willed to other persons. As the California attorney general indicated in a public speech, the intention was to limit the number of Japanese who would come to or stay in California (Kitano, 1969).

[1]Adapted from C. D. Garvin and F. M. Cox, "A History of Community Organizing since the Civil War with Special Reference to Oppressed Communities." In F. M. Cox, J. L. Erlich, J. Rothman, and J. E. Tropman (Eds.), *Strategies of Community Organization,* 3rd Ed. Copyright © 1979, pp. 47–49. Reprinted by permission of the publisher, F. E. Peacock Publishers, Inc.

Garvin and Cox note in Cultural Study 1-2 the response of Black, Mexican, Asian, and Native Americans to support systems.

Cultural Study 1-2

The Organization of Ethnic Minority Support Systems[2]

A variety of forms of organization among Black Americans was tested between 1865 and 1914 as Black people coped with their shifting status in American life. One of the earliest forms was developed by a group of prominent Black people in 1865 and led by Frederick Douglass and George T. Downing, who were "charged with the duty to look after the best interests of the recently emancipated" (Fishel & Quarles, 1967, pp. 259, 260). Nearly 25 years later, in 1883, a very different kind of step was taken by the Louisville Convention of Colored Men, which "concentrated on large issues of political, as distinct from partisan, rights, education, civil rights and economic problems" (Fishel & Quarles, 1967, p. 308). Five years later, the Colored Farmers Alliance and Cooperative Union came into existence. In 1890, the Afro-American League organized in another direction, emphasizing legal redress rather than politics (Fishel & Quarles, 1967, p. 312). In 1890, Blacks from 21 states and the District of Columbia organized the Afro-American League of the United States. Issues of concern to this group included school funds and legal and voting rights. In 1896, the National Association of Colored Women was formed.

Crosscurrents similar to those that affect the organizations of Black people today were operative between the Civil War and World War I. On the one hand, many efforts were under the influence of Booker T. Washington, who sought an accommodation with White interests in order to maintain their support. On the other hand, W. E. B. DuBois epitomized an opposition to that approach in 1905 when he called for "a conference 'to oppose firmly the present methods of strangling honest criticism'" (Fishel & Quarles, 1967, p. 357). The Niagara movement grew out of this meeting and by 1909 resulted in the formation of the National Association for the Advancement of Colored People. Such social workers as Jane Addams, Florence Kelly, and Lillian Wald assisted in these organizing efforts.

The Committee on Urban Conditions among Negroes in New York City, later to

(continued)

Cultural Study 1-2 (continued)

became the National Urban League, was another organization in which social workers were involved during this period. Its first executive, George Edmund Haynes, "was on the faculty of Fisk University and particularly interested in training black social workers" (Fishel & Quarles, 1967, p. 361).

Mexican Americans were confronted with successful efforts to take away their lands. One response to this situation was the development of small groups for protection and support. Some, for survival, became bandits. Organized protest for Mexican Americans, however, began in agriculture. In 1903, for example, Mexican–American and Japanese –American sugar beet workers struck in Ventura, California (Howard, 1970). In addition, throughout this period, but particularly from the 1880s on, many organizations came into existence whose function was, according to Alvarez (1971), to preserve a Mexican–American way of life through "celebrations, social events, provision of facilities, information and communication networks" (p. 209). The function of such organizations was to preserve a bicultural and bilingual existence.

The Native Americans during this period (1865–1914) continued to have well-developed forms of tribal organization, partly as a heritage of their early struggles for survival against White encroachment. However, the tribes were separated from one another geographically and structurally and thus were often easy prey for governmental manipulation. Nevertheless, the militancy of the period—the extent of actual warfare—as well as persistent legal action, represents an impressive, though unsuccessful, effort to secure a greater measure of justice from American society.

The early Chinese immigrants were organized into family or benevolent associations, tongs, or business interests. For the Japanese, the Japanese Association for Issei (first-generation Japanese in the United States) had some similar functions. Thus, for these Asian groups, a major function of community organizations during this period was mutual benefit and cultural participation.

[2]Adapted from C. D. Garvin and F. M. Cox, "A History of Community Organizing since the Civil War with Special Reference to Oppressed Communities." In F. M. Cox, J. L. Erlich, J. Rothman, and J. E. Tropman (Eds.), *Strategies of Community Organization,* 3rd Ed. Copyright © 1979, pp. 54–56. Reprinted by permission of the publisher, F. E. Peacock Publishers, Inc.

During the early part of the 20th century, people of color continued to experience oppression. The rejuvenation of the Ku Klux Klan, race riots, large-scale migration of minority laborers, the erosion of tribal government, and quota restrictions on minority immigration characterized this period. Garvin and Cox describe minimal minority gains at the expense of widespread oppression. Cultural Study 1-3 traces those trends from 1915 to 1929.

Cultural Study 1-3

Oppression and Social Conditions[3]

By 1920 more than half the population of the United States lived in cities. Industrial innovations were accelerated by the heavy demands on production created by World War I. The twenties formed a decade of confidence in the economic system.

Ironically, this period also brought some major crises in civil liberties. "After World

War I there was a wave of raids and deportations; it arose from the uneasy feeling that the Russian Revolution had caused a shift in the world balance of power and spawned a fanatic faith threatening American survival" (Lerner, 1957, p. 455). The period also witnessed the intensification of activities of groups such as the Ku Klux Klan, with antagonism directed against Blacks, Jews, and the foreign born.

Blacks

During the period from 1915 to 1929 Black Americans made strong attempts to improve their lives and were simultaneously subjected to major efforts at repression. Seventy-six Black people were lynched in 1919 (Fishel & Quarles, 1967), and "the white national secretary of the NAACP was badly beaten on the streets of Texas" (Fishel & Quarles, 1967, p. 403). Chicago experienced a severe "race riot" in 1919 that resulted in the death of 15 White and 23 Black persons, as well as injury to an additional 537 (Fishel & Quarles, 1967).

However, progress occurred in many spheres of American life. The term *the New Negro* became prevalent in the 1920s, and its popularity bore some relation to the increased self-respect of many Black war veterans. During this period, distinguished people such as Langston Hughes, Countee Cullen, and Paul Robeson began their careers. Black school attendance jumped between 1910 and 1930 from 45% to 60% of the eligible school population (Fishel & Quarles, 1967). In fact, in many ways the current emphasis on Black power and Black identity has ideological antecedents in this period.

Chicanos

These years saw a large immigration of persons from Mexico into what had become the United States. Between 1910 and 1919, nearly 225,000 persons came, and in the next decade the number was almost double (Lopez y Rivas, 1973, p. 85). The Mexican economy was in a poor state after the Mexican Revolution, while the Southwestern United States was experiencing considerable economic growth. There was a development and expansion of nonagricultural worker organizations during this period.

Native Americans

Between 1915 and 1929, the conditions of Native Americans continued to deteriorate as the government persisted in its policy of implementing the Dawes Act of 1887, which distributed land to individuals. The government sustained its effort to undermine the widely practiced custom of holding land in common for the good of all. The act not only created severe economic problems but eroded traditional tribal government (Taylor, 1972).

In addition to the effects of the Dawes Act, two other actions also diminished tribal ties. From 1917 to 1921, the trust on land allotments of Native Americans of less than one-half Native American blood was terminated. Many Native American agents were also eliminated and their wards placed under school superintendents and farmers reporting directly to the Commissioner of Indian Affairs (Taylor, 1972). This measure focused activities on individuals, not tribes, and presumably moved Native Americans as individuals into non–Native American education and agriculture.

Asian Americans

The Immigration Act of 1924 epitomized the attitudes of the American government, if not of the society, to the foreign born. No immigration was to be permitted for Asians; low

(continued)

Cultural Study 1-3 (continued)

quotas were set for southern Europeans and high ones for northern Europeans. This policy made it impossible, particularly for the Chinese who had not come as families, to form or reunite families. In Japanese communities, these years marked the birth and early development of many *Nisei,* or second-generation Japanese Americans. With great determination, many Nisei moved into middle-class occupations.

[3] Adapted from C. D. Garvin and F. M. Cox, "A History of Community Organizing since the Civil War with Special Reference to Oppressed Communities." In F. M. Cox, J. L. Erlich, J. Rothman, and J. E. Tropman (Eds.), *Strategies of Community Organization,* 3rd Ed. Copyright © 1979, pp. 57–58. Reprinted by permission of the publisher, F. E. Peacock Publishers, Inc.

The powerlessness of people of color persisted through the Depression and World War II. There were fair employment and housing laws but no significant changes affecting minority human rights. Illegal Mexican aliens were used as cheap laborers. Japanese Americans on the West Coast were detained in relocation centers (American concentration camps) as a consequence of war hysteria and economic reactions of White agricultural business interests. The resulting loss of property and income amounted to millions of dollars. It is an irony that Japanese Americans fought with distinction in European combat divisions and were used in intelligence units during the Pacific campaign. Garvin and Cox summarize that period in Cultural Study 1-4.

Cultural Study 1-4

Powerlessness and the Minority Condition[4]

Blacks

The creation of many New Deal agencies "added credence to the emergent fact that for the first time the federal government had engaged and was grappling with some of the fundamental barriers to race progress" (Fishel & Quarles, 1967, p. 447). There were, nonetheless, many times when Roosevelt, who was highly regarded by many Black leaders, failed to deliver on expectations because of political considerations. Where local control was strong, the effect of some of those programs was to continue the exclusion of Black people from necessary benefits.

It is undeniable, however, that important strides were made during this period (1929–1954). There was a considerable expansion of opportunities for Black people in important governmental positions. Civil service brought many Black people into white-collar positions in government. World War II increased this momentum. The Committee on Fair Employment Practice, established by Roosevelt in 1941 to improve employment opportunities in defense industries, was a significant development. In 1948, Truman created the civil rights section of the Justice Department and established the President's Committee on Equality of Treatment and Opportunity in the Armed Services. The courts struck down restrictive housing covenants and outlawed segregation on buses in interstate travel.

Chicanos

From 1929 through the early 1950s Chicanos began to move beyond the Southwest into many other parts of the United States. This relocation was due in part to the processes of acculturation, but was due also to the fact that new Mexican immigrants were willing to work for lower wages than second-generation persons, who then tended to move to new areas. Particularly in the North, jobs were more available and wages better. A pattern of migrant farm labor was also established, emanating from the Southwest and spreading to other parts of the country as Chicanos followed the crops.

Much of the immigration during this period was illegal but responsive to employers seeking cheap labor. Employers aided the smuggling in of such persons (Moquin with Van Doren, 1971). The need for labor was heightened as Asian immigration ended.

Native Americans

Early in this period the government adopted a new approach to Native Americans: the Indian Reorganization Act of 1934. The intent of this act was to reverse the land policy of the Allotment Act of 1887 and the intent of trying to "stamp out everything that was Indian" (Taylor, 1972, p. 20). The 1934 act specifically provided authorization for the purchase of new land, the initiation of tribal organization, and the creation of loan funds for individuals *and tribes,* and extended the trust of Indian lands "until otherwise directed by Congress" (Taylor, 1972, p. 20).

This new policy of a more humane concern for Native Americans was a part of FDR's New Deal. It may also have made a difference that the Commissioner of Indian Affairs from 1933 to 1944, John Collier, was an anthropologist with a long career of interest in Native American affairs. Collier was critical of many American values and was identified with the aspirations of many Native American groups, and he had some utopian ideas about the potential of Native American society (Taylor, 1972).

Tribal governments established under the 1934 act were helped to develop constitutions and carry on many operations required of modern governments, economic as well as political. In contradiction to this course of action, however, was the policy of promoting assimilation by urging states to provide the same services for individual Native Americans as for other citizens.

Asian Americans

Between 1929 and 1954 there was also a gradual improvement of the economic status of Chinese Americans, although not necessarily of their social status. Kitano states:

> In the late 1930's and during World War II the Chinese became our friends and allies, although the general tone of the friendship was condescending.... Their peace loving nature was emphasized; they had fought valiantly against the "sly, tricky Jap"; they were different from their more aggressive neighbor.... In many ways, this praise deflected from the everyday humiliation, harassment, and deprivation faced by many Chinese, even with the relatively favorable attitude toward all Orientals (except the Japanese) at this time [Kitano, 1974, p. 200].

The most devastating event affecting the Japanese–American community was the wartime evacuation of all persons with as little as one-eighth Japanese blood from the West Coast. By March 1942, 110,000 such persons, most of them citizens of the United States, were in virtual concentration camps in such states as Colorado, Utah, and Arkansas. Most Japanese Americans complied even though they had to abandon their homes and possessions. This terrible injustice continued until 1944, when the Supreme Court revoked the

(continued)

Cultural Study 1-4 (continued)

policy. Most families who survived the experience had to begin all over again. Little remained of their property or belongings.

⁴Adapted from C. D. Garvin and F. M. Cox, "A History of Community Organizing since the Civil War with Special Reference to Oppressed Communities." In F. M. Cox, J. L. Erlich, J. Rothman, and J. E. Tropman (Eds.), *Strategies of Community Organization*, 3rd Ed. Copyright © 1979, pp. 65–67. Reprinted by permission of the publisher, F. E. Peacock Publishers, Inc.

Social Work and Ethnic Minority History

Discrimination in Social Services

We now turn, from a level of general historical documentation, to a specific discussion of social work and minority history. The crucial question after this brief history of the minority experience in the United States is: What was the professional stance of social work toward minorities during these periods? Trattner (1979) reports that during colonial days Blacks were viewed by most colonists as uncivilized and inferior. They were children of Satan who were not entitled to the same rights as White people. Blacks were excluded from the social welfare system. Black slaves were the responsibility of their masters and could not receive aid under the poor laws. Freed Blacks were denied assistance and were forced to develop their own informal self-help network. Later, some settlement house workers played an important part toward the creation of the National Association for the Advancement of Colored People in 1909 and the National Urban League in 1911. They also served as delegates to the 1921 Pan-African Congress held in London, Brussels, and Paris under the leadership of William E. B. DuBois. There was a decline in settlement house support during the 1920s and 1930s as Latin Americans, Puerto Ricans, Native Americans, and Blacks moved to the central cities and as professional social workers turned increasingly to casework.

Solomon (1976) records that prior to the Civil War, Blacks were excluded from welfare services in many areas and were unable to enter poorhouses, orphanages, hospitals, and state facilities in various parts of the country. The Charity Organization Society provided family rehabilitation services almost entirely to White families, neglecting problems among Black families. Following World War I, social workers were influenced by concern with intrapsychic processes and insight and moved away from social, situational, and interpersonal factors in problem solving. Blacks were rarely perceived as amenable to such treatment since there were so many other survival issues that took precedence.

Dieppa (1983) points out that social work lost its minority perspective of cultural pluralism during its initial 50-year development:

Although the settlement movement seemed to advance the concept of cultural pluralism during the social reform period (1900–20), its goal in relation to the masses of poor immigrants who arrived in this country was assimilation. Consequently, the advent of psychoanalytic theory in the 1920s and its acceptance and adoption by social workers resulted in a loss of concern for issues related to cultural pluralism. From the 1930s to the 1950s the social work profession focused its knowledge and efforts on the intrapsychic aspects of human problems. The failure of ethnic minorities of color to assimilate was perceived as resulting from their own failings" [Dieppa, 1983, p. 116].

Morales (1976) reviews the early history of California social work and reports the following discriminatory and racist actions and attitudes:

1. social service discrimination (that is, total exclusion, limited access to services, or inequitable resource and outdoor relief) against Mexican–American families and children;
2. the 1927 California Conference of Social Work definition of the Mexican as an expendable and undesirable labor group, which provided a rationale for mass deportation of Mexican Americans (many being United States citizens) to Mexico and the withholding or denial of relief payments and welfare services;
3. the 1934 statement of Emory Bogardus, Dean of the University of Southern California School of Social Work, that on the whole Mexican children fell below "American" children in intelligence, and his advocacy of segregated schools so that Mexican children would not develop feelings of inferiority.

No doubt individual social workers and scores of social agencies assisted ethnic minority people and fought against unjust policies, laws, and practices. However, a brief examination of the history of clinical social work practice indicates that social workers were engaged in social diagnosis theory formulation; individual, family, and group work among poor and middle-class Whites; the formation of specialty associations; and the nature of generic casework (Northen, 1982). The focus of social work practice was the establishing of its own professional theory and trade union base.

With the passage of major civil rights and immigration legislation in the mid-sixties, the stage was set for a series of Black, Brown, Yellow, and Red Power movements that swept the country. Ethnic minority college students and young adults became visible on university campuses and in ethnic inner-city communities. They demanded and received from university administrators the establishment of ethnic minority study departments. These centers became the focal point for community development activities such as ethnic elderly programs, minority youth tutoring and drop-in centers, and political organizing for minority services. They served as knowledge bases for rediscovering cultural and ethnic roots, exploring service delivery systems, and generating social minority research. The country was aroused with a conscience for social justice and implemented legislation, policies, and programs for minorities.

Educational Inattention to Minority Practice

Ethnic minority social work knowledge and practice theory has lagged behind the national focus on people of color. For example, it was not until 1970 that the Council on Social Work Education (CSWE) stated that its number one priority was ethnic minority group concerns. CSWE inaugurated a program of minority student and faculty recruitment, scholarships, and grant monies (Pins, 1970). It mandated the integration of ethnic minority content into social work school curricula (Dumpson, 1970). Minority social work educators wrote a series of CSWE publications on the principal non-white minority groups. Many articles and several books appeared on ethnicity, racism, policy and program needs, and selected minority groups. Between 1969 and 1973, there was a

2.5% increase in the number of minority students seeking a master's degree in social work, followed by a minority student decline between 1973 and 1977. Full-time minority social work faculty registered a slight increase nationally (Ishisaka & Takagi, 1981). The publication of major social work practice books revealed an absence of significant minority principles that distinctly addressed people of color. There were scattered articles on minorities in practice anthologies (Compton & Galaway, 1979; Cox, Erlich, Rothman & Tropman, 1979; Munson, 1980). Professional social work commitment to ethnic minorities shifted with national concerns to women and gay rights, nuclear disarmament, and other social areas.

A study of eighteen social work practice texts written between 1970 and 1983 was undertaken to determine their ethnic minority content (see Table 1-1). An underlying assumption was that social work undergraduate and graduate students would be exposed to minority content through relevant reading of these books. This presupposition was based on the fact of social work minority interest and commitment in the 1970s. The number of minority-related chapters was compared with the total number of chapters, and the number of subject index pages related to ethnicity, culture, and minorities was compared with the total number of pages of each book. The following results were obtained from these comparisons:

Fifteen social work practice texts contained no specified minority chapter(s).
Eight social work practice texts contained no subject indexes on ethnicity, culture, and minorities.
Seven social work practice texts contained no minority chapter(s) nor any subject indexes on ethnicity, culture, and minorities.
Three social work practice texts contained minority articles or chapters, ranging in number from 1 to 7.
Two social work practice texts contained subject index pages related to ethnicity, culture, and minorities.
4% (13 out of 304) of the chapters in 18 social work practice texts were minority focused.
.6% (44 out of 7688) of the total pages were devoted to the subject of ethnicity.
1% (94 out of 7688) of the total pages were devoted to the subject of culture.
1% (57 out of 7688) of the total pages were devoted to the subject of minorities.
3% (195 out of 7688) of the total pages were devoted to the combined subjects of ethnicity, culture, and minorities.

This investigation revealed that leading social work practice theorists and texts have but minimally mentioned ethnic minorities and related areas. It is beyond the scope of this study to speculate on the reasons for such a marginal treatment of minority aspects of practice. However, social work students exposed to these thinkers and readings have not received adequate knowledge on ethnic minority practice principles.

Minimal Coverage in Journals

Related to the study of social work practice texts is a similar investigation of ethnic minority content in leading social work journals. The hypothesis was that, given minimal minority content in social work practice books, there would be an adequate number of minority social work articles to supplement that lack. An examination of

TABLE 1-1.   Ethnic Minority Content in Social Work Practice Texts, 1970–1983

Author(s)	Title of book	Publica- tion year	Minority chapters	Total chapters	Index pages, ethnicity	Index pages, culture	Index pages, minorities	Total pages
Roberts & Nee	*Theories of Social Casework*	1970	0	9	0	4	0	408
Pincus & Minahan	*Social Work Practice: Model and Method*	1973	0	13	0	0	0	355
Goldstein	*Social Work Practice: A Unitary Approach*	1973	0	9	0	0	0	288
Fischer	*Interpersonal Helping: Emerging Approaches for Social Work Practice*	1973	0	41	no index	no index	no index	668
Klenk & Ryan	*The Practice of Social Work*	1974	1 article	6 (29 articles)	no index	no index	no index	448
Siporin	*Introduction to Social Work Practice*	1975	0	12	0	0	0	468
Meyer	*Social Work Practice: The Changing Landscape*	1976	0	6	0	0	0	268
Fischer	*Effective Casework Practice: An Eclectic Approach*	1978	0	10	0	0	0	393
Compton & Galaway	*Social Work Processes*	1979	7 articles	16 (35 articles)	7	9	43	565
Jayaratne & Levy	*Empirical Clinical Practice*	1979	0	11	0	0	0	340
Gilbert, Miller & Specht	*An Introduction to Social Work Practice*	1980	0	12	1	0	0	336
Hollis & Woods	*Casework: A Psychosocial Therapy*	1981	0	20	14	11	0	534
Northen	*Clinical Social Work*	1982	0	10	13	20	0	369

(continued)

TABLE 1-1. (continued)

Hep-worth & Larsen	Direct Social Work Practice: Theory and Skills	1982	0	22	0	12	0	559
Gambrill	Casework: A Competency-based Approach	1983	0	18	4	4	0	448
Lowen-berg	Fundamentals of Social Intervention	1983	0	12	0	12	0	373
Johnson	Social Work Practice	1983	0	15	0	17	0	388
Morales & Sheafor	Social Work: A Profession of Many Faces	1983	5	20	6	5	14	480
Total			13 (4%)	262 (304)	44 (.6%)	94 (1%)	57 (1%)	7688
Combined Index Pages (Ethnicity/Culture/Minorities)						195 (3%)		

minority articles in *Social Casework, Social Service Review,* and *Social Work* was undertaken during the same time period (1970 to 1983). The number of articles related to minorities in general and to Black, Latino, Asian, and Native Americans in particular was compared with the total number of articles written in each of the three leading social work journals (see Table 1-2). The study revealed the following trends:

The journals contained 3% (54) general minority articles, 2% (44) Black American articles, 1% (27) Latino–American articles, 1% (26) Asian–American articles, and 1% (29) Native American articles.

The journals published 8% (180) articles on ethnic minority issues and groups out of 2078 total articles.

Social Casework published 12% (98) articles on ethnic minorities out of 827 total articles.

Social Work published 9% (71) articles on ethnic minorities out of 819 total articles.

Social Service Review published 4% (19) articles on ethnic minorities out of 432 total articles.

There were five years (1975, 1976, 1979, 1981, and 1983) in which *Social Service Review* published no articles on ethnic minorities.

There was one year (1971) in which *Social Work* published no articles on ethnic minorities.

There was one year (1980) in which the journals published no articles on Black Americans; four years (1970, 1978, 1980, 1983) in which there were no articles on Latino Americans; four years (1971, 1974, 1977, 1983) with no articles on Asian Americans; and five years (1970, 1974, 1979, 1981, 1983) with no articles on Native Americans.

The investigation of leading social work journals reflected a slight increase of minority

TABLE 1-2. Ethnic Minority Articles in Social Work Journals, 1970–1983

Journal	Year	General minority articles	Black American articles	Latino–American articles	Asian–American articles	Native American articles	Total minority articles	Total articles
Social Casework	1970	3	6	0	1	0	10	56 (133)
Social Service Review		1	3	0	0	0	4	26
Social Work		0	2	0	0	0	2	51
Social Casework	1971	1	0	9	0	0	10	59 (131)
Social Service Review		2	1	0	0	1	4	26
Social Work		0	0	0	0	0	0	46
Social Casework	1972	3	2	1	1	0	7	62 (163)
Social Service Review		2	1	0	0	0	3	25
Social Work		9	3	1	1	1	15	76
Social Casework	1973	4	0	0	0	0	4	50 (144)
Social Service Review		0	2	0	0	0	2	23
Social Work		1	3	2	2	3	11	71
Social Casework	1974	0	1	9	0	0	10	61 (154)
Social Service Review		0	1	0	0	0	1	25
Social Work		2	1	0	0	0	3	68
Social Casework	1975	1	1	0	1	0	3	57 (148)
Social Service Review		0	0	0	0	0	0	33
Social Work		0	1	1	0	1	3	58
Social Casework	1976	0	0	1	13	1	15	64 (157)
Social Service Review		0	0	0	0	0	0	36
Social Work		0	1	2	0	1	4	57
Social Casework	1977	2	0	2	0	0	4	57 (144)
Social Service Review		0	0	0	0	2	2	33
Social Work		3	1	0	0	1	5	54

(continued)

TABLE 1-2. (continued)

Social Casework	1978	2	0	0	1	1	4	59 (147)
Social Service Review		0	1	0	0	0	1	33
Social Work		1	0	0	0	0	1	55
Social Casework	1979	0	0	1	1	0	2	57 (151)
Social Service Review		0	0	0	0	0	0	34
Social Work		1	2	1	0	0	4	60
Social Casework	1980	1	0	0	1	12	14	66 (157)
Social Service Review		1	0	0	0	0	1	34
Social Work		1	0	0	0	3	4	57
Social Casework	1981	0	3	2	1	0	6	56 (142)
Social Service Review		0	0	0	0	0	0	33
Social Work		1	0	0	1	0	2	53
Social Casework	1982	2	2	0	1	1	6	63 (157)
Social Service Review		1	0	0	0	0	1	36
Social Work		7	4	3	1	1	16	58
Social Casework	1983	1	2	0	0	0	3	60 (150)
Social Service Review		0	0	0	0	0	0	35
Social Work		1	0	0	0	0	1	55
		54 (3%)	44 (2%)	27 (1%)	26 (1%)	29 (1%)	180 (8%)	2078

Journals	Minority Articles	Total Articles
Social Casework	98 (12%)	827
Social Service Review	19 (4%)	432
Social Work	71 (9%)	819

articles (8%) compared with 3% of the total practice text pages. However, the overall results reveal a dearth of literature on ethnic minorities in practice textbooks and professional journals over a period of 14 years.

Underemphasis in the Profession

Dieppa (1984) has amassed evidence from several sources of the following conditions:

1. There has been little indication that social work curricula are providing the

knowledge, skills, and intervention strategies required to work effectively with minority people.

2. The social work profession has become more conservative, reflecting American society.
3. Social work faculty and administrators do not know how to incorporate minority content into social work curricula.
4. There are doubts raised by ethnic minorities about the validity of ethnic minority information conveyed and the qualifications of faculty working in this arena.
5. The social work profession has made limited efforts to develop its own body of knowledge about ethnic minority groups and has relied on sociological, psychological, and literary materials.
6. There is a need for more research on specific practice situations and differences between workers and others in race, class, sex, and sexual orientation and on the life experiences, culture, strengths, and history of specific ethnic groups.
7. Professional publications have paid limited attention to important and timely contributions to knowledge about particular ethnic minority populations.

One could argue, however, that the presence in practice texts of general content applicable to minority clients compensates for the lack of content pertaining explicitly to people of color. For example, there has been recent emphasis on environmental stress, extended family, and natural support systems. These themes are minority relevant even though no application to ethnic minorities is made by standard social work practice texts. In these instances, it is left to the reader to make the connection to the particular cultural problem situation. Our point is that there is a shortage of minority-explicit content in existing social work practice books and articles during the seventies and eighties. To point out that there is minority-applicable content is to alleviate the ethnic minority responsibility that social work practice writers must assume in their publications. The social work practice assumption has been that practice principles are generic even in their application to minority clients. This position is no longer defensible.

There are some encouraging signs. First, with the social policies of the Reagan Administration, economic recession and massive unemployment have refocused national attention on the plight of poor people and of minorities in particular. Second, due to social work student recruitment, minority doctoral fellowships, and faculty affirmative action, minority practice faculty have appeared in many university social work programs. The 1984 Annual Report of the Council on Social Work Education Commission on Minority Group Concerns states that between 1974 and 1984, 178 students were supported through the CSWE Ethnic Minority Doctoral Fellowship Program. Other activities include the computerization of a categorized bibliography on ethnic minority groups relevant to social work education and practice, a minority faculty directory and regional listing of CSWE Minority Fellows, and minority tenure issues (*Commission, Committee and Task Force Reports*, 1984). Third, social work education practice material has moved away from generic interest, in the seventies, toward more specialized topics in the eighties. Focal interest on minority practice remains high among social workers who recognize the increase of minority clientele and wish to cultivate skills in minority social work. Moreover, there is hope for the immediate future in the quality of practice publications from minority faculty, students, and practitioners. Toward this end, a more promising chapter of historical development appears on the horizon than there has been in the past.

Conclusion

The intent of this chapter has been to present the case for minority social work practice with people of color. We have underscored the dearth of ethnic minority practice material and the need to formulate cultural knowledge and skills. We have defined the parameters of ethnic minority social work practice. Social welfare arose from religious and secular humanism and the social needs of the poor and disabled. However, it tended to exclude ethnic minorities, particularly Blacks, as a result of racism and segregation pervading White society. People of color suffered alienation, oppression, and exploitation. The early history of social welfare revealed the lack of involvement in altering effects of minority prejudice. As public opinion and federal legislation moved toward minority civil rights, the social work profession reflected a commitment to people of color. As a profession, it has served and advocated minority causes and clients during the past two decades. Social work education has published minority literature, promoted minority recruitment of students and faculty, and elected minorities to leadership positions. However, the conservative political atmosphere of the eighties has impeded the minority momentum. Social workers must sensitize the American public to minority social justice. They must be effective practitioners with their minority clients.

In subsequent chapters, we will explore the values and knowledge base of minorities and formulate a minority practice process model. This particular framework details the stages of contact, problem identification, assessment, intervention, and termination. Minority practice principles and case studies emerge in the various sections. Social workers will, we hope, be stimulated to apply these perspectives to minority persons in need.

References

Alvarez, S. (1971). Mexican-American community organizations. In O. I. Romano-V (Ed.), *Voices: Readings from El Grito, a journey of contemporary Mexican American thought, 1967–1973* (pp. 205–214). Berkeley: Quinto Sol Publications.

Chunn, J. C., II, Dunston, P. J., & Ross-Sheriff F. (Eds.). (1983). *Mental health and people of color: Curriculum development and change.* Washington, D.C.: Howard University Press.

Commission, Committee and Task Force Reports. (1984). New York: Council on Social Work Education.

Compton, B. R., & Galaway, B. (Eds.). (1979). *Social work processes.* Homewood, Ill.: Dorsey Press.

Cox, F. M., Erlich, J. L., Rothman, J., & Tropman, J. E. (Eds.). (1979). *Strategies of community organization.* Itasca, Ill.: F.E. Peacock.

Devore, W., & Schlesinger, E. (1981). *Ethnic-sensitive social work practice.* St. Louis: C.V. Mosby.

Dieppa, I. (1983). A state of the art analysis. In G. Gibson (Ed.), *Our kingdom stands on brittle glass* (pp. 115–128). Silver Spring, Md.: National Association of Social Workers.

Dieppa, I. (1984). Trends in social work education for minorities. In B. W. White (Ed.), *Color in a white society* (pp. 10–21). Silver Spring, Md.: National Association of Social Workers.

Dumpson, J. R. (1970). Special committee on minority groups. *Social Work Education Reporter, 18,* 30.

Federico, R. C. (1980). *The social welfare institution: An introduction.* Lexington, Mass.: D. C. Heath.

Fischer, J. (1976). *The effectiveness of social casework.* Springfield, Ill.: Charles C Thomas.

Fischer, J. (1978). *Effective casework practice: An eclectic approach.* New York: McGraw-Hill.

Fishel, L. H., Jr., & Quarles, B. (1967). *The Negro American: A documentary history.* Glenview, Ill.: Scott, Foresman.

Garvin, C. D., & Cox, F. M. (1979). A history of community organizing since the Civil War with special reference to oppressed communities. In F. M. Cox, J. L. Erlich, J. Rothman, & J. E. Tropman (Eds.), *Strategies of community organization.* Itasca, Ill.: F.E. Peacock.

Goldstein, H. (1973). *Social work practice: A unitary approach.* Columbia, S.C.: University of South Carolina Press.

Green, J. W. (1982). *Cultural awareness in the human services.* Englewood Cliffs, N.J.: Prentice-Hall.

Hepworth, D. H., & Larsen, J. A. (1982). *Direct social work practice: Theory and skills.* Homewood, Ill.: Dorsey Press.

Howard, J. R. (Ed.). (1970). *Awakening minorities: American Indians, Mexican Americans, Puerto Ricans.* New Brunswick, N.J. Transaction Books.

Ishisaka, A. H., & Takagi, C. Y. (1981). Toward professional pluralism: The Pacific/Asian-American case. *Journal of Education for Social Work, 17,* 44–52.

Jayaratne, S., & Levy, R. (1979). *Empirical clinical practice.* New York: Columbia University Press.

Kitano, H. H. L. (1969). *Japanese Americans.* Englewood Cliffs, N.J.: Prentice Hall.

Kitano, H. H. L. (1974). *Race relations.* Englewood Cliffs, N.J.: Prentice-Hall.

Klenk, R. W., & Ryan, R. M. (1974). *The practice of social work.* Belmont, Calif.: Wadsworth.

Lerner, M. (1957). *America as a civilization: Life and thought in the United States today.* New York: Simon & Schuster.

Lopez y Rivas, G. (1973). *The Chicanos: Life and struggles of the Mexican minority in the United States.* New York: Monthly Review Press.

Mehr, J. (1980). *Human services: Concepts and intervention strategies.* Boston: Allyn & Bacon.

Meyer, C. H. (1976). *Social work practice: The changing landscape.* New York: Free Press.

Moquin, W., with Van Doren, C. (1971). *A documentary history of the Mexican Americans.* New York: Praeger.

Morales, A. (1976). The Mexican American and mental health issues. In M. Sotomayor (Ed.), *Cross cultural perspectives in social work practice and education* (pp. 2–20). Houston: University of Houston Graduate School of Social Work.

Munson, C. E. (Ed.). (1980). *Social work with families.* New York: Free Press.

Northen, H. (1982). *Clinical social work.* New York: Columbia University Press.

Pincus, A., & Minahan, A. (1973). *Social work practice: Model and method.* Itasca, Ill.: F.E. Peacock.

Pins, A. M. (1970). Entering the seventies: Changing priorities for social work education. *Social Work Education Reporter, 18,* 2.

Reid, W. (1978). *The task-centered system.* New York: Columbia University Press.

Silva, J. S. (1983). Cross-cultural and cross-ethnic assessment. In G. Gibson (Ed.), *Our kingdom stands on brittle glass* (pp. 59–66). Silver Spring, Md.: National Association of Social Workers.

Siporin, M. (1975). *Introduction to social work practice.* New York: Macmillan.

Solomon, B. B. (1976). *Black empowerment: Social work in oppressed communities.* New York: Columbia University Press.

Taylor, T. W. (1972). *The states and their Indian citizens.* Washington, D.C.: United States Department of the Interior, Bureau of Indian Affairs.

Trattner, W. I. (1979). *From poor law to welfare state: A history of social welfare in America.* New York: Free Press.

Ethnic Minority Values and Knowledge Base

In the preceding chapter, perspectives on social work minority practice were presented as a starting point for investigation. These practice perspectives require an understanding of values, ethics, and minority knowledge theory, which are guidelines for practice process. Values influence how the minority client and the social work practitioner formulate and interpret social problems. Ethics determine the implementation of values in a choice decision and in resulting behavior. Knowledge is the systematic formulation of a body of facts and principles. The base of minority social work knowledge involves the interaction between social work practice approaches and the concepts of ethnicity, culture, minority, and social class.

Social work minority knowledge theory includes theories of human behavior and practice. Although knowledge theory is oriented toward practice in this chapter, there are minority behavior theories surrounding the concepts of ethnicity, culture, minority, and social class. The term *minority knowledge* involves the range of information, awareness, and understanding of the minority situational experience. It includes history, cognitive-affective-behavioral characteristics, and societal dilemmas of people of color. The term *minority theory* refines minority knowledge in a series of formulated general principles that tentatively infer or explain these phenomena in a systematic manner. It includes the examination of underlying dynamics that cause, for example, prejudice and that have been verified to some degree.

As a professional discipline, social work offers a value perspective and a code of ethics that advocate the social well-being of persons. However, do its beliefs and ethical code speak to ethnic minority values and ethical perspectives? Professions have value preferences that give purpose, meaning, and direction to professional workers. Hepworth and Larsen (1982) point out that professional values do not exist apart from societal values. Professions champion selected societal values and society gives legal, legislative, and program sanction and recognition to professions. A profession is linked to certain societal values and tends to serve as society's conscience for those particular values.

At its worst, social work has been identified with the dominant society and criticized as a social control agent against elements endangering the institutional status quo. At its best, it embraces values and ethics that reflect the moral good of a society committed to service, provision, and advocacy for the poor and oppressed. Social work must be aware of societal influences on its values and ethics. A middle-class social worker and a ghetto resident may respond to different physical, economic, and cultural realities. Likewise, social work knowledge tends toward Western social sciences. Unlike Third World thought, Western knowledge theory emphasizes the freedom and independence of the individual from behavioral dysfunction that impedes normal functioning. The client changes with the assistance of a helping person and reliance on verbal exchange and analysis. Minority knowledge theory, on the other hand, emphasizes the individual's membership and functioning within the collective (family, community, and ethnic group). Knowledge theory involves ethnic helpers, customs, and cosmic forces in the process of personal change. This chapter offers an alternative perspective on ethnic minority values and knowledge base.

Value Criteria

Social Work Values

According to Rokeach (1973), a value is a belief that a mode of conduct or end state is preferable to an opposite or converse one. Professional values refer to vested beliefs about people, preferred goals for people, means of achieving those goals, and conditions of life. They represent selected ideals as to how the world should be and how people should normally act (Hepworth & Larsen, 1982). Compton and Galaway (1979) list three social work values: respect for the dignity and uniqueness of the individual, client self-determination, and legal authority and self-determination. Northen (1982) identifies the values of the inherent worth and dignity of the individual and mutual responsibility or interdependence upon one another for survival and fulfillment of needs. The value ideology of social work is humanistic in that it is concerned about the welfare and protection of the client and the client's own participation in the helping process; scientific in that it prefers objectivity and factual evidence, rational practitioner's judgments and actions; and democratic in that it governs relationships with people by principles of reciprocal rights, obligations, and welfare of the individual, group, and society. Hepworth and Larsen (1982) stress access to life resources and opportunities to realize potentialities; the unique dignity, worth, and individuality of every person; the right to freedom that does not infringe on the rights of others and to independence and self-determination in transactions; and societal opportunities and citizen responsibility to participate in the democratic process. The emphasis on self-determination and individuality represents the tension between the rights of the individual and the demands of society. Keith-Lucas (1971) traces the periods of individual rights in the fifties and client social and psychological adaptation in the sixties.

Social work values are rooted in Judeo-Christian principles emphasizing justice, equality, and concern for others. Addams (1907) speaks about love and justice as regulators of human relations. She refers to the difficulties of life confronting immigrant groups who settled in the ghettos and to the principles of love and justice that were the motivating social work forces. Addams also alludes to the Judeo-Christian beliefs in the integral worth of man and one's responsibility for one's neighbor. In Christianity, love possesses qualities of devotion, loyalty, and social responsibility. Justice relates to actions that strengthen relationships in society. Social work operationalizes love through the expression of empathy, genuineness, warmth, and acceptance of the individual. Justice is demonstrated through social equality, rights, and responsibilities such as access to economic opportunities and education. Justice is the fulfillment of reciprocal expectations of fairness (Kent & Tse, 1980).

Social work values reflect humanistic and democratic concepts of freedom, individuality, and social concern. These precepts are implemented in an ethical code that governs professional social work spheres. In the following section, relevant components of the NASW Code of Ethics are examined to illustrate how social work values are translated into standards of conduct.

Social Work Code of Ethics

The 1980 National Association of Social Workers (NASW) Code of Ethics sets personal and professional standards of behavior for its members. It specifics rules of conduct for social workers in relationship to self, clients, colleagues, employers, and the social work profession, and ethical responsibility to society. Hepworth and Larsen (1982) point out that a code of ethics has formal functions:

1. accountability of the profession to society, consumers, and practitioners;
2. regulations to safeguard the professional behavior of members;
3. competent and responsible membership practices;
4. protection of the public from unscrupulous and incompetent practitioners.

Professional ethics involves translating values into a standard of practice governing individual and group character, actions, and ends.

Principles of the NASW Code

The NASW Code of Ethics establishes principles of ethical behavior, professional service, client well-being, and community action. The social worker's conduct involves the creative use of self. The social worker should maintain high standards of personal comportment and professional performance. The primary emphasis of the Code is on the service obligation of the profession toward persons. The social worker should act in accordance with the highest standards of professional integrity and impartiality. A social worker engaged in research should follow the conventions of scholarly inquiry and protect participants by securing their informed consent and ensuring confidentiality. The focus is the primacy of the client's interests, maximum self-determination for the client, respect for the client's rights and prerogatives, and confidentiality and privacy of information. The social worker should establish fair and reasonable fees that are commensurate with the services performed and the client's ability to pay.

Interprofessional ethics are the social worker's responsibility to colleagues. The social worker should treat colleagues with respect, courtesy, fairness, and good faith. It is his or her responsibility to relate to the clients of colleagues with full professional consideration. This obligation means nonsolicitation of colleagues' clients and communication with other agencies or colleagues involved with his or her clients. The social worker's responsibility to employers and employing organizations covers improving the agency's policies and procedures, upgrading the efficiency and effectiveness of services, and rejecting employment or student field placement in an organization under NASW sanction for violation of ethical standards.

The social worker is responsible for maintaining professional integrity, community service, and knowledge development of the profession. This requirement means upholding the values and mission of social work, making social services available to the general public, and utilizing current and emerging professional practice knowledge. Finally, the social worker should promote the general welfare of society. Among the crucial areas are the prevention of discrimination and the promotion of respect for diverse cultures; commitment to accessibility of resources, services, and opportunities; and support of policy and legislative changes to improve social conditions and to promote social justice.

Implications for Minority Practice

The NASW Code of Ethics has implications for ethnic minority clients and communities. There are clear statements against discrimination. The social worker should not practice, condone, facilitate, or collaborate with any form of discrimination on the basis of race, color, sex, sexual orientation, age, religion, national origin, marital status, political belief, mental or physical handicap, or any other preference or personal characteristic, condition, or status. The social worker should not engage in any action that violates or diminishes the civil or legal rights of clients. Beyond this, the ethical responsibility to ethnic minority clients involves a personal and professional exploration of the social worker regarding attitudes toward minorities, knowledge of minority client groups, and awareness of particular ethnic community needs. The social worker should acquire appropriate social casework knowledge and skills about working with minorities. Through demographic studies, contact with local minority neighborhoods, and practice workshops, the social worker develops ethnic expertise as an effective helping agent. The social worker's ethical responsibility to society reemphasizes nondiscrimination, equal opportunities, and respect for cultural diversity.

These principles set a tone for social work minority activities. The Code of Ethics implies a careful examination of the ethnic composition and distribution of social work staff in an agency. It means the exposure of subtle professional practices that could be interpreted as discriminatory with respect to minority clients, such as condescending attitudes toward minority concerns. It fosters the development of creative job training and employment programs for minority unemployed youth and adults in the local community. It encourages dissemination of professional information about minority cultures and social needs and about programs to facilitate culturally relevant helping strategies. To what extent are social worker and social service agencies creatively implementing the minority aspects of the NASW Code? The question is a crucial one. It is particularly serious in a social and political climate that has moved toward a conservative philosophy and away from a strong enforcement of affirmative action and nondiscrimination.

Ethnic Minority Values

The history of social work in the United States revolves around a concern for the poor and oppressed in physical, economic, and social need. Social workers administer survival services such as food, housing, and medical care on behalf of society. Social work has emphasized the values of the dignity and uniqueness of the individual, self-determination of the client, and accessibility of resources. These values tend toward a high regard for persons and individual rights and freedom. They form the basis for relating to clients in practice situations. In contrast, ethnic minorities espouse corporate values such as family interdependency and obligation, metaphysical harmony in nature or religion, and ethnic group identity.

Values are not either/or propositions. Persons may hold values that may be considered conflicting in his or her own belief system. For example, a person may affirm his or her individual freedom of choice and yet believe in the collective value obligation to his or her family. In some situations one value may have a priority over the other within a hierarchy of values defined by the minority person, family, or community. Value hierarchies may differ for various ethnic groups and individuals. Moreover, persons of color may be bicultural in the sense that they may endorse values held by the majority society as well as those considered important by their own group. The issue may be under what circumstances (that is, degree of acculturation) the majority or minority values will prevail. For example, a minority young adult may assert his or her freedom to socialize with and date people of many races. To a broad extent, the object is to experience many different kinds of people. However, due to the young person's ethnic upbringing, his or her collective family obligation is to marry a person of the same race. The marriage may be arranged by both sets of parents or by a professional matchmaker. To a certain extent, the potential value conflict has been set aside by the higher collective minority value of family obligation: namely, to marry a person of the same race and to preserve the family name and ethnic identity.

Although social work values are oriented toward client rights, social work should address and incorporate collective minority values. A minority value base for social work implies social policies, programs, and procedures that emphasize family unification, recognition of the leadership of elders and parents, and mutual responsibility among family members. Arising out of family values is a respect for religious institutions and spiritual practices. Black and Latino communities have tended toward Protestant and Catholic Christianity within their cultural adaptations. Asian Americans participate in Christian and Buddhist churches and are aware of the moral ethic of family honor. Native Americans have rediscovered spiritual values in native rituals.

Pedersen (1979) observes that Euro-American cultural values have dominated the social sciences and have been accepted as universal. In turn, they have been imposed on non-Western cultures. Recently there has been interest in examining non-Western value assumptions that offer alternatives to the dominant culture value system. Likewise, Higginbotham (1979) point out that psychotherapy is determined by culture-specific values. For example, the emphasis of psychoanalysis on individual growth is in contradistinction to kinship and group-centered cultures. In the following sections, three minority values related to family, spirituality, and identity are set forth as important elements for social work to incorporate into its value schema.

Minority Family Values

Patterns

Minority values revolve around corporate collective structures. For example, the individual wishes of a particular family member are subordinate to the good of the family as a whole. The family unit is considered the most important transmitter of cultural values and traditions. The value of the family is emphasized over that of individual members (Mokuau, in press). Argyle (1982) states that the family is more important in developing countries than in developed ones. It encompasses a wider range of relatives with closer relationships and greater demands than in Western countries. The family is the primary source of relationships and is called upon to pay for education, help get jobs, and assist when members are in trouble. Among ethnic minorities, a number of family functions are carried out:

1. *Maintenance of ethnic identification and solidarity.* Mindel and Habenstein (1981) point out that the family socializes its members into ethnic culture through family lifestyles and activities. Family gatherings and community celebrations of cultural holidays are examples of perpetuating ethnic awareness. Fritzpatrick (1981) further observes that in Latin America, the individual has a deep consciousness of family membership. Puerto Ricans in particular practice a deep sense of family obligation to the extent of using advancements in public office or private business to benefit their families. Alvirez, Bean, and Williams (1981) coin the term *familism* to emphasize the importance of this central point of reference and place of refuge. One turns to another family member for advice and help.

2. *Extended family and kinship network.* Minority extended family and kinship networks function on the principles of interdependence, group orientation, and reliance on others. For example, the Puerto Rican family has the institution of *compadres:* people are designated as "companion parents." These compadres become godparents of the child, particularly as sponsors at baptism and confirmation. In other instances, they are witnesses at a marriage or consider themselves compadres due to common interest or intense friendship. They feel free to give advice or correction and are expected to be responsive to the needs of the person. Among Blacks there is an extensive reliance on kinship networks, which include blood relatives and close friends called kinsmen. These networks arise out of mutual need of such things as financial aid, child care, advice, and emotional support. Furthermore, young Black children are taken into the household of elderly grandparents in informal adoption (Staples, 1981). The Hopi tribe practices bifurcate merging, meaning that the mother's and father's sides are divided into separate lineages and that relatives of the same sex and generation are grouped together in helping clusters. The mother's sister is close to her and the child and behaves toward the child as the biological mother would (Price, 1981). These models are variations on extended family and kinship networks.

3. *Vertical hierarchy of authority.* Minority families operate within parental authority structures. Jenkins (1981) states that ethnic minority parents value obedience to parental authority, particularly the father. Minority children, however, may be at odds with this hierarchy due to the influences of the dominant society. Alvirez, Bean, and Williams (1981) identify the principle of subordination of the younger to the older in the traditional Mexican–American family. The minority elderly receive respect from youth and children, who speak to them using the formal rather than the familiar form of address. Furthermore, the hierarchy of authority for Mexican Americans is male-centered. The older male children have a degree of authority over younger children and sisters. During the absence of the father the older son assumes authority or shares it with the mother. There are variations on a strict vertical hierarchy of authority in minority families who have become acculturated to the dominant society.

Variations

These principles of family function vary among the principal minority groups in the United States. For Native Americans, grandparents retain official and symbolic leadership in family communities, as witnessed by the behavior of children who seek daily contact with grandparents and by grandparents who monitor parental behavior. In this milieu, grandparents have an official voice in child-rearing methods. Parents seldom overrule corrective measures from their elders. Younger people seek social acceptance from an older member of the community. Because the acceptance of the elders is sought, their norm-setting standards are seldom ignored. Unrelated leaders are incorporated into the family. These functional and flexible roles of "grandparents," "aunts," and "uncles" establish an important structure of relationships (Red Horse, Lewis, Feit, & Decker, 1978).

In Black American families, there is a sense of corporate responsibility. Children of family systems belong to the extended family clan, not merely to the parents. The extended family is responsible for the care and rearing of children, teaching them appropriate skills and values. As a consequence, uncles, aunts, cousins, and grandparents have considerable power in the family. It is not uncommon for these relatives to "adopt" informally children whose parents are unable to care for them or for children to be given to relatives temporarily or permanently. Kenyatta states:

> As in past times, the extended family exists largely as a response to and, let it be stressed, as a triumph over the impact of racism. Within the extended family, bartering of goods and services helps to buffer against the sharp edges of economic insecurity. The extended family both strengthens and is often strengthened by broader social institutions within the black community, especially the black church. Extended families serve as grapevines for information of economic as well as affectionate significance and the extended family also serves as a reserve of affection, affirmation, encouragement, empathy, love, and sanity. It is "how we got over" and how we get over, one of various survival mechanisms to insure the continuity of black life [Kenyatta, 1980, p. 43].

Chief among the valued ties for many Black Americans are the mother-child and sibling relationships. In many families, the mother keeps the family together (Mendes, in press).

Asian–American families have specific roles and relationships. The family is patriarchal, with father as the leader of the family, mother as the nurturant caretaker, and sons of more value than daughters. The family relationship is based on filial piety and mutual obligation. The child is expected to be obedient to parents and elders. In exchange, parents are responsible for the upbringing, education, and support of the child (Kitano, 1974). Parents and children demonstrate respect for their ancestors and, in return, ancestral spirits provide protection for the family. These interdependent roles of family members are supposed to keep the family intact (Sue, 1973). Knowing one's place in the family arrangement is a primary value of group loyalty (Mokuau, in press).

Latinos value the extended family structure and interaction in their daily life. Ruiz and Padilla (1977) observe that family therapies probably yield higher success rates among Latinos than among non-Latinos, regardless of whether the problem is intrapsychic or extrapsychic. An understanding of Latino family dynamics is crucial for social work practice. In the Latino family, fathers have prestige and authority; sons have more and earlier independence than daughters; sex roles are rigidly defined; and the aged receive respect and reverence. Married sons visit their parents frequently, a custom that does not connote the pathological dependency implied in other cultures. It is not unusual in Chicano families for married children to move to a mobile home on the parent's land and share the same property. For Chicanos, staying close to home has a different meaning. The motivations may be positive: the desire to maintain contact with several generations, to accept responsibility for older people, and to guide and protect younger brothers and sisters (Roll, Millen, & Martinez, 1980).

Minority family values stress a sense of mutual obligation to support, care, and provide for each other. They emphasize family collectivity rather than individual independence. Social work should explore the meaning of family responsibility with minority clients.

Minority Religious and Spiritual Values

Religion and spirituality have external and internal values for ethnic minorities. Pedersen (1979) observes that non-Western cultures have an appreciation of religious and spiritual participation in the universe. Health and illness are defined in terms of harmony or disharmony with the universe. The concept of the spiritual is related to a metaphysical affinity with environmental forces in nature. Chestang (1976) offers a view of religion's role as sustaining an individual in adverse social stress and becoming a rallying point for social change. He states that the religious institutions "serve the psychological purpose of strengthening the individual in the face of his impotence against the social structure and the sociopolitical function of providing an outlet for his talents and abilities as well as furnishing a focal point for community organization" (Chestang, 1976, p. 72). Staples (1976) likewise asserts that religion has fortified Blacks against the destructive force of racism, providing a mechanism for reduction of tension and a defense against the white hostile world. It has given credibility to cultural heritage, validated the worth of Black people, and provided hope for the future.

Religion and the church have an extensive influence in the Black and Latino communities. Religion was an integral part of the lives of African slaves who were brought to the United States. Religion has historically sustained Blacks through the hardships of slavery, prejudice, and racism. The Black churches remain a strong force shaping civil rights and political justice for Black people. Black Protestant theologians have articulated liberation theology, which analyzes the sins of society as oppression and proclaim the good news of liberation and freedom in Christ. The influence of Biblical passages and stories, prayer, and the role of the Black clergy are powerful forces in the value structure of the Black community. Likewise, Latinos have historically been rooted in religious values. Latinos have a sense of morality and religious practice stemming from the church and their culture. In the Catholic Church, the priest participates in the life of the Latino community through religious observances and holidays, confirmations, children's classes, and social services. Catholic Social Services maintains an extensive Latino program and identifies with local barrio churches. Protestant Latino churches provide emergency financial aid, home visitation, care for the ill, newcomer services, housing, employment, and rehabilitation programs for addicts and other outcasts. For the Latino family the church is a moral force shaping the ethical behavior of family members and a spiritual influence for religious instruction and community change. To families who are involved in various church activities, it is also a social vehicle for meeting with friends and interacting with the community.

For Asian Americans, formal religions include Buddhism, Protestantism, and Catholicism. Asian Americans in the Catholic Church are generally integrated with other ethnic groups in a geographic parish. Protestant and Buddhist churches serve a single Asian group such as the Japanese, Chinese, Pilipino, Korean, or Vietnamese. Asian Americans tend to practice values such as respect for one's ancestors, filial piety, and avoidance of shame. These moral principles assist many Asian Americans in family and social functioning by defining their obligation, duty, and loyalty to others. Good performance and achievement bring honor to the family. Shame and dishonor are powerful motivators to minimize unacceptable behavior. Mental illness and retardation, criminal behavior, job failure, and even poor school grades are kept in the family. To share negative information outside the home is to bring disgrace on the family name. This standard of morality may seem harsh and rigid to the outsider, but to many Asian Americans it maintains honor and harmony in the family.

Native Americans probably have the closest relationship between spiritual realization and unity and their cultural practices, as illustrated in Cultural Study 2-1. While Catholic and Protestant clergy have sought to Christianize Native Americans, there has been maintenance of indigenous religious rituals and beliefs in the healing power of nature. Natural forces are associated with the life process itself and pervade everything that the believing Native American does. Community religious rites are a collective effort that promote this mode of healing and increase inward insight and experiential connection with nature. Native American individuals can utilize the positive experiences resulting from ceremonial events, power-revealing events (omens, dreams, visions), and contact with a tribal medicine man in the helping process. Helping to discover and reinforce the therapeutic significance of Native American religious and cultural events can be a learning task for social workers (Lewis, 1977).

Cultural Study 2-1

Plains Indians' Spiritual Retreat

Among the sacred ceremonies of the Plains Indians are the rites of purification, the annual tribal Sun Dance, and the individual spiritual retreat. The purification rites are centered in a dome lodge made of intertwined willows and covered over tightly with bison robes. In the circular form of the lodge and in the materials used in its construction, the tribesman sees a symbolic representation of the world in its totality. The lodge is the very body of the Great Spirit. Inside this lodge of the world, participants submit to intensely hot steam produced when water is sprinkled on rocks previously heated in a special sacred fire located to the east of the lodge. As the men pray and chant, the steam, conceived as the visible image of the Great Spirit, dissolves both physical and psychic coagulations, permitting a spiritual transmutation to take place. The elements contribute their respective powers to purification so that participants experience the dissolving of illusory separateness and the achievement of reintegration or harmonious unification within the totality of the universe. Going forth from the dark lodge, the men leave behind all physical impurities and spiritual errors and are reborn into the wisdom of the light of day. All aspects of the world have been witnesses to this cycle of corruption, death, wholeness, and rebirth. The cosmic powers have all contributed to the process.

The Sun Dance rites are performed annually by the entire tribe. This prayer dance is the regeneration or renewal of the individual, tribe, and entire universe. It takes place within a large circular pole lodge. At the center is a tall cottonwood tree representing the axis of the universe, the vertical link joining heaven and earth, and thus the path of contact with the solar power, the sun, symbol of the Supreme Principle or Great Spirit. Supported day and night by a huge drum beaten by many men and by heroic and nostalgic songs, the dancers hold eagle plumes and continually orient themselves toward the sacred central tree or toward one of the four directions of space. Blowing whistles made from the wing bone of the eagle, the men dance individually with simple and dignified steps towards the central tree, from which they receive supernatural power, and then dance backward to the periphery of the circle without shifting their gaze from the center. The power of the sacred center, realized within participants, remains with each individual and unifies the people.

The individual spiritual retreat or vision quest involves a total fast for a specified number of days at a lonely place, usually a mountain top. Alone and in constant prayer, the individual is in utter humility of body and mind and stands before the forms and forces of nature. He seeks the blessing of sacred power, which comes to him through a dream or vision of some aspect of nature, possibly an animal who offers guidance for the future direction of the man's life. These natural forces are an iconography that expresses the ultimate power or essence of the Great Spirit. In silence within the solitude of nature is heard the voice of the Great Spirit. Their quest for supernatural powers is essential to the spiritual life of the Plains Indians and influences their quality of life. The sacred tobacco pipe is central to all the rites and expresses sacrifice and purification, the integration of the individual within the macrocosm, and the realization of unity (Brown, 1969).

Social workers and other human service professionals should ascertain the meaning of religion or a spiritual perspective for particular clients. Gary (1978) remarks that mental health professionals often minimize the functional usefulness of religion for minority clients:

Unfortunately, there is a tendency for professionals to ignore or downplay the role of the Black church. One thing is apparent, many of these professionals, especially Whites, do not understand this religious orientation in the Black community. Some, because of their ethnic and religious backgrounds and for a variety of other reasons, have difficulties in advocating or emphasizing the positive role of religion (Protestantism) in mental health [Gary, 1978, pp. 31, 33].

Church-related social services can readily identify with the link between family and church in the Black and Latino communities. Moral values are also a strong influence among Asian Americans. Within the Native American community, the spiritual experience is closely identified with symbolic rituals, which have cultural meaning for behavioral renewal and change. Although not all ethnic minorities are influenced by the religious and spiritual, there are many who utilize this value system to sustain and nurture their existence. There is an increasing need for social workers to be aware of the functional value of religion for minority clients.

Minority Identity Values

Chestang (1976) defines individual identity as the conglomerate of consciousness, personality, attitudes, emotions, and perceptions that is termed the *self*. Identity is a result of interaction between the heredity of the individual and the life experiences determined by physical and social environment. Viewed from a developmental perspective, many people of color become aware of the negative societal attitudes toward their racial group, and those attitudes have a devaluing or destructive effect on their identity. Within their own ethnic community they find positive elements to reshape their minority identity.

In the past two decades, ethnic groups have rediscovered their cultural background. Ethnic history and cultural awareness are integral parts of university ethnic studies curricula. More recently, with the television series *Roots,* many ethnic minorities and others have researched their genealogies and the history of their ancestors and relatives. There are a number of variables common to minority identity values. The most obvious feature that distinguishes members of minorities from their White counterparts is skin color. All people of the earth have been classified according to color: white, brown, black, yellow, and red. Ethnic identity has been undermined by a color hierarchy. White symbolizes innocence, purity, and fairness. Black is associated with evil, darkness, and dirt. Yellow conjures up cowardice, impurity, and discoloration. Red is associated with rage and anger. The derogative tone of such idioms as "dirt black," "yellow belly," and "red skin" have caused them to become racist slurs and they are still with us. Moreover they depreciate ethnic identity value. In the 1960s the theme "Black is beautiful" was a way of reinforcing the positive physical appearance of ethnic identity.

Along with skin color, name and language are important. Many people of color have forgotten or changed their native names for Anglo-European ones. Black Americans adopted or were given the last name of their plantation owners. Some Black Americans have legally changed their English names to African ones, as Native Americans have done with their native ones. Latinos are named after relatives and ancestors and may have full names consisting of four or five words. Asian Americans have combined an English first name with their ethnic middle and last names. An ethnic native name has a significant cultural meaning for the person. For some cultures, the invested worth and life mission of the person are found in the given name. In other cultures, the name perpetuates the memory of important ancestors in the family. Akin to the name is the language of an ethnic minority group. Many minority immigrants are unable to speak English and converse in their native language at home. Within the ethnic community, language ability is a criterion of social acceptance. Inability to speak the language confers ignorance and shame. Language shapes unique patterns of thoughts, producing cognitive differences between English and, for instance, Spanish. Minorities think and express themselves in different ways from those who speak in English. Different language nuances influence behavior patterns.

There are a number of generic principles related to ethnic identity. DeVos and Romanucci-Ross (1982) categorize two types of ethnic identity: past-oriented cultural identity and expressive-behavioral cultural identity. Past-oriented identity involves four characteristics:

1. *Competence.* Ethnic identity determines a person's confidence to take on goal oriented activities, builds group competence based on collective confidence and supportive attitudes, and fosters independent capacities for status.

2. *Responsibility.* Ethnic identity defines ethical obligations and its moral code, has an internalized moral dimension of both negative and positive heritage, and sometimes causes conflict about ethical standards.

3. *Control.* Ethnicity places one's group in a superordinate or subordinate position with respect to other groups. Those in the superordinate status legitimate their authority and dominance when there is social insecurity or individual impotence. The subordinate group is subjected to pressures to demonstrate its submission based on survival or dependency. In other instances, the ethnic identity of the subordinates is a moral imperative to seek liberation, autonomy, and independence from the oppressor.

4. *Mutuality.* Ethnic traditions define modes of competition and cooperation expected by the group. In-group activities may demand concerted behavior and mutual trust to act together, emphasizing cooperation and minimizing competition. In other instances, competition is directed toward people outside the ethnic group.

Ethnic identity factors that influence the expression and understanding of behavior include five traits:

1. *Harmony.* Peace is maintained at the expense of conflict in ethnic group relationships. Harmony is used to maintain group continuance, whereas hostilities are projected onto outsiders in the form of scapegoating.

2. *Affiliation.* An ethnic group maintains mutual contact and communication based on sharing common past experiences. In some instances, ethnic peers maintain more intimate companionship than do family members of different generations. Loss of a sense of belonging—social isolation or the threat of separation—are social sanctions against violators of group norms.

3. *Nurturance.* Ethnic identity forms the basis for interdependency in terms of caring,

help, and comfort. Ethnic membership fosters benevolent care of one generation for another. Professionally trained members of an ethnic group have an advantage of reaching their own people who need help because of their ethnic identity.

4. *Appreciation.* Ethnic identity fosters pride in one's group, creating a sense of humanity, dignity, self-respect, and proper status. The danger is apparent when highly positive cultural traits are devalued by others or when a group is forced to acknowledge the merits or superior technology of an alien group.

5. *Pleasure and suffering.* Ethnic identity is related to a person's social satisfaction in terms both of personal identity and of one's relation to a group, and to tolerance of suffering and death. Ethnic beliefs, cultural knowledge of history, and other systems form the basis for meaning in life.

These ethnic identity themes are useful to our understanding of common meanings that apply to a psychocultural theory of particular groups. To a certain extent, the nine variables listed apply to cultures in general. However, in the case of ethnic minorities, these factors are crucial to self-survival and group sustenance. For this reason, it is important for social workers to locate and mobilize these centers of ethnic identity.

Social Work and Minority Values

The preceding sections have examined traditional social work values and ethics and minority values centering on family, spirituality, and identity. Social work values and ethics have been based on individualistic democratic ideals of self-determination, freedom of choice, and social responsibility. Minority values deal with collective entities such as the family, church, and nature. The individual derives his or her point of reference from these ethnic structures. In order to bridge the gap between individuality and collectivity, social work must incorporate a cosmological orientation that accounts for the importance of family, spirituality, and nature. The individual draws meaning, relationship, and direction from these areas. These concepts should be reflected in broader social work definitions of values and ethical code. Among the crucial minority values are the following, which could be incorporated into the NASW Code of Ethics:

  Social work values family unification, parental leadership, respect for the elderly, and collective family decision making.
  Social work encourages the healthy application of religious and spiritual beliefs and practices, which join the individual and family to collective institutions and cosmic forces in the universe, resulting in harmony, unity, and wholeness.
  Social work seeks to use family kinship and community networks as supportive means of treatment for persons who are able to benefit from collective helping.
  Social work values the rediscovery of ethnic language and cultural identity, which strengthen a person's relationship to his or her heritage.

These propositions serve as useful bridges to link traditional social work values with minority ones. The next two parts of this chapter deal with the knowledge theory dimension of social work practice and with minority theory issues that have implications for understanding people of color.

Social Work Knowledge Theory

In order to implement these applied values, the social worker needs a body of knowledge from which an ethnic theory base can be developed. It is important to address the particular societal needs and problems of minority people that impede social change. Surveying these knowledge parameters and then detailing appropriate theory is the task of this section.

Social Work Practice Theory

General systems theory has been applied to social work practice in the past decade (Pincus & Minahan, 1973; Goldstein, 1973; Compton & Galaway, 1979). In general systems theory, complex adaptive systems describe relationships between individuals and other subsystems such as family, relatives, neighborhood, school, job, church, and community. People's problems are viewed as a product of transactions between systems. Systems theory has provided social work practice with a new set of terminology. For example, *boundary* is a semipermeable demarcation line that defines the components of a system. Boundaries define individual and relational components. They filter information entering or leaving the system. The term *equifinality* refers to accomplishment of similar outcomes by different developmental routes from different initial conditions. Individual systems are in the process of change and seek multiple goals. Equifinality is concerned with emergence, purpose, goal seeking, and self-regulation. Social work practice theorists have utilized systems theory as the knowledge theory base to explain interaction of person and environment (Meyer, 1976; Germain & Gitterman, 1980).

Roots in Psychoanalysis

In contrast to systems theory, social work practice has drawn on psychotherapeutic personality theories as its knowledge theory underpinning. Freudian psychoanalytic theory formed the basis of psychodiagnostic casework in the twenties and thirties. It explained purposeful and goal-directed behavior, which has causal connection and continuity between past events and present behavioral actions. Unconscious, preconscious, and conscious forces motivate thought, feeling, and action. Behavior is shaped by a personality self composed of the id (the biological instinctual force), the superego (the moralistic societal force), and the ego (the mediator between id and superego). Psychodiagnostic casework applied psychoanalytic theory to the individual in a social work context. Social diagnosis consisted of detailed histories of the individual, parental relationships, and significant events in the childhood and adolescence of the client. Social intervention involved the caseworker's interpretation and formulation of intervention plans based on present action to resolve past conflicts.

Ego psychology.   Ego psychology arose as a revision to psychoanalytic theory. It conceived of the ego as the major integrating force of the personality, bringing the internal person into relationship with the external world. The ego assumes the major functions of perception, adaptation, and equilibrium between the psychophysical needs and outside demands. The major contribution of ego psychology was the notion of the ego as an autonomous self that functioned independently of instinctual drives. Ego psychology categorized ego development according to successive life stages. The ego adapts or misadapts at crucial stage periods. During the life development stages, the ego relates early and past experiences to present and future anticipatory states. Mastery or failure at earlier stages affects the present course of the life crisis. At each stage there is normal stress, which could result in crisis overload. Ego mastery involves mobilizing adaptive coping mechanisms to deal with stress. Crisis intervention theory is derived from ego psychology.

Existential-humanistic theory.   Functional casework was the forerunner of humanistic and existential theory, which emphasized growth potential. Functional casework held a high view of man and societal relationships. There is an implicit faith in the innate striving of each person to be human and healthy in social growth. There are time phases of beginning, middle, and ending. Agency structure defines purpose and goals for the worker-client relationship. Freedom of choice involves the client's choosing to grow and change according to inner resources. The purpose of functional casework is to release human power, for individual fulfillment and social good, and social power, for social institutions and social policy.

Cognitive theory.   Cognitive theory focused on conscious thinking, which controls feeling and behavior. The client conceptualizes and verbalizes problems through thought processes. Language is the vehicle for reasoning, communication, and problem solving. Human beings process phenomena, which are translated into perceptions. Problem solving and task-centered casework have drawn on cognitive theory. In problem-solving, the worker helps the client to think through a problem situation. The problem-solving process consists of problem definition, cause and effect history, range of problem alternatives, choice selection solution, and feedback. Task-centered casework extends the problem-solving approach with empirical measurements. It uses a time-limited structure with task planning and implementation. Tasks are selected according to the unsatisfied wants of the client. Task work is based on specific goals and the contract plan. Major elements are problem specification, contracting, task planning, task review, task completion and goal resolution, and termination (Reid, 1978; Berlin, 1982).

Behavioral theory.   Behavioral theory has given social work practice a set of specific indicators for measuring client change in the practice process. It focuses on the selection of learned behavior, identification of behavioral antecedents and consequences, and behavioral change intervention. Behavior casework identifies dysfunctional behavior factors, formulates specific goals and contract negotiation, and establishes baseline and intervention measurements. It has influenced practice theory selection. Hepworth and Larsen (1982) ask:

> How then does one decide which theories to study in depth? The most important criterion to consider is *the extent to which a given theory has been supported by empirical research.* Obviously theories whose tenets have been affirmed through research and whose efficacy ha[s] likewise been established are preferable to theories that have not been subjected to rigorous empirical testing. [p. 10].

Social work practice is aware of empirical validation of client intervention when change procedures are implemented.

Applications to Minority Practice

Casework practice theories are applicable to minority clients. Psychodiagnostic casework is relevant when exploring past role relationships and significant family events. Themes such as prejudice and racism, generational differences, and cultural adjustments have past linkages to present cognitive, affective, and behavioral states. Ego psychology is helpful when a minority individual under stress and crisis discovers cultural values as a means of restoring coping mechanisms. For some minority clients, reconstruction of the crisis event involves working through cultural conflict and finding a resource in a significant-other person of the client's community. Existential-humanistic theories are useful with minority individuals who are in the midst of an identity crisis. Time limits and agency boundaries provide structure for direction and guidance. Cognitive problem solving with a task-centered approach fits the need for structure, logical planning, and concrete action. This practice strategy is effective with problems such as finding a job, parent and child conflicts, relocating after moving to the United States from another country, and other life adjustment areas. Behavioral casework affords an opportunity for clients to identify and relate specific behavioral indicators to a set of life issues. Pinpointing antecedents and consequences, formulating concrete goals and contracts, and instituting monitors to count behavior frequencies are steps that workers and clients can take.

Knowledge Theory and People of Color

Community Level

Because the ethnic minority experience is a multifaceted problem configuration, it is important to conceive of a range of knowledge theories that are applicable on several levels. On the community level, conflict theory speaks to the domination of the "haves," who have power and authority over the "have-nots." Murase (in press) explains that proponents of conflict theory view inequality as resulting from a struggle or competition for resources, privileges, and rewards that are in short supply. In this struggle, the groups in power get what they want and prevent the less powerful from getting what they want.

Racial minorities are kept in a subordinate position because it serves the interests of the dominant groups to maintain such a stratified system. Domestic colonialism is an ethnic minority application of conflict theory. It states that Whites utilize culture as an instrument for dominating minorities. White Americans in the 18th, 19th, and early 20th centuries sought to impose Euro-American family patterns on minority families while attempting to destroy minority family systems. Implicit in the application of conflict theory to ethnic minorities is the knowledge of minority history, which illustrates the conflict between the minority and majority society, particularly oppression and exploitation suffered by people of color. Institutional racism and blaming the victim are practices that reflect conflict and power dominance. In the process of being dominated, ethnic minorities have been relegated to a position of underdevelopment and dependency on a social structure similar to a colony in the classic sense. Conflict between the dominant society and colonized minorities occurs when the latter attempt to break those controls (Murase, in press).

On the basis of these observations of minority communities, social work has been cast as the social control arm of society. Minority clients seek out public welfare workers, who offer limited cash and material assistance in accordance with social regulations. Naturally, people of color are suspicious of social workers, who represent the distributors of human resources. Social workers should personalize their contact roles with poor and minority clients and learn to be advocates of social justice and equity in human services.

Family Level

On the minority family level, systems theory explains the individual within the family social system. A social system is a configuration of identified subsystems with prescribed roles and functions. The minority family is the major integrative entity for individual participation and interaction. It prescribes individual role performance within the values and beliefs of the family. A natural support system involves a network of individuals and groups brought together by a common bond. The extended family, friends, neighbors, minister, and community comprise an extensive support network.

The concept of psychohistorical experience is appropriate to minority family theory. Minority history involves a series of events that affect ethnic group development. The major emphasis of psychohistory is cultural intrusion, which has disrupted family systems. Red Horse is a particular proponent of this view with respect to Native Americans. Most Native American families have suffered from a psychohistorical experience that separated whole generations from the family system. For example, Native American children have been removed from natural family systems for what the U.S. government termed "protection from abusive environments" and "cultural enrichment." The government's rationale was to provide socioeconomic opportunities and education programs away from the nuclear family. Young adults were removed from kin systems for employment training programs at urban industrial sites. The elderly were isolated on reservations from younger generations or placed in long-term care facilities far from their homes. As a result, most Native American families strive to preserve culture and are suspicious of outside authorities and human service professionals (Red Horse, in press).

The same psychohistorical experience applies to Black, Latino, and Asian Americans, who historically have suffered cultural family intrusion. Poor Black families have been fractured by economic stress. Public assistance, loss of job, alcoholism, spouse and child abuse, and desertion are elements in the intrusive cycle. Latino Americans have felt the effects of economic cultural intrusion. Fathers and brothers of Mexican families have left their homes, crossed the border, worked as farm and sweat shop laborers, and suffered exploitation. The fracturing, disruption, and plight of these families attest to the psychohistorical experience of poor Latinos. Asian Americans have historically experienced family intrusion through a series of immigration exclusion acts during the first part of this century. As a result, many Chinese, Japanese, and Pilipino elderly are single men who came to this country as laborers and were unable to marry women of their ancestry because of immigration quota restrictions. These elderly men are now isolated individuals in urban and rural ghettos and have lost contact with relatives in their native countries.

Individual Level

On the minority individual level, role theory is useful to understand interactional behavior. George Herbert Mead developed the concepts of role and generalized other. The self is composed of attitudes of various individuals with whom the person interacts in his or her sphere. It reaches full development when a person's self comprises attitudes of particular individuals and the internalized attitudes of the community, the generalized other. In many minority communities, individuals learn family and community role relationships. The oldest son or daughter is invested with the role of a surrogate parent to younger brothers and sisters. The role of the father is authoritative in decision making, while the role of the mother is mediator between the wants of the children and the authority of the father. Role diffusion occurs when individual prescribed roles are rejected and the generalized other of the ethnic community is set aside. Role conflict arises between community role expectations and the wishes of the individual. The intent of role reintegration is to reach a balance between intended roles and personal choices.

Issues in Minority Knowledge Theory

The social worker often encounters the minority individual client who presents differential manifestations of minority group membership. Against the backdrop of ethnicity, culture, minority, social class, racism, prejudice, and discrimination is the minority individual who may or may not have been affected by those phenomena. The minority client is a unique representative of a corporate personality ethnic group. The social worker must carefully construct with the minority client the basis for which each factor—for example, ethnicity—influences the client's psychosocial identity as a person and as a member of a particular minority group. An awareness of the range of minority knowledge theory is the first step in subsequent utilization of relevant ethnic dimensions that impinge on the particular client.

It is crucial to delineate minority knowledge theory issues that address the situation of people of color. Rather than drawing implications for minorities from existing social work knowledge theories, there is a case for developing a minority theory base that influences social work practice thought. This section deals with issues of minority knowledge theory related to ethnicity, culture, minority, and social class. Each concept contains a body of knowledge crucial to understanding people of color. Social work theorists should integrate these themes into practice knowledge.

Ethnicity

The concept of ethnicity is fundamental to knowledge theory of minorities. Davis (1978) defines ethnicity as a sense of identity based on loyalty to a distinctive cultural pattern related to common ancestry, nation, religion, and/or race. Mindel and Habenstein (1981) explain the ethnic group as those who share a unique and social cultural heritage passed on from generation to generation and based on race, religion, and national identity. DeVos (1982) further places ethnicity in a time frame: (1) present-oriented membership as a citizen of a particular state or a member of an occupational group, (2) future-oriented membership in a transcendent, universal, religious, or political sense, or (3) past-oriented self defined by ethnic identity based on ancestry and origin. Ethnic definitions, according to DeVos, refer to an independent past culture that holds in common religious beliefs and practices, language, historical continuity, and/or common ancestry or place of origin.

Ethnicity is a powerful unifying force that gives one a sense of belonging based on commonality. Gordon (1964) observes that an ethnic group possesses a feeling of peoplehood. Likewise, Green (1982) states that members of an ethnic group have a sense of sharing. Recently there has emerged a sense of ethnic consciousness—that is, an awareness of distinctive ethnic culture. This influence was particularly strong in the 1960s and 1970s within the Black civil rights movement, which affected group mobilization of ethnic minorities. It also gave rise to a new awareness of White ethnic consciousness (Mindel & Habenstein, 1981). Ethnicity has become an organizing force that has provided a sense of community, a way of coping with an impersonal world, and a means of social mobilization in a minority context (Greeley, 1969).

Aspects of Ethnicity

There are numerous aspects of ethnicity that must be understood by social work practitioners. Green (1982) differentiates two dimensions of ethnicity: categorical and transactional. Categorical ethnicity refers to the manifestation of specific and distinctive traits, such as color, music, food, and socioeconomic status. Transactional ethnicity is concerned with the ways people behave and communicate their cultural distinctiveness. It defines social boundaries in terms of ceremonies, technology, language, and religion. Furthermore, Green (1982) argues that these idiosyncratic differences in ethnicity between the worker and client become the basis for a healthy sense of individual identity and capability. He refers to such ethnic resources as culturally based communication styles, healthy cultural values, and family and peer support. DeVos and Romanucci-Ross (1982) categorize four approaches to ethnicity:

1. ethnic or social behavior that ranges from organization to disorganization within social structure and produces social change;
2. patterns of social or ethnic interaction, including patterns of conformity and deviancy in ethnic behavior and social conflict accommodations;
3. focus on the self as the subjective experience of ethnic identity in terms of adaptation and maladaptation and changes in the life cycle or in social conditions;
4. personality patterns in ethnic behavior that emphasize adjustment and maladjustment as well as psychosexual and cognitive development.

These views of ethnicity tend to emphasize the ethnic person, ethnic social influence, or an interaction between the two.

Harwood (1981) points out that there are differences among people in a given ethnic group but its members nevertheless have common origins, a sense of identity, and shared standards of behavior to which professional providers from still other ethnic groups may be unable to respond appropriately. He further identifies three aspects of ethnicity that form the basis for collectivities or groups:

1. ethnic social ties of common origins;
2. ethnic shared standards of behavior or norms shaping the thoughts and behavior of individual members;
3. ethnic collective participation with one another in a larger social system.

There is a distinction between behavioral and ideological ethnicity. According to Harwood, behavioral ethnicity refers to distinctive values, beliefs, behavioral norms, and languages learned by members of an ethnic group during the socialization process. These distinctive cultural standards serve as the basis for interaction within the group and with members of other ethnic groups and for participation in the mainstream social institutions. Ideological ethnicity is based on customs such as special food preferences, the celebration of certain holidays, or the use of dialectal phrases or words from an ancestral language in speaking English. McGoldrick (1982a) identifies seven factors influencing ethnicity:

1. the stresses of migration to a new situation and the potential abandonment of much ethnic heritage;
2. the preservation of the languages spoken in the home;
3. the identity of race and country of origin;
4. the family place of residence in an ethnic neighborhood;
5. the socioeconomic status, educational achievement, and upward mobility of family members and the relationship of these factors to ethnic dissociation (the process of severing this and reducing identification with one's ethnic group as one moves up socioeconomically into the dominant society);
6. the emotional process (loyalty, ambivalence) in the family;
7. the political and religious ties to the ethnic group.

Behavioral Characteristics of Groups

There has been an effort to differentiate the behavioral characteristics of various ethnic groups. McGoldrick (1982b) has made preliminary observations on seven ethnic groups that tend toward stereotypic generalizations. However, they are useful in a continuing discussion of ethnic group behavior. The following is McGoldrick's tentative typology, derived from working with ethnic groups in a Bowen[1] family systems therapy approach:

Irish. The Irish rely on personal responsibility, privacy, and humor. They often have difficulty with closeness and tend to be cut off emotionally. There is a need to respect their personal boundaries and privacy. However, they may respond minimally but significantly. Humor is often used to create distance. The Irish tend to do silent cut-offs without discussing the issues, submerging the emotional response. They need individual encouragement, particularly feedback about continued work on their own.

[1] Murray Bowen's approach emphasizes interaction among family systems. See his *Family Therapy in Clinical Practice* (New York: Jason Aronson, 1978).

Italian. The Italian family is extremely enmeshed within family subsystems and has personal relationships with extended family. Separation is perceived by the family as betrayal. Small independent moves of family members may create great waves in the family. The disclosure of family secrets and breaking taboos can be problematic. Fathers may be threatened with losing their position when children, especially daughters, separate. There is a need to maintain family unity and strength.

Jewish. Jews tend to have extremely close and supportive relationships, tend to understand themselves, and are family oriented. They have positive value of Jewish heritage, but many Jewish families have closed off their feelings about experiences in the holocaust. Trips to Israel can put them in touch with cut-off aspects of family and culture. Family conflicts tend to center around money, family businesses, and attendance at family gatherings. Complaints about family members that are meant to help may instead escalate the problem. It is helpful to work with Jewish families around planning for gatherings (for example, a Bar Mitzvah or wedding).

WASP. WASPs (White Anglo-Saxon Protestants) are interested in family genealogy and background. There is a need for personal space, distance, and boundaries. Family triangles and issues tend to be covered over for reasons of respectability. It is difficult to get families to talk about feelings, particularly negative ones. Everyone keeps up appearances. Whites of this background respond to personal responsibility and privacy, being an individual in the family, and independent thinking and planning ahead.

Puerto Rican. Puerto Ricans are attached to the informal kinship network of extended kin, godparents, and neighbors who assist with childrearing. It is important to be connected with one's family. Enmeshment and the lack of differentiating from the family, particularly for the daughter, can create problems.

Black. Pride and a sense of connectedness with family and culture have special meaning for Blacks. It is important to ask about informal kinship systems and significant family connections. At times it may be difficult for Blacks to find out about their history. There may be anxiety about relating to certain dysfunctional family members and shame about aspects of family history.

Greek. Greeks have a strong sense of ethnic pride and cultural heritage. There is often much jealousy and competitiveness among family members. Rigid family roles lead to cultural conflict, particularly as the younger generation differentiates itself and becomes acculturated in this country. Individual work is preferred, since it would be difficult for them to expose themselves as a group.

Chinese. Chinese family structure focuses on a formalized family system with deep historical roots, unlike the family emotional system of Americans. An emphasis on the natural system and its allegiances would fit this formal family generational system.

As previously indicated, ethnicity is the basic foundation for individual and group identity. It is the unifying force that brings a people together on the basis of race, ancestry, nation, and/or religion. Social work practice utilizes these aspects of ethnicity to help a person "belong to," "relate to," and "take pride in." There are also ethnic characteristics and qualities that tend to differentiate groups: behavioral reactions, family structure, sense of cohesion, interactional intensity, and other aspects. Further investigation of ethnic dynamics and working with particular minority groups would be helpful to social workers and other human service professionals.

Culture

Culture deals with the social heritage of man. Gordon (1978) defines culture as the way of life of a society, consisting of prescribed ways of behaving or norms of conduct, beliefs, values, and skills. Brislin (1981) views culture from a cross-cultural contact perspective in terms of interaction with unfamiliar people and focusing on people's characteristic behavior, ideas, and values. Hodge, Struckmann, and Trost (1975) refer to culture as the sum total of life patterns passed on from generation to generation within a group of people. Culture includes institutions, language, values, religious ideals, habits of thinking, artistic expressions, and patterns of social and interpersonal relationships. Green (1982) explains culture as elements of a people's history, tradition, values, and social organization that become meaningful to participants in an encounter. The essential idea of these explanations is that culture reflects the lifestyle practices of particular groups of people who are influenced by a cultural pattern of values, beliefs, and behavioral modalities.

Cultural Pluralism

Cultural pluralism is a reality confronting current society. Pantoja and Perry (1976) define cultural pluralism as "a societal value and a societal goal [that] requires that the society permit the existence of multicultural communities that can live according to their own styles, customs, languages, and values without penalty to their members and without inflicting harm upon or competing for resources among themselves" (p. 81). Gordon (1978) observes that American society is a composite of groups who have preserved their own cultural identity. Within the cultural patterns of the national society is the cultural diversity of the ethnic subsociety. Gordon refers to this as the subculture of the ethnic subsociety. Within cultural pluralism are ethnic groups who maintain their own communal social structure and identity, values, and behavior patterns. In group relations there is a level of tolerance that holds as long as there is no conflict with the broader values, patterns, and legal norms of the entire society. McLemore (1983) has further distinguished two major forms of cultural pluralism: (1) conformity and merger with assimilation and (2) separation and antiassimilation. He depicts the range of cultural pluralism as extending from a high degree of assimilation of the majority culture and the retention of native heritage through middle-range assimilation of certain majority and minority areas to low social and marital assimilation. Figure 2-1 illustrates the span of cultural pluralism that McLemore describes.

Arising from this context of cultural pluralism is the problem of biculturalism and marginality. Gordon (1978) explains the dilemma of the marginal individual who stands on the border or margins of two cultural worlds and is a member of neither. This person may be from a racially mixed or interfaith marriage or may have personality and experiences that place him or her between the majority and minority groups. There are a number of directions for the marginal person: remain in the marginal position for an indefinite period, return to ethnic group of origin, or participate in a subsociety of marginal people who have a commonality of lifestyle. However, cultural resolution, whether it be with the majority, minority, or another subculture, is vital for the well-being and purposeful direction of the individual.

	Complete Anglo conformity	Complete separation
Cultural assimilation:	X (high acceptance of host culture)	X (low rejection of native culture)
Secondary structural assimilation:	X (high "integration" in education, occupations, residence, political participation, and mass recreation)	X (low "integration" in religious, health and welfare, and "social" recreational activities)
Primary structural assimilation:		X (low in out-group friendships)
Marital assimilation:		X (no out-group marriages)

Figure 2-1.   The range of assimilation within a context of cultural pluralism. *(From* Racial and Ethnic Relations in America, *2nd Ed., by S. D. McLemore, p. 99. Copyright ©1983 by Allyn and Bacon, Inc. Reprinted by permission.)*

Behavioral Effects of Culture

Various functional characteristics of culture underscore its importance as a major behavioral influence. Price-Williams (1979) believes that culture is a qualifying variable representing the mainstream of cross-cultural study. As such, the cultural factor is central to an understanding of the dynamic ways people function and interact in their primary environment. Bilmes and Boggs (1979) view culture as the intersubjective phenomenon connecting the individual as the bearer of culture with the group as the locus of culture. A major implication is that without a cultural tie the individual is unrelated to his or her primary group, from which identity and meaning derive. With the cultural linkage as the interface, the individual is able to relate to and communicate with his group locus. Figure 2-2 illustrates this foundation of culture.

Bilmes and Boggs (1979) state that culture governs behavior in that it is synonymous with conduct, habit, and customs. Likewise Draguns (1979) asserts that culture shapes behavior and personality and that behavior rooted in individual personalities produces

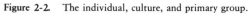

Individual ◄─────────────── Culture ──────────────► Group
(bearer of culture)   (intersubjective factor)   (locus of culture)

Figure 2-2.   The individual, culture, and primary group.

degrees of cultural change. Furthermore, culture is conceived as a code that guides interpretation of behavior. It is a primary element of the cognitive system that makes actions intelligible to others (Bilmes & Boggs, 1979) and provides ways of communicating, thinking, and interacting with one another and one's environment (Ciborowski, 1979). Finally, culture is a system of knowledge: parts of the behavior code exist in the minds of some members of the cultural group (Bilmes & Boggs, 1979).

The foregoing discussion has established the primary role of culture as a mechanism for functioning. However, there are certain elements of culture that interact in clusters. These components of culture can be classified according to the following (Cuellar, 1984):

1. collective cultural influences (ways of relating within the group view and use of time, language, beliefs, group experience, group identity, and way of life);
2. cultural choices (food, dress, accepted norms and values, lifestyle, religion, emphasis on education);
3. cultural arts (music, dancing, architecture, and other forms of expression);
4. cultural coping systems (child rearing practices, family structure and network, ways of identifying problems, ways of problem-solving, and use of available resources).

Theories of Culture

In order to amplify the importance of culture, we present three theories of culture with brief explanations: cultural system, cultural duality, and cross-cultural relations. These theories represent particular cultural emphases affecting human behavior and social functioning. As such, they underscore the primary influence of culture as an essential part of the client's make-up.

Culture-centered systems theory.   Bates and Harvey (1975) present a culture-centered systems theory that highlights the essential core of culture as society in a latent state. Culture is society stored in the memories of society's members or latent behavior patterns awaiting the conditions that will reactivate that portion of the social system. Personality combined with culture produces certain individual capabilities:

1. organic capacities, disabilities, drives, or motivations;
2. perception mechanisms and equipment;
3. organic memory, recall, and associational mechanisms;
4. neurological motor control mechanisms;
5. learned memory content, such as experiential and factual information and learned attitudes toward culture, self, and others.

Society is the social system. Situational and interactional factors account for the way latent behavior becomes active. They serve as the mechanism whereby society as stored cultural patterns meets society as actual action. Figure 2-3 illustrates the relationship among culture, personality, and society. In the view of Bates and Harvey, culture consists of behavioral rules that are stored as a learned program for action. Culture interacts with personality to result in overt behavior. In turn, society is the behavior performed by members in relation to one another.

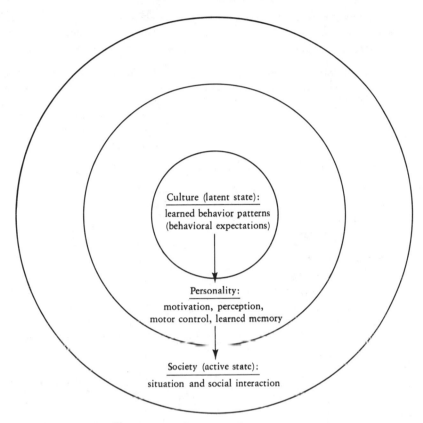

Figure 2-3. Culture-centered systems theory.

Cultural duality theory.   Chestang (1976) has presented a social work knowledge theory that relates to the role of environment as an influence on social functioning. Affecting the Black experience (which is applicable to minorities in general) are three social-environmental conditions that have an impact on the person: social injustice, societal inconsistency, and personal impotence. Social injustice is the denial of legal rights and as such is a violation of social agreements. Social inconsistency is the institutionalized disparity or contradiction between word (affirmation of self-worth and esteem) and deed (societal rejection, demeaning of minority culture and ethnicity). Personal impotence is the sense of powerlessness to influence the environment. Furthermore, the Black person is tied to the larger society through incorporating its values, norms, and beliefs. The incorporation of the dominant culture means that the individual has been acculturated by the prevailing social system. The social conditions confronting Blacks cause a split in the acculturative process, resulting in a cultural duality.

In consequence, the Black person has established a cultural duality consisting of sustentative and nutritive aspects of culture. Sustentative aspects consist of tools, weapons, shelter, material goods and services for livelihood, physical comfort, and safety. They pertain to the instinct for survival. Nutritive aspects relate to attitudes and beliefs, ideas and judgments, codes, institutions, arts and sciences, philosophy, and social organization for expressive thinking, feeling, and behavior. They fulfill needs for psychological and social gratification, identity, intimacy, and emotional support. Brown (no date) has applied the dual perspective concept to Native Americans:

> Native Americans, as other ethnic minority populations, have experienced much incongruence between the two systems. The nurturing culture has validated the individual and family and generally produces feelings of positive self-worth and being valued. The sustaining system has given messages and structural rigidity which devalued Indian people and their ways. The difference between these two systems has led to institutional racism. To cope with the situation, it becomes necessary for Indians to develop two ways of relating and coping: one set of behaviors for the nurturing system and another set for use in the sustaining system. In the nurturing system, one can have status, respect and clearly-defined roles and contributions. In the sustaining system, the same person or family may roleless and be judged as worthless, resistant, inadequate or problematic. Self-esteem is high in one system; it is challenged and eroded in the other [p. 114].

The duality of culture has an impact on character development, which is an adaptation to the sustaining and nurturing environments. There are two types of character development. The depreciated character incorporates society's negative attributions and emerges from the sustaining environment. The transcendent character incorporates positive ethnic community images and is supported by the nurturing environment. Culture plays a strategic role in both types of character development. From Chestang's perspective, culture in the form of the cultural duality is a response to social environmental conditions and results in character development adaptation (see Figure 2-4).

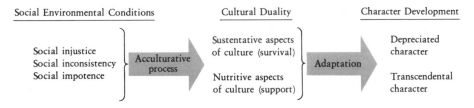

Figure 2-4.   Cultural duality theory.

Cross-cultural relations theory. Bochner (1982) presents a cross-cultural relations theory that begins with the premise that human beings are social creatures who interact as individuals, as groups, and as societies. Individuals belong to family, work, recreational, worship, artistic, and political groups. These groups tend to be hierarchically organized. Social groups reflect culturally homogeneous and heterogeneous societies. In the United States, there are culturally diverse groups composed of many different ethnic subgroups. Societies and cultures can be compared internally and externally with others. Societies differ internally in cultural homogeneity and externally in terms of cultural dimensions.

Given these groups and subgroups, there are major differences between interactions among members of the same society and interactions that cross group boundaries. Race, skin color, language, and religion are determining factors. In-group and out-group ("us" and "them") differentiation suggests that out-group members are seen in more stereotypic terms than members of the in-group. Bochner asserts that discrimination against out-group members could be reduced by individuating them. He summarizes research that explains reductions and increases in prejudicial attitudes, social perceptions, attributions, and behavioral indexes. When contact occurs between groups within the same society or between two or more societies, the range of possible outcomes includes genocide, assimilation, segregation, and integration. Genocide is the systematic and ruthless killing of members of a group by a majority or technologically superior group. Assimilation takes place when a group or society gradually adopts or is forced to adopt the customs, beliefs, and lifestyles of a dominant culture. Minority members become culturally and physically indistinguishable from the mainstream after a few generations. The working assumption of the dominant group seems to be that assimilated groups are inferior and self-rejecting and the majority culture is superior to the minority. Segregation occurs when the dominant majority or minority group adopts a policy of separatism (with respect to one or more areas such as geography, culture, schools, marriage) to keep unwanted people, ideas, and influences out. Integration happens in a culturally pluralistic society when different groups maintain their cultural identity and yet merge into a single group. Differences in worship, politics, recreation, occupation, and other areas coexist within a broad framework of identity, values, and goals. There are examples of different cultures coming into contact geographically and politically. On the individual level, the outcome of cultural contact can range from cultural rejection to acceptance, each having its effects on the person.

Bochner suggests that cross-cultural relations can be enhanced if each person can regard the other as a different but interesting person. Contact with an outsider is an opportunity to learn about the world at large and another culture in particular. Both parties must be sensitive to the impact that they have on each other and each must make an effort to learn about the other's culture. Figure 2-5 explains the dynamic elements of cross-cultural relations theory.

Minority

Along with the concepts of ethnicity and culture, the term *minority* is central to a discussion of issues in ethnic minority theory. Davis (1978) defines a minority as a group that is discriminated against or subjected to differential and unequal treatment. It is characterized as subordinate, dominated, relatively powerless, and unequal in other ways. Traditionally the term *minorities* has referred to racial, national, and religious groups but it has recently been applied to women, the aged, the physically handicapped, and the behaviorally deviant. Mindel and Habenstein (1981) view a minority as having unequal access to power and as being stigmatized for traits perceived by the majority as inferior. (According to these definitions, a minority group may not always be smaller *in number* than the dominant majority; a larger population may still be subordinate or disadvantaged, hence a minority).

Longres (1982) analyzes the dynamics of minority versus majority. Majority and minority interest groups differ in power and influence as well as in position of dominance or subordination. Minority group members tend to have fewer rights and less power than the majority, to have a history of disadvantage, and to lack privilege. Under

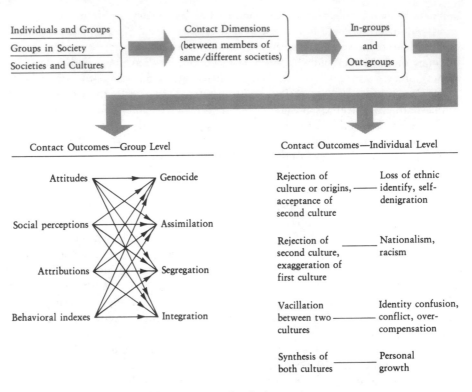

Figure 2-5.   Cross-cultural relations theory.

these conditions, minorities seek to eliminate the domination of the majority. The success of minority groups in overcoming subordination depends on their capacity to work on their own behalf and on the response of the majority.

Davis (1978) likewise points out the discrimination of the dominant community against minority groups. Discrimination is manifested through the control of businesses, occupations, choice property, government, public facilities, and exclusive organizational membership. Dominant groups value their sense of superiority and perceive action toward the improvement of minority status as a threat to peace and order. It is therefore important to estimate the possibilities and probabilities of change.

Minority Relationships with the Dominant Culture

There are several points of group contact and interaction at which minority status is particularly significant. At the time of immigration, racial and cultural groups enter another's territory as minorities. Racial and cultural minorities are formed when political boundaries are created during territorial expansion and when war and peace treaties are signed. Shifts of political power occur when a former minority becomes politically dominant and the ascendant group loses its controlling power, as, for example, at the decolonization of a country and the transfer of power and government to a formerly subjected people. Social groups also emerge with distinctive beliefs and practices in lifestyle, religion, or politics. Homosexuals, the Mormons, and the American Communist Party are diverse groups who created new subcultures with marked differences from the dominant social patterns. Finally, minorities differentiated biologically (on the basis of sex, age, or physical condition) are assigned socially discriminatory status and are given prime attention in the public media.

Minority groups interact with the dominant society through competition and conflict. Groups compete for scarce resources such as jobs, housing, welfare, and other essentials. Conflict occurs when groups meet in direct rivalry ranging in form from verbal exchanges to eliminating the other group from competition. However, "small groups may become powerful if they have sufficient economic resources, unity, organization, coordination with other groups, community prestige, access to the mass media and to political decision makers, and other advantages" (Davis, 1978, p. 30). Social workers should assess the particular situations of contact for ethnic minority clients in terms of the conflict and competition between dominant and minority groups.

Cultural Assimilation

Cultural assimilation is related to the concept of minority. Davis (1978) defines assimilation as a process whereby a group gradually merges with another, losing its separate identity and pride in distinctive cultural traits. The degree of assimilation is based on the modification of cultural traits (such as native language, naming system, traditional values, and model personality characteristics). Partial assimilation refers to selective participation in the dominant culture (for example, job occupation in the dominant society, ethnic community activities in one's own minority group) (Brislin, 1981). Full assimilation is achieved when immigrant minorities and their children leave behind their ethnicity and blend fully into the majority group (McLemore, 1983).

Related to the degree of assimilation are two basic dimensions: cultural and structural assimilation. The former refers to acculturation, or the replacement of minority group cultural traits with those of the dominant community. The latter deals with integration of social interaction, or the replacement of minority group institutions and informal social patterns with participation in the dominant community. The dominant society is more apt to allow minority assimilation on a cultural than on a structural level. It resists the assimilation of minorities into social institutions (intermarriage), organizations (social club, church), and social primary groups (family) (Davis, 1978). Although assimilation of dominant values and practices does occur, ethnic minorities increasingly are maintaining their own culture. Assimilation, in this sense, relates to our previous discussions of ethnic distinctions and cultural pluralism.

Social Class

A final issue in minority knowledge theory is social class. Gordon (1978) defines social class in terms of social hierarchical arrangements of persons on the basis of differences in power, political power, or social status. Gordon (1978) has coined the term *ethclass* to relate ethnic minorities and social class status. Ethclass refers to the social participation or identity of persons who are confined to their own social class and ethnic group. Ethclass is a subculture that falls under the social structure of a society. It is a set of social relationships within which members relate to each other and to major social institutional activities.

Willie has conducted recent research on ethnic minorities, particularly Black families, and social class. Willie (1979) views social stratification in terms of a horizontal dimension of class behavior and a vertical dimension of caste groups. Occupation, education, and income constitute the important horizontal variables of social class. Race or ethnicity, sex, and age make up the principal vertical categories of social caste. Furthermore, Willie (1981) asserts that racial discrimination, not limited education, contributes to minority inequality in employment and income. He presents case studies of affluent, working-class, and poor Black families.

Affluent Blacks are termed the conformists and belong to middle-class families with both husband and wife employed. Both rely on the public sector for jobs, women as teachers in the public schools and men in postal, business, and professional positions. Both spouses cooperate on work at home, encourage education, and are involved in community affairs. They are achievement and work oriented and upwardly mobile, and they own personal property.

Working-class Blacks are the innovators who struggle for survival and depend on the cooperative efforts of husband, wife, and children. Income is just above the poverty line. Families include five or more children. Parents are literate but have limited education. As a result, racial discrimination and insufficient education delimit the employment opportunities for working-class Blacks. Long working hours and two jobs, after-school and weekend jobs for children, stable work history, and long-term neighborhood residency characterize this group. They own their own home, raise their children with a strong sense of morality, and are self-reliant.

Poor Blacks are termed the rebels; they cope with low income status through extended households. Families subsist at near or below the poverty level and are often part of broken homes. Jobs, houses, communities, spouses, and friends are in flux. Unemployment is a constant threat, with women in service occupations and men employed as unskilled factory workers and maintenance men. Marriage and child-rearing occur during the middle teenage years. Some families have eight or more children. First marriages may dissolve, with other marital arrangements taking their place. Parents of this group are grade school or high school dropouts. Juvenile delinquency may occur as a result of unstable parental relationships. There is fierce loyalty between mothers, children, and grandmothers. Brothers and sisters may loyally help maintain family functions when both parents work outside the home. Because of this situation, poor Black families rebel and reject society and experience failure and disappointment. When their hope is taken away, violent rebellion is a means of resistance.

Harwood (1981) observes that there is a relationship between ethnicity and social class:

> Within the larger American social system, some ethnic groups are to a significant degree confined to lower-class positions because of barriers to both power and economic resources that are built into the status system by informal and, to some extent still, legal norms. Individual mobility in the class system is also limited for members of these groups. Although the reasons for these political and economic barriers may be explained differently by social scientists of various theoretical persuasions, few would deny that Blacks, Native Americans,

and Hispanics in the United States disproportionately occupy the lowest strata of the class system and have historically been restrained within these strata by legal and economic means [p. 5].

For ethnic minorities, social class is influenced by racial discrimination and socioeconomic constraints. Although people of a particular minority group may occupy different social class levels, coping with survival and the reality of racism are forces that bind people of color together.

Conclusion

We started with an examination of traditional social work values, ethics, and knowledge theory that are familiar to social work practitioners. However, along with these concepts are discussions of ethnic minority values and knowledge issues that clearly point to an alternative direction. Minority values tend to be collective, centering on family, authority hierarchy, spirituality, and identity. Issues in minority knowledge are concerned with ethnicity, emphasizing ethnic group behavior, cultural pluralism, minority versus majority dynamics, and social class. These value and knowledge components form the basis for an orientation to minority social work practice.

The following chapter builds on this foundation, constructing the framework for ethnic minority social work practice. Process stages, worker-client interaction, and task-oriented action are components of this approach.

References

Addams, J. (1907). *Newer ideals of peace.* New York: Chautauqua Press.

Alvirez, D., Bean, F. D., & Williams, D. (1981). The Mexican American family. In C. H. Mindel, & R. W. Habenstein (Eds.), *Ethnic families in America: Patterns and variations* (pp. 269-292). New York: Elsevier.

Argyle, M. (1982). Inter-cultural communication. In S. Bochner (Ed.), *Cultures in contact: Studies in cross-cultural interaction* (pp. 61-79). Oxford: Pergamon Press.

Bates, F. L., & Harvey, C. C. (1975). *The structure of social systems.* New York: Gardner Press.

Berlin, S. B. (1982). Cognitive behavioral interventions for social work practice. *Social Work, 27,* 218-226.

Bilmes, J., & Boggs, S. T. (1979). Language and communication: The foundations of culture. In A. J. Marsella, R. G. Tharp, & T. J. Ciborowski (Eds.), *Perspectives on cross-cultural psychology* (pp. 47-76). New York: Academic Press.

Bochner, S. (1982). *Cultures in contact: Studies in cross-cultural interaction.* Oxford: Pergamon Press.

Brislin, R. W. (1981). *Cross-cultural encounters: Face-to-face interaction.* New York: Pergamon Press.

Brown, E. G. (no date). Social work practice with Indian families. In E. F. Brown, & T. F. Shaughnessy (Eds.), *Introductory text: Education for social work practice with American Indian families* (pp. 109-152). Tempe, Ariz.: Arizona State University School of Social Work, American Indian Projects for Community Development, Training and Research.

Brown, J. E. (1969). The persistence of essential values among North American Plains Indians. *Studies in Comparative Religion, 3*, 216–225.

Chestang, L. (1976). Environmental influences on social functioning: The Black experience. In P. San Juan Cafferty & L. Chestang (Eds.), *The diverse society: Implications for social policy* (pp. 59–74). Washington, D.C.: National Association of Social Workers.

Ciborowski, T. J. (1979). Cross-cultural aspects of cognitive functioning: Culture and knowledge. In A. J. Marsella, R. G. Tharp, & T. J. Ciborowski (Eds.), *Perspectives on cross-cultural psychology* (pp. 101–116). New York: Academic Press.

Compton, B. R., & Galaway, B. (Eds.). (1979). *Social work processes.* Homewood, Ill.: Dorsey Press.

Cuellar, B. (1984, March). *Components of culture.* Paper presented at the meeting of the Council on Social Work Education, Detroit.

Davis, F. J. (1978). *Minority-dominant relations: A sociological analysis.* Arlington Heights, Ill.: AHM Publishing Corporation.

DeVos, G. (1982). Ethnic pluralism: Conflict and accommodation. In G. DeVos & L. Romanucci-Ross (Eds.), *Ethnic identity: Cultural continuities and change* (pp. 5–41). Chicago: University of Chicago Press.

DeVos, G., & Romanucci-Ross, L. (1982). Ethnicity: Vessel of meaning and emblem of contrast. In G. DeVos & L. Romanucci-Ross (Eds.), *Ethnic identity: Cultural continuities and change* (pp. 363–390). Chicago: University of Chicago Press.

Draguns, J. G. (1979). Culture and personality. In A. J. Marsella, R. G. Tharp, & T. J. Ciborowski (Eds.), *Perspectives on cross-cultural psychology* (pp. 179–207). New York: Academic Press.

Fritzpatrick, J. P. (1981). The Puerto Rican family. In C. H. Mindel & R. W. Habenstein (Eds.), *Ethnic families in America: Patterns and variations* (pp. 189–214). New York: Elsevier.

Gary, L. E. (1978). *Support systems in Black communities: Implications for mental health services for children and youth.* Washington, D.C.: Howard University Mental Health Research Center, Institute for Urban Affairs and Research.

Germain, C. B., & Gitterman, A. (1980). *The life model of social work practice.* New York: Columbia University Press.

Goldstein, H. (1973). *Social work practice: A unitary approach.* Columbia, S.C.: University of South Carolina Press.

Gordon, M. M. (1964). *Assimilation in American life.* New York: Oxford University Press.

Gordon, M. M. (1978). *Human nature, class, and ethnicity.* New York: Oxford University Press.

Greeley, A. M. (1969). *Why can't they be like us?* New York: Institute of Human Relations Press.

Green, J. W. (1982) *Cultural awareness in the human services.* Englewood Cliffs, N.J.: Prentice-Hall.

Harwood, A. (Ed.) (1981). *Ethnicity and medical care.* Cambridge: Harvard University Press.

Hepworth, D. H., & Larsen, J. A. (1982). *Direct social work practice: Theory and skills.* Homewood, Ill.: Dorsey Press.

Higginbotham, H. H. (1979). Culture and mental health services. In A. J. Marsella, R. G. Tharp, & T. J. Ciborowski (Eds.), *Perspectives on cross-cultural psychology.* New York: Academic Press.

Hodge, J. L., Struckmann, D. K., & Trost, L. D. (1975). *Cultural bases of racism and group oppression.* Berkeley: Two Riders Press.

Jenkins, S. (1981). *The ethnic dilemma in social services.* New York: Free Press.

Keith-Lucas, A. (1971). Ethics in social work. In R. Morris (Ed.), *Encyclopedia of social work* (pp. 324–328). New York: National Association of Social Workers.

Kent, R., & Tse, S. (1980). *The roots of social work in Christianity.* Unpublished master's thesis, California State University, Sacramento.

Kenyatta, M. I. (1980). The impact of racism on the family as a support system. *Catalyst,* *2,* 37–44.

Kitano, H. L. (1974). *Race relations.* Englewood Cliffs, N.J.: Prentice-Hall.

Lewis, R. (1977). Cultural perspective on treatment modalities with Native Americans.

Longres, J. F. (1982). Minority groups: An interest-group perspective. *Social Work, 27,* 7–14.

McGoldrick, M. (1982a). Ethnicity and family therapy; An overview. In M. McGoldrick, J. K. Pearce, & J. Giordano (Eds.), *Ethnicity and family therapy* (pp. 3–30). New York: Guilford Press.

McGoldrick, M. (1982b). *Notes on Bowen systems therapy with different ethnic groups.* Unpublished discussion paper.

McLemore, S. D. (1983). *Racial and ethnic relations in America (2nd ed.).* Boston: Allyn & Bacon.

Mendes, H. A. (in press). Black American families. In D. Lum & M. Zuniga (Eds.), *Ethnic minority social work practice: Individual, family, and community dimensions.*

Meyer, C. H. (1976). *Social work practice: The changing landscape.* New York: Free Press.

Mindel, C. H., & Habenstein, R. W. (1981). Family lifestyles of America's ethnic minorities: An introduction. In C. H. Mindel & R. W. Habenstein (Eds.), *Ethnic families in America: Patterns and variations* (pp. 1–13). New York: Elsevier.

Mokuau, N. (in press). Asian American individuals. In D. Lum & M. Zuniga (Eds.), *Ethnic minority social work practice: Individual, family, and community dimensions.*

Murase, K. (in press). Asian American communities. In D. Lum & M. Zuniga (Eds.), *Ethnic minority social work practice: Individual, family, and community dimensions.*

Northen, H. (1982). *Clinical social work.* New York: Columbia University Press.

Pantoja, A., & Perry, W. (1976) Social work in a culturally pluralistic society: An alternative paradigm. In M. Sotomayor (Ed.), *Cross cultural perspectives in social work practice and education* (pp. 79–94). Houston: University of Houston Graduate School of Social Work.

Pedersen, P. (1979). Non-Western psychology: The search for alternatives. In A. J. Marsella, R. G. Tharp, & T. J. Ciborowski (Eds.), *Perspectives on cross-cultural psychology.* New York: Academic Press.

Pincus, A., & Minahan, A. (1973). *Social work practice: Model and method.* Itasca, Ill.: F.E. Peacock.

Price, J. A. (1981). North American Indian families. In C. H. Mindel & R. W. Habenstein (Eds.), *Ethnic families in America: Patterns and variations* (pp. 245–268). New York: Elsevier North Holland.

Price-Williams, D. (1979). Modes of thought in cross-cultural psychology: An historical overview. In A. J. Marsella, R. G. Tharp, & T. J. Ciborowski (Eds.), *Perspectives on cross-cultural psychology* (pp. 3–16). New York: Academic Press.

Red Horse, J. G. (in press). Native American families. In D. Lum & M. Zuniga (Eds.), *Ethnic minority social work practice: Individual, family, and community dimensions.*

Red Horse, J. G., Lewis, R., Feit, M., & Decker, J. (1978). Family behavior of urban American Indians. *Social Casework, 59,* 67–72.

Reid, W. J. (1978). *The task-centered system.* New York: Columbia University Press.

Rokeach, M. (1973). *The nature of human values.* New York: Free Press.

Roll, S., Millen, L., & Martinez, R. (1980). Common errors in psychotherapy with Chicanos: Extrapolations from research and clinical experience. *Psychotherapy: Theory, Research, and Practice, 17,* 156–168.

Ruiz, R. A., & Padilla, A. M. (1977). Counseling Latinos. *Personnel and Guidance Journal, 55,* 401–408.

Staples, R. (1976). *Introduction to Black sociology.* New York: McGraw-Hill.

Staples, R. (1981). The Black American family. In C. H. Mindel & R. W. Habenstein (Eds.), *Ethnic families in America: Patterns and variations* (pp. 217–244). New York: Elsevier.

Sue, D. W. (1973). Ethnic identity. In S. Sue & N. Wagner (Eds.), *Asian Americans: Psychological perspective* (pp. 140–149). Ben Lomond, Calif.: Science and Behavior Books.

Willie, C. V. (1979). *Caste and class controversy.* Bayside, N.Y.: General Hall.

Willie, C. V. (1981). *A new look at Black families.* Bayside, N.Y.: General Hall.

3

A Framework for Social Work Practice with People of Color

How far has ethnic minority social work practice progressed in the human services? Jenkins declares: "the social welfare field, although deeply involved in serving ethnic clients and training ethnic workers, has only recently and in peripheral ways acknowledged the need for ethnic content in therapeutic and service approaches" (Jenkins, 1981, p. 4). There are a number of reasons for this lag. Green (1982) cites major theoretical and methodological deficiencies in areas such as training techniques, evaluation schedules, and systematic case studies; abstract directives; and the anecdotal nature of minority data. Cheetham (1982) further criticizes the response of social work to multiracial communities for being patchy, piecemeal, and lacking in strategy. It has relied on generic problem analysis and treatment to the exclusion of recognizing ethnic and racial differences. A starting point for remedying the shortcomings is to develop a practice typology or framework that serves as a guideline for minority groups, settings, and service patterns.

A framework for direct practice is designed to orient social work practitioners to working with people of color in a systematic and effective manner. As a result, the social worker has a perspective on direct practice (working directly with clients as opposed to working in administration) from which to operate as a helping person. A framework sets an operational perimeter and identifies certain procedural principles to be followed in the helping effort. It provides the social worker with a degree of flexibility within guidelines. It also emphasizes specific ethnic minority subthemes that are unique to working with people of color.

In this chapter, we begin by considering existing minority frameworks in relation to the current state of the field. Next we present an overview of a model for the direct practice of ethnic minority social work that is the basis of this book. Particular practice process-stage issues are explained in detail. Subsequent chapters cover the various stages, with detailed ethnic practice principles, case illustrations, and procedural recommendations.

Existing Frameworks for Minority Social Work

Minority social work practice frameworks have emerged in the decade of the 1980s as a result of individual and group efforts. In this section, we plan to cover a traditional social work practice ethnic-sensitive approach and a cross-cultural awareness practice perspective. These treatments are preliminary background to the development of our ethnic practice framework model.

Framework for Traditional Ethnic-Sensitive Practice

In 1981 Devore and Schlesinger wrote the first book on ethnic social work practice; such a work was long overdue in the field of direct practice. In the broadest sense, it covers ethnicity, social class, and social work practice and adopts sociological and psychological insights to practice needs. Its particular emphasis is the delineation of how class and ethnic factors contribute to the process of assessment and intervention. Two basic themes underlie the need to relate traditional social work practice to ethnic content: (1) that ethnicity and social class shape life's problems and influence problem resolution and (2) that problem-solving social work must simultaneously focus on micro and macro problems. These emphases draw heavily on human behavior and practice approaches of social work.

Foundation

Devore and Schlesinger place an emphasis on understanding ethnic reality on the basis of general knowledge of human behavior and specific knowledge of ethnic group and social class. Ethnic reality is composed of ethclass, ethnicity, and social class. Human behavior is explained in terms of Erik Erikson's theory of the life cycle focusing on specific stages with ethnic minority content. Together with ethnic reality, there are layers of understanding that form the foundation of social work practice. The first layer is a basic knowledge of human behavior, incorporating human development and the life cycle, social role, systems theory, and understanding of personality, and knowledge of agency structure, goals, and functions. These subjects are generally covered in social work courses on behavior and reflect human, social, economic, and cultural influences on people and the environment. The second layer involves self-awareness in terms of the client's ethnicity and its influence on practice. The emphasis is on cultivating the client's ethnic "who am I" awareness from the dual standpoint of the parents' ethnicity and the client's religious heritage. The third layer is the impact of ethnic reality on the client's daily life. Work, housing, marital and family relations, child-rearing, health, food, and institutional assistance interact with ethnic background.

Ethnic-sensitive social work practice draws on an understanding of human behavior, clarifying its relationship with problem causation and practice application. There are no new approaches to social work practice in Devore and Schlesinger. Rather there is an effort to evaluate the dimensions of ethnic reality found in the psychosocial, problem-solving, social provision and structural, and systems approaches. Part of the problem in adapting traditional social work practice theory to minority practice is the peripheral treatment it gives to cultural content. Due to its limited focus on ethnic issues, it leaves most minority content to inference. Consequently, few principles for practice with people of color can be drawn from traditional schools of practice.

Working Principles

Unique to the framework for ethnic-sensitive social work practice are assumptions, principles, and skills related to working with minorities:

- History has a bearing on the generation and solution of problems. The history of minority group oppression and the experience of migration into the United States have an effect on individual members of the group. This ethnic history has an effect on personality and lifestyle.
- The present is affected by the past and accompanying problems. Ethnic group history may influence perception of present problems. The ethnic reality of minority environmental conditions shapes the scope of the problem.
- Ethnic reality is a source of cohesion, identity, and strength or strain, discordance, and strife. Minority family values, extended family structure, cultural and religious rituals and celebrations, ethnic schools, and language are sources of support or conflict. These variables have an influence on individual behavior patterns.
- Nonconscious phenomena affect functioning, particularly cultural routines and dispositions toward life. They are part of the self and evoke emotional response.
- Simultaneous attention to micro and macro issues requires the integration of individual and systematic change. Economic and social inequity in the form of racism, poverty, and discrimination underscores the structural source of the problem and the effect on the individual.
- Understanding of the ethnic community means that the social worker should be familiar with population characteristics, availability of resources, and neighborhood networks that can assist clients. Census material, community publications, and interviews with community leaders are ways of uncovering and mastering community dynamics.
- Knowledge of human behavior and self-awareness focuses on ethnic family life trends and group cognitive, affective, and behavioral responses. Particular class and ethnic dispositions about language, culture, and social problems have a bearing on how clients respond to workers. Workers must likewise recognize how their own ethnic background affects their behavior.
- Gathering data prior to the worker-client encounter is a way to review, synthesize, and order information about the client, problem, and referral. It is particularly important to have information on ethnic background, social class, and issues of racism or prejudice involved.
- Problem identification consists of setting the stage, utilizing empathetic community responses, and specifying or particularizing the problem. Some suggestions for the worker are to draw on available information as much as possible before the encounter; to alternate between open-ended and closed questions; to reflect facts and expressed feelings; to share feelings appropriate to the situation and offer opinions and ideas that will increase knowledge of the situation; to be responsive to requests for concrete services; to move slowly toward reaching for feelings; to

convey facts readily; to be imaginative in finding ways to learn about the problem; to understand who are the appropriate actors; to start with the client's perception of the problem; and to ascertain the link between individual functioning and the social situation.

- Contracting occurs when there is agreement on how to proceed, what might be accomplished, and what are the goals.
- Problem solving consists of ongoing reassessment of the problem, subdivision of the problem into manageable parts, identification of obstacles, obtaining and sharing of information, review of progress or setback, and termination.

The framework of Devore and Schlesinger was a preliminary effort to introduce ethnic and cultural meaning into social work practice and to interpret the minority implications of existing modalities of social work practice. Relationship building, problem identification, contracting, and problem solving are traditional concepts of social work practice and were applied to ethnic situations. This approach demonstrated that traditional social work practice could be infused with ethnic meaning.

Framework for Cross-Cultural Awareness Practice

Following the publication of Devore and Schlesinger, Green (1982) published his book *Cultural Awareness in the Human Services* as a group effort of the University of Washington social work faculty. Committed to a multiethnic perspective on the delivery of human services, it places a major emphasis on cultural awareness, or the background of cultural groups. The cross-cultural framework draws on the anthropological theories of Barth (ethnic group), Kleinman (health-seeking behavior), and Spradley (ethnosemantics and ethnographic interviewing). It recognizes that ethnic minority clients are entitled to competent social services but that social work has been insensitive to cultural differences and rarely considered its relation to minority communities. A cross-cultural model of social work is designed to apply to cross-cultural encounters, organize ethnographic client information, and be useful to a range of social service activities. *Ethnicity* is a key term in this approach. *Categorical ethnicity* refers to manifest cultural differences of individuals and groups, whereas *transactional ethnicity* denotes the ways in which people communicate to maintain their sense of cultural distinctiveness.

Help-Seeking Behavior

Green adopts a model for what he terms *help seeking behavior;* his model recognizes the diverse perceptions of ethnic groups in a pluralistic society. Language is a key communicative modality to explain and evaluate experience. A problem is both a personal and a social event. It elicits individual reactions and requires confirmation from others before action takes place. The model has four major components:

1. the client's definition and understanding of an experience as a problem;
2. the client's use of language to label and categorize a problem;
3. the availability and use of indigenous community resources and the decision making involved in problem intervention strategies;
4. the client's cultural criteria for determining problem resolution.

As a support to the model of help-seeking behavior, cross-cultural social work utilizes ethnographic information in planning, delivery, and evaluation of ethnic minority social services. The emphasis is on the cross-cultural learning and ethnic competence of the social worker. The worker must learn about another culture in terms of its cognitive beliefs, affective expression, and behavioral relationships. Ethnic competence involves awareness of cultural limitations, openness to cultural differences, opportunity to learn about client experience, utilization of the cultural network of community resources, and acknowledgment of cultural values of morality, honesty, and integrity within each ethnic group. This knowledge is fundamental to procedural steps. Learning about and entering an unfamiliar community is achieved through studying background information, visiting the community, and making a social map of ethnic groups, social organizations, community beliefs and ideology, distribution of resources, patterns of mobility, and access to and utilization of human services. Contact with key ethnic leaders or gatekeepers who are willing to share community knowledge provides the worker with information and an ongoing relationship. Practicing participant observation is a means of collecting data with the notion of what ought to be observed and why a particular topic is important.

Delivery of Social Services to People of Color

The cultural awareness framework further delineates social services to Black, Asian, Native, and Chicano Americans. An aspect of help-seeking and help-providing activity is examined in terms of community, family, and urbanization. Each of the principal ethnic minority groups is presented to familiarize the reader with a specific cultural context.

Black Americans. Leigh and Green (1982) trace the historical relationship of social work to the Black community and criticize the profession for its neglect of relevant intervention strategies, family role, and indigenous community institutions. From a historical perspective, the Black family has long existed within a well-defined, close-knit system of relationships. Authority and responsibility have been clearly assigned and complex rules of behavior have embedded them in village and regional linkages. Family life in the United States was impaired by slavery, but the Black community has survived as an active unit for meeting the needs of its members. The church has remained a central institution in the community. There have been underlying coherent themes such as strong bonds of household kinship, an orientation to work for the support of family, flexible family roles, occupational and educational achievement, commitment to religious values, and church participation. Black families participate in extended family networks, which pool resources and provide economic and emotional security. These interdependent relationships form a system of mutual aid in such areas as finances, housing, and child rearing. Social workers have a responsibility for becoming familiar with Black community and family dynamics. Cultural sensitivity in the form of awareness and knowledge is the first step toward assisting Black clients.

Asian and Pacific Americans. Ishisaka and Takagi (1982) use the term *Asian and Pacific Americans* as a collective designation of numerous, disparate, and self-contained groups whose ancestry is in Asia and the Pacific Islands. They trace the history of immigration and patterns of resettlement of Chinese, Japanese, and Pilipino Americans. Although Asian communities have been remarkably self-sufficient as a result of mutual-aid associations, social service statistics have documented needs in the areas of unemployment, economy, health, and mental health. Asian Americans have characteristically placed strong emphases on cultural values and family structure. The Chinese–American family is, for the individual members, a reference group and source of personal identity and emotional security. It exerts control over interpersonal conduct, social relations, and occupational and marital selection. Japanese Americans are traditionally influenced by strong values of filial piety, respect and obligation, harmony, and group cooperation. There have been changes in values and family relationships toward increasing individualism. However, avoidance of shame, indirect communication, self-effacement, and modesty appear to be maintained in recent generations. Among Pilipino Americans, there are strong family-centered values and extended kinship relationships. Respect is given to the head of the family and to the elderly. Marriage is an alliance between kin networks. The values of group cooperation, mutual obligation, and personal pride and integrity combine to create an interdependent society and conflict-free relationships. Asian Americans represent diverse subgroups with profound language and cultural differences from mainstream American culture. Practice with Asian Americans must take into account length of stay and country of origin (foreign born versus American born), socioeconomic status, fluency in English, and history of intergroup conflict. The foreign-born generally require information referral and concrete services, while American-born seek counseling and treatment. There is a movement toward multiservice indigenous social service organizations in the Pacific-Asian communities.

Native Americans.   In contrast to Black and Asian Americans, Native Americans represent the minority with needs in the areas of income, education, health, and mental health. There are higher rates of arrest, drinking, and unemployment among Native Americans than among other ethnic groups. Of Native Americans, one-third live on reservations, one-third live in urban areas, and one-third move between reservations and cities. The children of urban Native Americans have few contacts with traditional life and require coping skills to survive city life. Miller (1982) examined the following nine cultural traits in relation to social services:

Suspicion and distrust of White professionals and institutions
Passive nature, avoiding or withdrawing from assertive or aggressive situations
Shyness and sensitivity to strangers, resulting in low verbal behavior
Short-term orientation
Fatalistic view of life
Respect for individuality reflected in lax child rearing
Casual time orientation
Strong family obligations and extended family relations
Noninterference with others

Her conclusions are that these traits have not been defined operationally and often result in generalizations and stereotypes. Two traits were highly evident in her study: passivity in seeking services and shyness in interaction with the research investigator and professionals. These seem to be natural responses to outside institutions. On the whole, there is a wide variety of personality traits, cultural practices, and lifestyles.

The study also revealed that Native Americans had difficulty utilizing services and were dissatisfied with the services they received. Part of the reason was institutional barriers, such as direct and indirect cost, ambiguous agency procedures, transportation, lack of child care, waiting time, impersonal interaction, distance, and limited opening hours. A satisfactory contact was one that involved a professional who was sincere, had a sense of humor, spent time, and was nonjudgmental.

Miller (1982) summarizes the literature on delivery of transcultural services. It points out that mental health professionals do not have adequate knowledge of transcultural client interaction. Professional providers do not traditionally receive training in the delivery of transcultural services such as the need to discuss the family's Native American background and culture, to explore relevant areas, to ask questions that elicit information without causing discomfort, and to utilize cultural information in assessment. Social workers should employ strategies of cultural assessment that recognize biculturality, relevant values and lifestyles, and cultural strengths and show empathy.

Chicanos. Aragon de Valdez and Gallegos (1982) trace the historical oppression and powerlessness of Chicanos by White Americans, imposed from the time of the Treaty of Guadalupe Hidalgo (1848) to the present. As a response to their situation, Chicanos have relied on the church, service organizations, and political movements. The Catholic Church has not unified religion and ethnicity for Chicanos and has taken an antagonistic social stance subordinating Chicanos. Clearly the Church should engage in social involvement and advocacy on behalf of the Chicano community. Community-controlled service organizations and mutual aid societies have provided services and emergency assistance. Chicano political organizations have made an educational contribution to community life. Local and national voting drives, lobbying, campaigning, and endorsing candidates have characterized such groups as La Raza Unida, League of United Latin Citizens, and El Congresco.

The socioeconomic, educational, and cultural needs of Chicanos congregate in the areas of English language skills, poverty, cultural coping mechanisms, racism and discrimination, and substandard housing. Delivery of human services continues to be inaccessible, class-bound, culture-bound, and caste bound, and monolingual. Social services need to regear and rely on culturally specific treatment models. There are three components relevant to social work practice: (1) bilingual/bicultural staff and indigenous paraprofessionals; (2) procedural protocols emphasizing *personalismo* and a medical examination process; and (3) intervention based on active goal-oriented problem solving, family support networks, and family interaction and interdependence.

The framework for cross-cultural awareness practice is based on cultural awareness and sensitivity to minorities in general and to the unique characteristics of the major ethnic groups. The uniqueness of this approach has been the application of anthropological theory emphasizing problem investigation and community learning strategies. It stands in contrast to traditional social work practice, which has drawn on psychotherapy and has been treatment oriented. Green and his associates have demonstrated the need to continue dialogue on designing minority services, learning about ethnic clients and agencies, and using the ethnographic setting for problem solving.

Framework for Ethnic Minority Social Work Practice

There are similarities and differences between the frameworks for ethnic-sensitive practice, cultural awareness practice, and ethnic minority social work practice. Devore and Schlesinger's ethnic-sensitive practice approach delineates the human behavior and practice scope and boundaries of working with minority clients. Green's culture aware-ness orientation further specifies minority practice steps and treats the uniqueness of the principal minority groups. The framework for ethnic minority social work practice recognizes the groundwork of establishing a basis for minority social work practice and furthers the development of this field in three ways. First, it conceptualizes a systematic process-stage approach to minority practice, following the classic formula of beginning, middle, and end. Second, it offers generic principles of practice universal to people of color and supports them with examples from each of the key minority groups. Third, it uses a representative sample of case material from the ethnic clinical literature and develops direct practice continuity through a single family case study in the various process stages.

Theoretical Foundation

The framework for ethnic minority social work practice is based on the notion that there are common themes that pertain to working with people of color. At the same time, we recognize that each of the largest minority groups (Black, Latino, Asian, and Native American) has its own unique cultural history, socioeconomic problems, and treatment approaches. The concepts of *cultural commonality* and *cultural specificity* reflect these emphases. The question is, can one articulate, from a social work perspective, a framework for ethnic minority practice that is applicable to minorities in general and that recognizes minority subgroups in specific? There is a vigorous debate on this methodological issue, which is known as *etic versus emic goals.*

Etic versus Emic Goals

The term *etic* comes from the linguistic study of sounds and refers to the categorization of all the sounds in a particular language. The term *emic* refers to all the *meaningful* sounds in a particular language. From a cross-cultural perspective, these two concepts have been used to describe behavior in cultures. The etic goal documents principles valid in all cultures and establishes theoretical bases for comparing human behavior. The emic goal documents behavioral principles within a culture and focuses on what the people themselves value as important and familiar to them (Brislin, 1981). It is important to maintain both emphases in social work practice—that is, to focus on culture-common characteristics of minorities and on culture-specific traits of particular ethnic groups.

The objective of this book is to further the etic goal of establishing practice principles for people of color in general. A companion volume, *Ethnic Minority Social Work Practice: Individual, Family, and Community Dimensions,* edited by Lum and Zuniga (in press), pursues the emic goal of delineating individual, family, and community perspectives for Black, Latino, Asian, and Native Americans.

The etic aspect of social work practice is based on a number of factors. Cross-cultural psychology and anthropology assume that cognitive processes are universal and have common denominators (Lonner, 1979). Our intention is to set forth a process model for social work direct practice with people of color that draws universal or common principles across cultures. Cross-cultural psychology asserts that its major function is to formulate laws that hold for human nature based on findings with a specified number of individuals who represent a logical class (Price-Williams, 1979). Similarly, a priority of cross-cultural social work is to identify a number of practice principles that are applicable to all minorities before proceeding to delineate specific ones for each major ethnic group.

The Framework

Table 3-1 shows the four categories within the framework for ethnic minority social work practice: practice process stages, worker system practice issues, client system practice issues, and worker-client tasks. There are five process stages, which are used as major divisions of the framework. Practice process stages focus on the step-by-step

TABLE 3-1. Framework for Ethnic Minority Social Work Practice

Practice process stages	Worker system practice issues	Client system practice issues	Worker-client tasks
Contact	Delivery of services Understanding of the community Relationship protocols Professional self-disclosure Style of communication	Resistance, Communication barriers Personal and family background Ethnic community identity	Nurturing Understanding
Problem identification	Problem orientation Problem levels Problem themes Problem area detailing	Problem information Problem area disclosure Problem understanding	Learning Focusing
Assessment	Assessment dynamics Assessment evaluation	Social-environmental impacts Psycho-individual reactions	Interacting Evaluating
Intervention	Joint goals and agreement Joint interventional strategies (planning, selection, and implementation) Micro/meso/macro level interventions		Creating Changing
Termination	Destination, recital, completion Follow-up strategies		Achieving Resolving

logical sequence of worker and client movement in the helping process. Social work process has traditionally been characterized in terms of beginning, middle, and end. In this minority direct practice framework, the beginning process stages are *contact* and *problem identification;* the middle stages consist of *assessment* and *intervention;* and the ending is *termination.*

The terms *worker system* and *client system* refer to those substructures ("systems") of the framework that pertain to the individual person within the direct practice relationship: the worker, on the one hand, and the client, on the other. Practice issues are issues of concern within the context of practice. Worker and client systems practice issues are relevant to guiding both parties through the various stages. There are specific issues that must be highlighted and emphasized when the client is a person of color. For example, many of these practice issues (for example, problem area detailing, assessment evaluation, and joint goals and agreement) relate to all or most social worker-client encounters. However, there are practice issues (such as delivery of service, professional self-disclosure, problem orientation, and social-environmental impacts) that are unique to minority social work practice.

Worker system variables represent the crucial functions that the worker must undertake in order to move the client through the process stages. Client system variables are concerns with which the client must deal as a collaborator with the worker and as a person who is in the midst of a growth experience. Worker-client tasks entail the obligation of the social worker to nurture, understand, learn, and focus. Throughout the middle and ending stages, however, the client increasingly interacts, evaluates, creates, changes, and achieves, and, in the process, resolves. In the following sections, the process stages are explained in terms of the framework.

The Process-Stage Approach

Contact

Practice process stage.   Basic to the contact phase is the establishment of the relationship between the social worker and the minority client. Relationship is the primary requisite for retaining the client. Fischer (1978) describes this stage as experiencing and exploration. The client and worker engage each other in the effort to develop a mutually trusting relationship. The worker responds to the client with empathy, warmth, and genuineness. Fischer suggests: "the more positive the emotional responses in the client as evoked by the worker, i.e., the more he or she is liked, the greater will be the client's willingness to participate and be influenced" (1978, p. 247). The social worker demonstrates listening and understanding, respect and concern for the client as a human being, openness and spontaneity in the situation.

Worker system practice issues.   It is important for the social service agency to set up a responsive system of service delivery to meet the needs of minority clients. The use of bilingual/bicultural workers, community education and prevention outreach programs, accessible facility location, and minimal fees are ways to increase the use of services by people of color. The shaping of delivery of services is a result of understanding the community. Social service agency administrators should meet with ethnic community leaders and groups in their catchment area (mandated service area) to ascertain social needs, determine composition of the staff, and plan relevant programs. Social service staff should be oriented to various ethnic client communities and their socioeconomic needs, lifestyle, and other key elements. This groundwork must be performed before actual contact with clients.

When the social worker engages the minority client, he or she must observe certain relationship protocols, such as addressing the client with his or her surname, making formal introductions, acknowledging the elderly or head of household as the authority, and conveying respect through other means. Rather than focusing initially on the problem, the social worker should practice professional self-disclosure, whereby a point of interest common to the client and the worker becomes a means of forming a relationship. Further efforts to discover the ethnic family background of the client help the worker to gain a sense of familiarity. The worker should also structure the initial session by explaining the functions and procedures of the agency, the purpose of the sessions, and the range of problem areas that are encountered among a broad spectrum of clients.

The social worker's style of communication should convey friendliness, interest, and empathetic understanding. It is important to make the client feel at ease. The worker's modeling of a relaxed and open personal attitude evokes a similar response on the client's part. The worker should take cues communicated by the client, who eventually will allude to the reason for coming to the agency. At the point of disclosure, the content of communications moves from becoming acquainted with the client and his or her background to the presenting problem.

During the contact phase, the social worker gains a preliminary perspective on the client's psychosocial functioning. It is based on the information flowing from the reciprocal interaction between the client and his or her environment. The basic demographic information on the intake form includes indicators of psychosocial state such as place of residence, occupation, health status, family, and other distinguishing variables. For example, onset of a major illness, recent loss of job, or change of address is an indicator of concern. The social worker should note the client's attitude toward such particulars. In this first stage, however, the emphasis is on obtaining a sense of adequate functioning or dysfunctioning as the person-in-the-situation emerges. The worker overviews the biopsychosocial dimensions of the client (physical, cognitive-affective-behavioral, and environmental forces affecting the client) and picks up on the significant relationships and events, life experiences, and cultural/ethnic levels.

Client system practice issues.   There is a natural resistance on the part of minority clients who are entering the formal helping system. Suspicion and mistrust based on previous institutional contact, anxiety about the unknown, and shame about admitting the need for assistance are natural feelings of clients generally. For people of color, those feelings are exacerbated by racism and discrimination. The client often engages in testing the worker to determine whether he or she has racist values and biases. Social workers should examine themselves for traces of racism and prejudice and evaluate their attitudes toward particular minority groups.

Personal and family background play a major role in the contact stage. Asking about ethnic family background may be an important signal to a minority client that his or her ethnicity is valuable information for the social work practitioner. The worker might ask: How do you identify yourself as a member of an ethnic group? What are the important ethnic customs and beliefs that you and your family observe and practice? Are you a participant in several ethnic organizations? What are your favorite ethnic foods? Whom do you consider to be a local spokesperson or leader in your ethnic community? Are there any ethnic groups or individuals that you would approach for assistance? These are some areas for preliminary conversation that may or may not be relevant, depending on the client's reaction and the direction of the initial session.

It is important to determine the degree of acculturation affecting the minority client. For decades, the United States has been termed "the melting pot" of all races. Unfortunately, the result has been the abandonment of foreign influences, such as native language and dress, and the adaptation to Americanized behavior patterns. To be Americanized meant to discard vestiges of past culture and custom and adopt the language idioms, mannerisms, dress, and mentality of the majority culture. Acculturation is the process of adapting to a new or different culture, especially one with advanced patterns. The term's implication is that a person who is becoming acculturated is from an inferior cultural background. The majority culture applies pressure toward social conformity, which affects children who are conditioned to the patterns of the new culture and parents who maintain ethnic cultural values. Fortunately, with the rise of ethnic awareness in the past two decades, many third- and fourth-generation minorities are rediscovering their past cultural heritage and learning the history and language of their forefathers. These later generations have embraced cultural pride and identity, which have formed an ethnic life pattern. Some new immigrants are moving toward partial assimilation of American lifestyle and behavior patterns, which are in conflict with traditional cultural values. Parents tend toward preserving authoritarian family roles and traditional values, and they are thus at odds with their children, who are exposed to the independent and individualistic lifestyles of their school and neighborhood peers. Underlying the adjustments demanded by acculturation is the displacement of parents who must cope with a new society filled with economic and social uncertainty.

Another example of personal and family background is the client's sense of ethnic community identity. Does the client feel related to the ethnic community and participate in its activities? Are there ethnic community resources that are available to the client? Helping a minority client or family adjust to life in this country, to sort out cultural values and traditions, and to stabilize family beliefs and practices are starting points for contact in practice with people of color. For clients who have grown up in this country and are aware of their own cultural identity issues, social work may focus on rediscovery of past cultural values and tradition and the meaning of their ethnicity.

Worker-client tasks.   Crucial to the contact stage is nurturing on the part of the worker. By "nurturing" we mean contributing to the growth process facilitated by the mutual involvement of the worker and client. Offering food and drink as one begins a session communicates the idea that physical refreshment and sustenance are important.

Translating this symbolic act into emotional nurturing involves healthy doses of empathy, warmth, and genuineness, which develop into rapport, trust, and openness. A minority client may reciprocate by inviting the worker to his or her home for a social activity or by bringing fruit, candy, or a token of appreciation. If the meaning of this act can be recognized and accepted, it can shape a mutually giving process.

Understanding is an important worker-client task. The worker should use open-ended reflection, recognizing the primacy of the client's feelings and thoughts. Understanding develops through careful listening and paraphrasing the client's expressed thoughts and feelings to clarify or acknowledge the message communicated. It is further expressed through the worker's support of the client in confronting the issues that concern him or her. These responses at the contact stage open up the minority client, releasing pent-up emotions and thought-remnants that require later follow-up.

Problem Identification

Practice process stage.   Once the dynamics of contact are set in motion, a problem area invariably emerges in the course of the worker-client relationship. Some minority clients continually face basic problems of survival such as unemployment, poor health, substandard housing, and other chronic issues. These problems are often caused by inadequate funding for existing services. Federal and state program budget cuts, for example, have affected AFDC and Medicaid, sending shock waves through the minority community, where marginal-income single mothers and elderly are now under slim economic and medical coverage.

Worker. system practice issues.   In the present framework, problems are regarded as unsatisfied wants. This problem orientation is in contrast to the pathological viewpoint, which is detrimental to people of color. Rather than uncovering the dysfunctional aspect of the problem, the worker interprets a problem as symptomatic of a positive striving that has been hindered by an obstacle in the client's life. This perspective casts a new light on the identification of problems.

There are various problem levels and themes that are useful in categorizing the multifaceted problems of ethnic minority clients. Recognition of micro (individual, family, and small group), meso (ethnic/local communities and organizations), and macro (complex organizations, geographical populations) levels comprises part of problem identification. Oppression, powerlessness, exploitation, acculturation, and stereotyping are problem themes for people of color.

In the problem identification stage, the psychosocial perspective focuses on the environment bearing on the minority client. Detailing of the problem area occurs when there is a match between the appropriate problem level(s) and theme(s). A minority client tends to confront multiple problems. For example, Black and Latino Americans in urban industrial jobs have been laid off on account of economic recession. Depression, loss of self-esteem, and family conflict have led to behavioral problems such as alcoholism, child abuse, and attempted suicide. Blue-collar minorities and Whites have also been affected by the economy. Detailing these problems implies matching macro (state of the economy) and micro (unemployed worker and his family) levels with the problem theme of powerlessness.

Client system practice issues.   During the stage of problem identification, the minority client reaches a point of having conveyed preliminary information to the worker about the problem. It may take time for the client to develop trust and overcome shame. Once the client can be assured that information about the problem will not be used against him or her, disclosure of the problem area ensues as a part of the process. Sharing a problem with the professional gives a minority client the opportunity to understand it from another perspective. Defining the chronological development of a problem aids understanding and allows the worker to gain individual and corporate insight.

Worker-Client Tasks

Throughout the problem identification stage, the tasks of the social worker and the minority client are learning and focusing. Learning consists of uncovering essential problem themes and then detailing them with facts. Learning occurs when the worker and client decide to settle on a particular problem that is considered primary by both parties. As the worker probes and the client responds, both learn about dimensions of the problem. The worker describes the problem as a logical sequence of events on the basis of information supplied by the client. The client has new insights into the problem area. Which segment of the problem seems most manageable to the worker and client? What portion of the problem can most readily be detailed, studied, and analyzed? What is the sequence or pattern of problem events? Who are the actors involved? When does the problem occur? Where is the problem located? Problem identification moves from general learning about problem issues to focusing on a specific problem.

Assessment

Practice process stage.   In social work practice, assessment generally involves an in-depth study related to a psychosocial problem affecting the client. Its purpose is to analyze the interaction of client and situation and to plan recommendations for intervention. How does the problem affect the client? What resources are necessary to respond to the problem? With a minority client, it is useful to identify cultural strengths, significant others, and community support systems. Interactions of client and environment can change. It is important at each session for the client to brief the worker and for the worker to ask the client what has happened since the last session. The focus of the problem may have changed. New factors may have been introduced. Strategies for change may need revision.

Worker system practice issues.   The psychosocial perspective on assessment focuses on the interaction of client and environment. On the cognitive level, the ethnic mind-set of the person of color affects thought patterns learned from minority parents, experiences, and formal and informal learning in his or her ethnic group. The minority person incorporates a past, present, and future life script of his or her ethnic history. For example, the person of color experiences institutional racism through various early childhood stages. The location of the home, racial composition of the neighborhood and school, and social segregation situation all play a part in the constructs incorporated into a person's ethnic experience. These learning situations form the basis of the person's cognitive mind-set. In subsequent interactions with people, past experiences color a person's cognitive perception and response. Hepworth and Larsen (1982) observe:

> Perceptions, of course, do not exist separate and apart from meanings that are ascribed to them; hence, we have considered perceptual and cognitive functioning as a single entity. It is the meanings or interpretations of events, rather than events themselves, that motivate human beings to behave as they do [p. 182].

Assessment categories of cognition focus on intelligence, judgment, reality testing, coherence, flexibility, and self-concept. Assessment of the cognitive level ascertains to what extent these variables are within an acceptable range of functioning. The worker must begin to assess the extent to which a minority person recognizes and analyzes the actions of a racist society and still functions with ethnic-oriented ideas and beliefs about living. The duality of an ethnic frame of reference and intellectual comprehension and judgment is the basis for sound reality-tested decision making, logical and coherent thinking, and a self-concept influenced by ethnic values and history. A person of color can cope by means of cognitive thinking about who he or she is and the reality of a racist society.

Affect for the minority person involves the extent to which feeling states are expressed or masked to a range of persons: family, friends, acquaintances, people of color, and nonminority persons. It is not unusual for minority people to change their affect responses according to their degree of familiarity with others present. For example, it is interesting to observe that when members of the same ethnic minority group gather together informally, there is a spirit of camaraderie. Bantering, jokes, and ethnic slang often characterize these moments. The affect is warm and open and the person feels at ease. However, the affect of the group members may change when a nonminority person appears on the scene. The group becomes quiet and affect remains low. This reaction may be due to the fact that minorities feel uncomfortable with nonminorities and tend to mask and seal over this aspect of affect in their presence. Only after considerable relating, testing, and trust can positive affect occur between minority and nonminority persons. Part of the reason for this guarded affect is that people of color do not want to place themselves in vulnerable positions by disclosure of genuine affect. Nonminority helping persons must not use affective disclosure as a means of confrontation with minority clients. The loss of rapport and trust between a nonminority worker and a minority client may ruin the potential relationship with that person or with the local minority community.

There are cultural limits on the extent to which some feelings can be expressed. Some minority groups vary in the degree of control they exercise over the disclosure of certain emotional states. To impose demands to "be totally open and let it all hang out" may be to ask for something beyond the cultural capacity of certain minority clients. Recognizing and respecting those limits and striving to work with clients on recognition and disclosure of feelings is a realistic goal for the social worker. For some minority groups, affect is expressed through concrete action. For example, unable to express the rage and anger of years of economic exploitation by local merchants, police harassment and brutality, and inadequate human services, Black Americans in the middle sixties took to the streets in a series of urban riots. Those destructive actions of protest expressed a corporate feeling of frustration and exasperation over society's indifference to their plight. Surprisingly, after civil unrest, federal and local funds, social programs, and national attention were focused on the predicament of inner-city Blacks.

Social workers must look beyond the traditional diagnosis of affective states. Affect is generally assessed according to the appropriateness of the client's functioning state vis-à-vis his or her clinical predicament. The psychiatric social worker looks for affective signs of depression and abnormality described as "flat or inappropriate affect." Although it is important to differentiate these affective categories, it is also necessary to consider the ethnic and cultural dynamics involving disclosure. How affect is expressed in nonverbal communication is a crucial consideration in assessment of minority clients.

Akin to the cognitive and affective states are the actions of the minority person that are the results of conscious decision making. There is a reason why an individual does what he or she does. Behavioral therapy teaches that there are antecedent events that precipitate behavior and resulting effects. In a threatening situation, a person of color may respond passively and stoically. A minority client may choose to exhibit a cognitive and affective reaction based on environmental threats. Sometimes strategies for ethnic survival have given rise to racial stereotypes. For example, the seemingly happy-go-lucky and obedient Black slave behaved in such a manner to avoid the wrath and whip of the owner. The quiet and smiling Asian American exhibited a survival behavior to avoid being attacked and lynched by angry White mobs at the turn of the century. The sleepy Mexican American, sombrero over his face, epitomized the maxim "hear no evil, speak no evil, see no evil" in the midst of vigilante rule. The stoic Native American with an expressionless face, wrapped in a blanket, concealed feelings of defeat and frustration over reservation restrictions. These minority behavioral responses are masks covering ethnic despair over social, economic, and political oppression suffered at the hands of a racist society.

A client may feel threatened in an unfamiliar and foreign setting or thoroughly at ease in a familiar environment oriented to his or her culture. The social worker can create the sort of environment that puts clients at ease. Green (1982) terms this behavioral awareness *ethnic competence*. He states:

> The definition implies an awareness of prescribed and proscribed behavior within a specific culture, and it suggests that the ethnically competent worker has the ability to carry out professional activities consistent with that awareness. It does not propose that trained individuals are those who can mimic the behavioral routines and linguistic particularities of their minority clients. Nor does it rule that out. Its emphasis is on the trained worker's ability to adapt professional tasks and work styles to the cultural values and preferences of clients [pp. 52–53].

The psychosocial perspective on the cognitive, affective, and behavioral dimensions of the minority client brings unique cultural knowledge to bear on clinical situations.

Client system practice issues.   Psychosocial assessment is concerned with the impacts of social environment on the individual client. Social environmental conditions affect and produce psycho-individual reactions. There are numerous examples of the cause-and-effect relationship between the person and the environment. The influence of society is a strong force that shapes minority reaction. For instance, societal caricatures about minorities forced Blacks toward behavior patterns that confirmed the stereotype in the minds of nonminorities. Leigh and Green (1982) observe:

> Yet, as stereotypes, these notions of restricted development persisted in popular ideas of racial differences. The belief that black people were conditioned by their genetic inheritance to develop only an inferior culture suggested that there was really very little justification for attempts to change, through social services, what seemed to have been established in nature [p. 96].

Similarly, Wise and Miller point out that the media continue to perpetuate the image of the Native American either as a romantic, mystical figure of the past, with a primitive and savage temperament, or as a displaced, drunken individual. These stereotypes confuse the development of Native American self-esteem and identity (Wise & Miller, 1981).

Positive social environment affects psycho-individual reactions in terms of self-esteem and ethnic strength. To what extent does a particular client value and maintain his or her culture? For many people of color, cultural preservation and endorsement are fundamental values. For Black Americans, extended family, church, art, music, and poetry are mobilizing forces. For Asian Americans, kinship and family ties, mutual obligation, and family welfare are elements of significant-other resources to be assessed. For Native Americans, respect for individuality, strong family relationships, and attendance at pow-wows are crucial to cultural development. For Latino Americans, family cohesion and helping networks, family interdependence, and respect for the elderly are factors in the assessment of cultural maintenance.

Minority clients should be aware of the range of effects that the social environment may have on them. The ethnic cultural environment and the discriminatory racist society are two forces that cause individual reactions. Social workers should assess the extent to which minority clients have cultural assets with which to fortify themselves.

Worker-client tasks.   In the assessment stage, the worker-client tasks consist of interacting and evaluating. In the interaction process, the worker and client sort through multiple cultural environmental factors and settle on those that have an effect on the problem. Performance of the interacting task is based on a unique relationship between the worker and the client. The worker is the inquirer and learner, while the client is in the teaching and clarifying role. This philosophy is patterned after Green's understanding of the ethnographic interview (Green, 1982). The evaluating task identifies individual and environmental factors that are useful in designing an appropriate intervention strategy. Evaluation appraises the changes necessary to alter the client's situation. It assembles detailed information about the problem, the client's cultural resources, and the community support system. It leads to the establishment of intervention goals, contract, and procedural strategies to implement changes. It focuses on present conditions, selected past events influencing the current problem, and the client's capabilities and motivation to work on the problem.

Intervention

Practice process stage.   Social work intervention is a strategy for change that modifies and resolves the problem situation. Intervention occurs when the biopsychosocial needs of the client are met through material and supportive resources in the minority family community and through social or religious organizations. Turner (1978) identifies three contexts for psychosocial functioning: the medium of human relationships, the availability of material and service resources, and the client's significant environment. The purpose of intervention is to effect change in the client and in the environment for mutual improvement.

Worker and client systems practice issues.   The worker and the client participate jointly in the formulation of goals, the contract agreement, and the matching of intervention levels and strategies. Bloom and Fischer (1982) define goals as "statements of what the client/system (and practitioner and perhaps relevant others) would like to happen, do, or be when intervention is completed" (p. 64). Goals are terminal or ultimate outcomes that the client and worker would like to have achieved upon completion of the intervention phase. Objectives are intermediate subgoals or developmental procedures, a series of steps beginning with concrete action and ending with the accomplishment of outcome goals. The statements of goals and contract should be brief and prescriptive directions.

Intervention is a strategy introduced to cope with and change the problem. The selection of interventional modality depends on the nature of the problem, the background of the client, and the professional judgment of the worker. The choice of a particular intervention should be based on certain objective criteria:

1. that the intervention should examine and resolve the problem;
2. that the intervention focuses on immediate past and present time sequences related to the problem;
3. that the intervention alters the psychosocial dimensions of the problem;
4. that the intervention requires tasks to mobilize the client in focused positive action;
5. that the intervention demonstrates in measurable terms that change has occurred in the problem area.

Levels of intervention are the same as the problem levels already named: micro, meso, and macro. These levels are matched with a number of interventional strategies: liberation, empowerment, parity, maintenance of culture, and unique personhood. Direct social work practice tends to operate in the levels of micro and meso interventions. For example, within the family and community there are natural helping resources that have an impact on the environment. Medicine (1981) advocates a psychosocial intervention based on extended family aid and corporate survival. This kinship strategy results in the family's cooperation for the purposes of economic and social well-being. Medicine describes examples of reciprocity, such as joint use of an automobile, hauling water, cutting wood, doing errands, exchanging child care services, caring for the elderly, and other adaptations.

As an interventional strategy for minority clients, liberation is the experience of release or freedom from oppressive barriers and control when change occurs in a client's life. For some, it is the realization of growth and decision making: the client has decided that oppressive circumstances and persons will no longer dominate him or her. This happens when the client is able to implement alternative choices in his or her situation. For others, liberation occurs when there is environmental change that influences the course of action for the client. Examples are the introduction of a job training program and the election of an ethnic minority mayor who makes policy, legislative, and program changes on behalf of people of color.

Another minority intervention is empowerment: "a process whereby persons who belong to a stigmatized social category throughout their lives can be assisted to develop and increase skills in the exercise of interpersonal influence and the performance of valued social roles" (Solomon, 1976, p. 6). It is the ability to experience power in the sense of rising up and changing one's situational predicament. It focuses on the assertion of the human right to resources and well-being in society. How can the minority client achieve empowerment? For a start, by gaining information about resources and rights and going through an experience in which the exercise of power results in a benefit to the minority client. Voting, influencing policy, and initiating legislation on the local level are practical avenues to empowerment.

Parity as an interventional strategy relates to a sense of equality, or having the same power, value, and rank as another. For a person of color, it is the feeling that he or she is being treated as a person equal to others in value. Its focal theme is fairness and entitlement to certain rights. Concrete examples are entitlement programs (Social Security, Medicare), income maintenance, adequate health care, and other resources that guarantee an adequate standard of living.

Maintenance of culture is a strategy that asserts the importance of the ideas, customs, skills, arts, and language of a people. It is particularly useful to trace the history of an ethnic group to identify moments of crisis and challenge through which it survived and triumphed. Applying such lessons of history to the present situation inspires the client to overcome obstacles. It is a source of strength on which the client draws as a resource. From maintenance of culture the minority person derives his or her identity as an ethnic individual.

Unique personhood is an interventional strategy that speaks to transcending stereotypes. It affirms the value held in social work that each person is unique in the helping relationship. There is something extraordinary in each person. Functional casework holds this high view of the individual person. When a person of color acts to gain freedom from social stereotypes, he or she asserts his or her unique personhood and discovers his or her own humanity.

Worker-client tasks.   The worker-client tasks of the intervention stage revolve around creating and changing. In formulating new ways to deal with existing problems, the worker and client are creating. Like the God of the Old Testament, whose words and orderly actions produce creation, the worker and client are engaged in originating a series of acts that they hope will result in the creation of a new system. By words, the worker and client communicate with each other and with their respective networks: family, extended support system, agency, and community resources. By action, the worker facilitates movement and direction to implement the creative formulations devised in collaboration with the client. The concept of creativity brings a new dimension to worker-client tasks. No longer is the worker going through the same motions and procedures again and again with the same type of client. Rather, each client poses a unique set of problems and interventional formulations that require creative imagination. The interweaving of worker, client, community, and service in infinite variations means that each case is a new creation.

The task of changing provides movement from one situation to another. Ethnic minorities have advocated changing their situation. Rather than talking to the client about the general idea of change, the worker provides specific courses of action that alter the situation. Task-centered casework moves the client and situation from point to point in a series of goal-oriented changes. Behavioral casework alters or modifies the behavior of the client and the antecedents and consequences of the environment. These are examples of approaches in clinical practice that emphasize change and measure its effects on the client. The minority community must change unjust and exploitative social policies, regulatory laws, and institutional practices. Intervention, in minority practice, must cover clinical and community dimensions.

Termination

Practice process stage.   Termination denotes a closure of the present relationship between the client and the worker. The manner and circumstances of termination shape the future growth patterns of the client. Termination is the tentative ending of sessions that have focused on the identified problem(s). There has, one hopes, been resolution of the problem in an agreed-upon number of sessions. Termination also means major adjustments of goals and interventional approaches, resulting in a new series of sessions. It is time to redefine the problem and renegotiate new goals and interventional strategies. In some instances, termination is the result of counterproductive factors such as numerous absences of the client or lack of significant movement on the problem. They may be due to unresolved resistance on the part of the client, dissonance between the personalities of the worker and client, cultural and personal barriers, or events beyond the control of the worker or client.

Worker and client systems practice issues.   Successful termination assumes arrival at destination points. Among them is mature growth. The client and worker are able to measure the difference of growth between the contact and termination stages. To differentiate the two stages as "before" and "after" is to recognize the changes that have occurred in the interval. Recital is an ingredient of termination: the client recites back the positive change that has occurred in the helping process. The client reflects on what has happened at certain points in his or her life. Completion is understood as achievement of goals and resolution of issues, attended by a sense of accomplishment.

Follow-up strategies involve maintaining contact with the client after the conclusion of the practice sessions. Telephone contacts and periodic follow-up meetings over the course of some months are helpful in evaluating the progress made by the client after completion of social services. Minority clients are known to have a high dropout rate for human services. Research is needed to determine which components of social treatment are responsible for premature closure.

Worker-client tasks.   In terms of worker-client tasks, achieving has the connotation of accomplishing and attaining a certain goal. For the worker, achieving consists in attaining the desired aim of helping the client through a problem situation. For the client, achieving means successfully sustaining the effort to change a psychosocial situation. Resolving places closure on decision making. There is a sense of finality in resolving.

Conclusion

This chapter has laid out a general framework for social work practice with people of color. Major categories were practice process stages, worker system practice issues, client system practice issues, and worker-client tasks. Social work practice principles were integrated with insights into issues concerning ethnic minorities. In the succeeding chapters, we will elaborate on the principles relevant to various process stages. The aim is to help social work practitioners implement this framework in their encounters with ethnic minority clients.

References

Aragon de Valdez, T., & Gallegos, J. (1982). The Chicano familia in social work. In J. W. Green, *Cultural awareness in the human services.* Englewood Cliffs, N.J.: Prentice-Hall.

Bloom, M., & Fischer, J. (1982). *Evaluating practice: Guidelines for the accountable professional.* Englewood Cliffs, N.J.: Prentice-Hall.

Brislin, R. W. (1981). *Cross-cultural encounters: Face-to-face interaction.* New York: Pergamon Press.

Cheetham, J. (1982). *Social work and ethnicity.* London: George Allen and Unwin.

Devore, W., & Schlesinger, E. G. (1981). *Ethnic-sensitive social work practice.* St. Louis: C.V. Mosby.

Fischer, J. (1978). *Effective casework practice: An eclectic approach.* New York: McGraw-Hill.

Green, J. W. (1982). *Cultural awareness in the human services.* Englewood Cliffs, N.J.: Prentice Hall.

Hepworth, D. H., & Larsen, J. A. (1982). *Direct social work practice: Theory and skills.* Homewood, Ill.: Dorsey Press.

Ishisaka, H. A., & Takagi, C. Y. (1982). Social work with Asian-and-Pacific-Americans. In J. W. Green, *Cultural awareness in the human services.* Englewood Cliffs, N.J.: Prentice-Hall.

Jenkins, S. (1981). *The ethnic dilemma in social services.* New York: Free Press.

Leigh, J. W., & Green, J. W. (1982). The structure of the Black community: The knowledge base for social services. In J. W. Green, *Cultural awareness in the human services.* Englewood Cliffs, N.J.: Prentice-Hall.

Lonner, W. J. (1979). Issues in cross-cultural psychology. In A. J. Marsella, R. G. Tharp, & T. J. Ciborowski (Eds.), *Perspectives on cross-cultural psychology*. New York: Academic Press.

Lum, D., & Zuniga, M. (Eds.). (in press). *Ethnic minority social work practice: Individual, family, and community dimensions*.

Medicine, B. (1981). American Indian family: Cultural change and adaptive strategies. *Journal of Ethnic Studies, 8*, 13–23.

Miller, N. B. (1982). Social work services to urban Indians. In J. W. Green, *Cultural awareness in the human services*. Englewood Cliffs, N.J.: Prentice-Hall.

Price-Williams, D. (1979). Modes of thought in cross-cultural psychology: An historical overview. In A. J. Marsella, R. G. Tharp, & T. J. Ciborowski (Eds.), *Perspectives on cross-cultural psychology*. New York: Academic Press.

Solomon, B. B. (1976). *Black empowerment: Social work in oppressed communities*. New York: Columbia University Press.

Turner, F. J. (1978). *Psychosocial therapy*. New York: Free Press.

Wise, F., & Miller, N. (1981). The mental health of the American Indian child. In G. Powell, A. Morales, & J. Yamamoto (Eds.), *The Psychosocial development of minority group children*. New York: Brunner Mazel.

Contact

Contact involves the establishment of a relationship between the social worker and the minority client. But even before the actual face-to-face encounter, the social service agency should carefully prepare its staff and its procedural policy for working with ethnic minorities. To create a system of service delivery for minority clients, it is important for the administrative director and staff to have conducted an agency self-study, gathered relevant data on the minority population, and trained staff on approaches to minority practice. The purpose of this chapter is to identify and explain the major subsystems comprising worker-client contact. Figure 4-1 represents the major elements of worker and client systems practice issues in the contact stage. Under client system practice issues, there are sections on the minority client's resistance, barriers to communication, personal and family background, and ethnic community identity. We then move to worker system practice issues: understanding the minority community, relationship protocols, professional self-disclosure, and style of communication. We suggest practical ways to implement them in a planned strategy for people of color.

Client System Practice Issues

Resistance

A person of color often approaches a formal professional social service organization with varying degrees of resistance. There may be feelings of anxiety and uncertainty over the unknown, shame and guilt over failure to solve his or her own problems, or anger when there is legal coercion to use the service. Moreover, going to a helping agency may represent the last resort, after going through family, friends, and the community's natural support systems.

Causes

Resistance has traditionally been understood from the psychoanalytic perspective as opposition to the bringing of unconscious, repressed material to consciousness. The therapist generally confronts the patient early in the interpretive process, since resistance builds from an unwillingness to accept insights into the problem. Resistance has recently

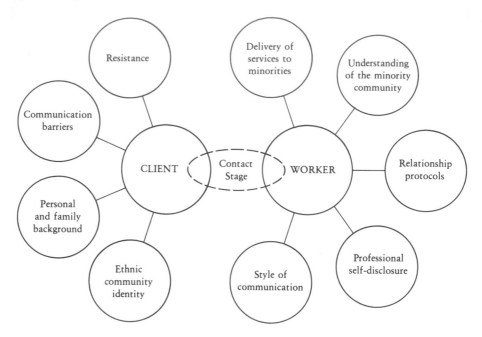

Figure 4-1.   Contact stage: Client system and worker system practice issues

been recognized as a natural reaction to coming to the helping process. Clinicians are taught to ask, as a part of the initial session, "How do you feel about coming here?" in order to deal with natural resistance. This open-ended question is a tactful way of exploring with the client any negative feelings that he or she may have. It is also designed to clear the atmosphere and to motivate the client. It seems natural to apply these principles to all clients.

However, understanding and coping with the resistance of minority clients calls for an alternative perspective, which must be differentiated for social work practice. Clear distinctions are made between minorities and nonminorities in social contexts. Bochner (1982) observes that in situations of cross-cultural contact people distinguish between hosts or owners, and visitors or newcomers, who are from dissimilar societies. These are labels that refer to in-group and out-group designations. Members of minority groups are particularly distinguished by highly visible characteristics of race, skin color, and language. Green (1982) uses the *cultural boundary* for the line that separates the professional social worker, organizational structure, and operational procedures from the minority client, community, and history. People of color reluctantly approach human service agencies that are controlled and dominated by Whites. The resistance of minority clients must be overcome through the establishment of trust.

Overcoming Resistance

A minority client must undertake the process of working through his or her resistance. Leigh (1984) describes how an ethnic minority person sizes up the helper. At first, he or she has minimal involvement and may be aloof, reserved, or superficially pleasant. He or she shows no overt interest in or curiosity about the worker. Then the client checks out the helper by asking about his or her personal life, background, opinions, and values. These probes are intended not only to evaluate the worker but also to become acquainted and to establish a personal relationship. Fritzpatrick (1981) points out that the basic value of the Puerto Rican culture is personalism—the focus on the individual's inner qualities, which determine his or her goodness or worth as a person. What makes a person good and respected is an inner dignity (*dignidad*). He remarks: "they are unusually responsive to manifestations of personal respect and to styles of personal leadership by men who appeal to the person rather than a program or a platform" (Fritzpatrick, 1981, p. 201). Perhaps the minority client instinctively searches for the inner qualities of the worker. Finding these traits, the client begins to lower his or her resistance and opens up to the worker. Otherwise, the client maintains resistance and drops out after an initial session or seeks another helping resource.

Velez (1980) further believes that *confianza en confianza* (trusting in mutual trust) is important to the extent that there is *deutro-learning,* a term that denotes mutualistic generosity, intimacy, and personal investment in others. Deutro-learning occurs when there is reciprocity of friendship, food, visits, labor, and other activities. Thus, the worker invests himself or herself in the client through the interpersonal helping process, while the client often reciprocates by bringing vegetables, fruits, candy, and other gifts of appreciation. *Confianza en confianza* further implies trusting in the trustworthiness of self and others. That is, the minority client trusts in the trustworthiness of the worker to an extent that eliminates the need for resistance. Not only does the client evaluate the character of the worker but reciprocal positive acts confirm the trust that has been established.

Lee (1981) observes that Indochinese are reluctant to disclose problems to strangers. Generally Indochinese share their problems and feelings with their families. Because of this cultural standard, Indochinese have to establish a vicarious family relationship with the worker. The process may involve assigning the worker a family kinship position. The worker is given a highly respected title, such as uncle or aunt, elder brother or sister, while the client speaks of himself or herself as nephew or niece (a younger, lower rank in the family). For some cultures, the implication is that the worker is adopted into the family as an honorary member, and therefore one with whom the minority client is able to share feelings and problems.

An ethnic minority client overcomes resistance by finding out about the worker, evaluating the worker's inner character, and perhaps bestowing family kinship. Social work practice should be aware of these alternative ways of dealing with resistance from the minority client. Rather than impeding the process, the social worker should participate in this reality-testing and demonstrate genuine caring and empathy.

CASE STUDY

The Hernandez Family

Mr. Hernandez is a 38-year-old Mexican American who is a gardener. He and his family are making an inquiry at the Family Service Association Agency regarding a problem one of the children is having in school. He speaks some English in his business because much of his clientele is middle- and upper-class Whites. From morning to evening he drives his truck and maintains yards and landscapes of many professional and wealthy Whites who live in the exclusive sections of the city. He is a hard worker who is friendly to his customers. During the holidays, many give him extra money and gifts for his family. After a hard day of work, Mr. Hernandez returns home tired. He has a few friends in the *barrio* who visit him in the evenings. He enjoys playing cards with them at home and drinking beer. He is reluctant to talk about personal and family problems to outsiders. Rather, he confides in his wife on the rare occasions when he is deeply troubled over a situation.

Task Recommendations

It is important to enter the world of a minority person. For 30 minutes you are to become Mr. Hernandez. Role-play him getting up in the morning before dawn, eating his breakfast, and leaving for a full day of gardening. Imagine his feelings about his work, his gardening skills, his conversations with some of his customers during the day, and his evenings at home with family and friends.

Over the course of several months, Mr. Hernandez tries to cope with a family problem involving his eldest son. He and his wife are unable to solve the problem. What would you do if you were Mr. Hernandez?

Would you approach a formal social service agency with your problem?

What would be your feelings during the opening session?

What kind of worker would you like to have help with your problem?

What would you do in order to determine whether the worker is a person whom you are willing to trust and in whom you are willing to confide?

Communication Barriers

Social work practice generally teaches communication skills based on the assumption that worker and client communicate through primary verbalization and secondary nonverbal cues. Devore and Schlesinger (1981) suggest tuning-in empathy to get in touch with feelings, attending skills focusing on verbal and nonverbal behavior, open- and close-ended questioning, and reaching for facts and feelings in a sensitive manner. However, there are a number of qualifications that must be made for people of color. Otherwise barriers to communication may form unbeknownst to the worker.

Special Concerns with People of Color

Valle (1980) suggests that to facilitate communication, the worker and client should begin *platica,* or friendly conversation. Latinos are used to mutual extended discussion, which is a recognized form of relationship building. *Platica* stresses mutuality and reciprocity, meaning an open and free exchange of information between the two parties. Helper-initiated friendly conversation about the weather, humorous incidents, or recent activities sets the stage for the development of a relationship. Brislin (1981) carries this good-will approach a step further when he observes that one must gear the conversation to the level of the client's background:

> Much cross-cultural contact involves communicating with people who do not share the same types of information. People who personalize knowledge are able to judge the amount of information the other person possesses and are able to communicate their knowledge through appropriate examples based on the background which the other person brings to the learning situation [p. 59].

It is important to find the personal fit between the communication levels of the worker and the client. As significant as the matching of levels of communication is appropriate content. Talking prematurely about taboo topics can hinder the flow of communication. Brislin (1981) speaks about conversational currency, or the range of topics that are considered proper subjects for conversation. They differ from culture to culture. Familiarizing oneself with those topics is necessary for the worker as conversation shifts to serious issues. Allowing the minority client to lead the way into a restricted topic is a safe rule of thumb. At times, a minority client may introduce a problem area in a subtle manner and wait for the worker to open up the dialogue around it. An impasse could form if the worker does not realize that this is happening. Leigh (1980) reminds us that a minority person often communicates latent content:

> Case workers will pick up on latent communication messages only if they have been trained to listen for such content and feelings. Racial references are probably passed by or when noted by the caseworker they will intervene and give another interpretation to the overt content. This action has the message in it that the subject is too dangerous, or immaterial to the process of help, or that the caseworker is too threatened by the mere perception of racial content in the relationship to manage his or her own feelings about the subject [p. 1].

The social worker must recognize that the person of color may be cautious about sharing his or her innermost thoughts and must adjust to indirect expression or allusions.

Educational Outreach

To increase communication and to promote mental health, educational media programs have been designed for minority community outreach. When ethnic minorities are exposed to cultural presentations, they are responsive to the helping process. Boulette (1980) offers four ways to present mental health concepts to Latinos; the methods are applicable to people of color in general. Spanish-language radio and television programming is a major vehicle of communication to the Chicano/Mexicano community. A series of 50 five-minute Spanish radio programs entitled *Una Familia Sana* ("a healthy family") focused on child-rearing practices; child development, discipline, and conflict resolution; and constructive parenting and cultural practices. The material was transcribed to cassettes, which were made available to organizations for parent-education discussion groups. A bilingual manual of preventive health care was written in Spanish and translated into English to retain a Chicano/Mexicano viewpoint. The manual was distributed to Spanish-speaking physicians, lawyers, public health nurses, welfare case aides, Headstart workers, and others. Educational coffee klatches and teas, called *Meriendas Educativas,* were organized to promote group mental health among low-income Spanish speaking women. These gatherings were designed to share information about primary prevention, reduce the social distance and distrust between staff and clientele, impart information about available services, and encourage resolution of child-rearing and marital problems. Learning fairs—*Fiestas Educativas*—were all-day health workshops for high-risk Latino parents. The goals were to recruit distressed parents; offer support in building strong, healthy families; encourage the sharing of language, traditions, and values; and provide medical, psychological, and resource information. These are examples of successful communication outreach programs in the area of mental health that target selected ethnic minority population groups.

Along with an awareness of overcoming communication barriers in a practice agency setting goes the complementary approach of educational outreach in the community. In working with minority clients, both strategies may be helpful in communicating problem-solving information on individual and community levels.

CASE STUDY

The Hernandez Family

Mr. Hernandez tends to be a quiet man who demonstrates his feelings through hard, methodical work on the gardening route. Because his English is limited, he is accustomed to communicating in Spanish with his family and friends. He does converse in English with his customers in order to maintain his business. In front of a helping professional such as a social worker, Mr. Hernandez is reserved and shy. He speaks only when it is necessary to answer questions asked by the worker. He does not initiate the conversation. Communication barriers are present.

Task Recommendations

Continue your role-playing of Mr. Hernandez, who has come to a family social service agency with a problem about his son. Place yourself in his position as a reserved man who is able to speak some English but who feels more comfortable communicating in Spanish. If you were Mr. Hernandez, what thoughts would be running through your mind about communicating with the worker?

What would be the best way to begin the conversation?
When would be the appropriate time to talk about the problem that I am having with my son?
How can I maintain my role as a strong father when my son has a problem?
Will I be blamed for my son's troubles?

Are there other Mexican–American families in similar situations?

These questions are pressing issues for Mr. Hernandez. How would you communicate effectively with him and lower some of the barriers that have been set up?

Personal and Family Background

It is important to cover information on personal and family background during the contact stage. Fritzpatrick (1981) points out that the solidarity of the family is the major psychosocial support for its members. The family provides a helping resource, particularly for minority individuals. Marsella (1979) observes that family structure and relationship patterns minimize depression in non-Western societies. Minority families have a support system composed of extended family and ethnic neighborhood community agencies. Among Latinos and other minority groups, there is a strong obligation to help each other as family members (Gonzales & Garcia, 1974). Personal and family background about the client is gathered to build a psychosocial information profile. Minority clients tend to be cautious about sharing information because it may have been used against them in the past. It is critical for the worker to develop information-gathering approaches that recognize this reality and to work with the minority client.

Solomon (1983) asserts that the traditional mode of gathering data during the initial interview may not be advantageous for minority clients. She indicates that clients are invariably required to answer questions that have little relevance to the problem-solving process. Examples are length of time in the community, place of employment, amount of family income, and religion. Some information, such as that pertaining to divorces, evictions, and last job held, reinforces the client's sense of personal deficiency. Solomon suggests that social workers ask questions that have direct bearing on the problem-solving work.

An alternative is to take down basic information over the telephone, such as name, address, phone number, and reason for coming to the agency. The worker allows essential information to emerge during the first few sessions and records relevant data after the client has left. Among the crucial areas of personal and family background are family structure, socioeconomic living conditions, and natural support system.

CASE STUDY

The Hernandez Family

Mr. Hernandez has been under increasing pressure during the past few months to support his family and several in-laws who have moved to Los Angeles from Mexico. Since unemployment is high, these recent immigrants are having a difficult time supporting themselves. Mr. Hernandez feels responsible and is working two jobs. As a result, he is gone from early morning to late night and is extremely tired when he arrives home. He is therefore unable to help his son Ricardo with his homework or play with him, and Mrs. Hernandez, who works in a laundry part time, cannot speak or read English. Moreover, the father has been under extreme stress and takes it out on the children. Ricardo has become disruptive in class. His grades have been poor in the last six weeks.

Task Recommendations

Obtaining personal and family information to increase knowledge of psychosocial interaction is important for the social worker. Some minority clients live in constant fear of revealing information that could be used against them in ways such as deportation from the United States. Disclosure of information should focus on relevant aspects of the problem.

> Review your agency's format for intake information. Discuss the possibility of revising it so that essential information is condensed to one page.
> Reflect on information that is essential to the problem-solving process.
> Use the first two sessions to obtain necessary information, which emerges during worker-client interaction.
> Find out about helping resources that the minority client has used in the ethnic community.

Ethnic Community Identity

It is important to determine whether the minority client is related to his or her ethnic community. Jenkins (1981) reports that minority people voiced positive feelings about going to their own community center staffed by bilingual/bicultural workers and having culturally oriented outreach programs. The choice of a worker was dependent on language fluency and cultural awareness. These findings support the need for establishing ethnic social service agencies that have capable ethnic staff, are located in a geographic area accessible to the ethnic population, and stress preventive educational programs.

Helping Networks

Within an ethnic community are natural helping resources that the minority client utilizes in his or her search for help. There are ethnic neighborhood networks that operate on many levels:

> Ethnic neighborhoods . . . were formed as places of refuge and protection in an alien world. The immigrants needed the support and assistance of others like themselves in order to establish a foothold in the new country. The ethnic neighborhood provided an economic base for the struggling newcomers. It also facilitated their efforts to organize and to participate collectively in the political system of America. In the neighborhood, they could

exchange information concerning the location of jobs and the views of various candidates for political office. Through neighborhood organizations, they could combine their forces to combat discrimination in employment or to negotiate with "city hall." In the neighborhood, they could engage in deeply satisfying human relationships with others who shared their language, religion, cuisine, and memories of the old country. The ethnic American neighborhood, in short, has been a device to enable immigrants to come to grips with the new while preserving many of the psychological satisfactions of the old. [McLemore, 1983, p. 382].

Various subsystems function within the networks to attend to particular needs. Newcomer services are vital to the constant influx of immigrants in many ethnic communities. Classes in English as a second language, job-finding employment services, reasonable and clean housing, native-language newspaper, and media programs are essential to making the adjustment to the new environment. Fritzpatrick (1981) cites the role of the Puerto Rican Family Institute, founded by Puerto Rican social workers, who identified and matched well-established and newly arrived families with each other. The former served as *compadres* to the latter in the New York City area in the early 1960s.

The *tanda* or *cundina,* a rotating credit association, is an example of a related support system. A number of invited participants contribute an agreed amount of money over a period of time. The total amount rotates to each participant within a time limit. Entrance into the *tanda* is based on mutual *confianza* relations and is designed to assist members with their financial needs.

Vega (1980) describes an integrated natural health delivery system composed of three layers with distinct functions. Revolving around a natural-healer support system, the primary level is composed of a network of individuals and families who have reciprocal exchanges with natural healers. The second level is the natural healing/coping community system whereby community residents are exposed to information about the healer. The third tier is made up of formal health service providers who are linked to the healer through treating the same individuals, having contact with each other, and having working arrangements for cross-referral and consultation.

Designated Helpers

Basic to the helping networks of an ethnic community are designated helpers who assist with a variety of local needs. In the Latino community, these persons are called *servidores.* Mendoza (1980) has classified *servidores* according to their roles:

1. historian *servidores,* who have resided in the community for 45 years or more and who have historical knowledge of the area and its actors;
2. young cohort *servidores,* who help their age peers in their 30s and 40s and the elderly Latinos;
3. resident and mobile *servidores,* who either operate in one location or travel throughout the county assisting persons;
4. program director *servidores,* who organize outreach group activities and are active on boards, in policy-making matters, and in advocacy;
5. casework counselor *servidores,* who work with individual clients as outreach workers and information and referral aides;
6. neighborhood caretaker *servidores,* who engage in supportive roles and make referrals to other *servidores* employed in agencies.

Servidores have established a community reputation for helping, building trust, resolution of problems, a willingness to give and provide for the needs of others, planning, information, outreach, and services to the elderly. The extent to which a minority client maintains a relationship with a *servidore* is an indication of the client's use of natural community resources.

Within an ethnic community, multiple service resources are available to a minority client. Whether or not a particular person is identified with a neighborhood or an ethnic population is important to determine at the beginning of the contact stage. Involvement in a specific ethnic community presupposes the client's strong identification with the ethnic community, which can be drawn upon for support systems.

CASE STUDY

The Hernandez Family

Mr. Hernandez is marginally involved with the local Mexican–American community. His wife is more involved in community affairs. She attends mass regularly at the neighborhood Catholic church. Apart from seeing his close friends and meeting his family responsibilities, Mr. Hernandez scarcely has time for community activities. He arrives home tired after working two jobs. Sunday is the only day he is off work. He usually goes fishing with his friends or with the children. He could be characterized as a person with a few close acquaintances who is trying to survive and meet the basic needs of his family.

At the same time, Mr. Hernandez is friendly and approachable in his community. He relates well to his neighbors and gives them advice about their landscape and gardening.

Task Recommendations

If Mr. Hernandez is open to help with family problems, ethnic community resources should be employed while guarding his confidentiality. There must be a guarantee that the whole Mexican–American community does not find out about his family problems. That would mean a loss of face.

What are some community resources potentially available to Mr. Hernandez to help him and his relatives with their job situations?
How would these resources be interpreted to Mr. Hernandez?
How could confidentiality be maintained if Mr. Hernandez decided to use a particular community service resource?

Worker System Practice Issues

Delivery of Services to Minorities

Central to an understanding ot minority social work practice is the effective design of a service delivery for ethnic clients. Watkins and Gonzales (1982) have summarized major barriers to utilization of social services by minority clients. In their review of the literature regarding Mexican Americans, they identify the following factors:

1. past compliance of social welfare agencies in identifying undocumented Mexicans for deportation;
2. perception of the public health worker as a representative of the government and therefore a potential threat;
3. group tension between Whites and Mexican Americans, especially when the worker is White;
4. fear of discrimination in treatment and high sensitivity to criticism from White health personnel;
5. differences in culture and language;
6. previous demeaning contact with mental health agencies;
7. lack of mental health facilities in the Mexican–American community;
8. differences in class-bound values of clients and agency staff;
9. biased diagnosis resulting in the assumption of high incidence of psychopathology among Mexican Americans;
10. the absence of bilingual and bicultural staff.

Other minority groups may voice similar reasons. The crucial question is: How can social work practitioners begin to lay foundations for contact with minority clients that will remove such barriers as those just listed? Fortunately, research in minority social services has uncovered certain principles in the utilization of services by minority clients.

Location and Pragmatic Services

Public and private agencies offering health care, employment, housing, day care, and other tangible and practical services should be located in or near large minority population areas. Arroyo and Lopez (1984) underscore the importance of geographic location of the social service agency;[1]

> Locating services in the *barrio* can be advantageous to a family service agency because of the high concentration of Chicanos; it is beneficial to the community because the services are physically accessible to the people who are to be served. It also indicates that the agency is sensitive to the importance of the *barrio* to Chicanos and the Chicano culture [p. 65].

There is good utilization of services by minority clients when facilities are located in their immediate neighborhood and are not advertised as mental health or counseling services (Catell, 1962; Yuen, no date). A home or storefront center, a unit of a multi-purpose community complex, or a component of a community medical facility

[1]From "Being Responsive to the Chicano Community: A Model for Service Delivery," by R. Arroyo and S. A. Lopez. In B. W. White (Ed.) *Color in a White Society*, pp. 63–73. This and all other quotations from this source are reprinted by permission of the National Association of Social Workers.

are appropriate choices for an accessible location. Agencies stand a better chance for steady utilization if they offer concrete, pragmatic aid. Mental illness or emotional disturbance carries a social stigma and disgrace for some minority cultures. After the agency has gained credibility and community trust, social and family casework can be applied to individual and group problems.

Staffing

Bilingual/bicultural workers should be employed for non–English-speaking minority clients. Arroyo and Lopez (1984) explain the strategic importance of a bilingual approach to minority clients:

> The significance of the Spanish language cannot be overemphasized, for Spanish has been instrumental in maintaining personal, meaningful relationships that have provided emotional stability for many Chicanos. Even Chicanos who are bilingual often revert to Spanish because it is their first language—their mother tongue—and it has great emotional significance for them. Moreover, Chicanos frequently think in Spanish even when they speak English. It is important to remember this phenomenon, particularly when providing counseling services to Chicanos, because when people experience stress, they tend to regress and use their primary language to express fully their worries, anxieties, fears, and concerns. Furthermore, it must be kept in mind that language reflects an individual's philosophy of life, value system, and (most important) aspects of the personality that one may find difficult to understand or even may not notice without knowledge of the language [p. 68].

Recent immigrants and elderly members of ethnic minorities have difficulty understanding and communicating in English when they seek public services (Lee, 1960; Chen, 1970; Campbell & Chang, 1973; Sue & Wagner, 1973). Bilingual and bicultural workers should be fluent in the language dialects of clients and familiar with child-rearing and family practices, ethnic customs and beliefs, and other cultural nuances. In the absence of bilingual/bicultural staff, a community case aide with language and cultural skills may be utilized as a co-caseworker with staff and client.

Crucial to the matter of staffing are a vigorous program for training staff in language and culture of the ethnic community populations and case consultation with a clinical resource in ethnic minority social work. Kahn, Williams, Galvez, Lejero, Conrad, and Goldstein (1975) describe a staff training experience that included on-the-job and university sessions on Papago Indians. Cultural Study 4-1 illustrates minority mental health training.

Cultural Study 4-1

Minority Staff Training[2]

I had first heard about mental health through a friend who was working as a Community Health Representative. She had asked if I would be interested in a position in the mental health field. Although I really didn't know much about mental health, it sounded interesting, so I applied and was surprised that I was hired.

I learned the job mainly from on-the-job training, dealing with cases at the same time that I was learning and getting experience. We started with an introduction from the mental health staff that included the professional staff and the one already trained Papago mental health worker.

We then paired up with the trained people and learned as we went along. We had a lot of training sessions in the beginning, which included role playing and explanations of things. The most important thing I think a mental health worker needs to learn is to develop a trusting relationship with people with whom he is working. Being honest with people about what you are trying to do and how you are trying to find ways to help them and maintaining confidentiality are important. Confidentiality is particularly sensitive on a reservation, where many people are related or know each other. The villages are very small and things can get around rapidly. Developing the interviewing skills is also quite important, as well as knowing what kind of information you need to have in order to understand the problem. Things like observing people's behavior and expression during the interview and getting them to talk about their feelings and to trust you enough to tell the details of the problem are other important skills. We had to learn about neurosis and psychosis, and how these conditions can be changed or helped.

Our program tries to build ongoing training sessions using the professional staff to have regular weekly sessions about different topics in the field. We spend a lot of time learning about abnormal psychology and having in-depth case conferences. We also try to have a training session for the whole staff at the University of Arizona at least once every several months, where we can take up a topic sometimes through a film and discuss it.

We have developed our skills in helping people, both in Anglo ways and in Papago cultural ways and sometimes with a combination of both. While we see a good variety of types of cases, I tend to work a lot with couples with marital problems and often these involve problems of alcoholism. I've learned it's important when I work with a couple that I also involve a female mental health worker so that I'm not biased for the man.

It's also important in many of the Papago marital situations to get the husband to show the wife some affection. Papagos aren't people who show others their feelings very readily and this is often a problem in marital situations. Take, for example, the case of a middle-aged couple I worked with recently. The case involved alcoholism, as do many cases on the reservation. The husband had been intoxicated for some time, seemingly ignoring his spouse's feelings. This came to our attention as a result of his spouse being admitted to the hospital because of acute depression. I worked extensively with the wife providing supportive therapy while attempting to contact the husband.

We finally managed to get the couple together. I then enlisted the aid of a female mental health worker to provide marital counseling. There was a misinterpretation by the couple that the other member did not wish to continue the marriage. Our first task was to get the couple together to assure that each wanted to continue the marriage. Our second task was to get the couple to express their feeling for one another. After many sessions the couple began to realize that their situation was not as hopeless as it seemed. Since then they have been able to resolve some of their problems.

[2]From "The Papago Psychology Service: A Community Mental Health Program on an American Indian Reservation," by M. W. Kahn, C. Williams, E. Galvez, L. Lejero, R. Conrad, and G. Goldstein, *American Journal of Community Psychology*, 1975, 3, 88–90. Reprinted by permission of Plenum Publishing Corporation.

Community Outreach Programs

Community outreach programs are effective with persons who are hesitant about coming to a social service agency for help. Outreach programs offer preventive education in schools, family associations, ethnic churches, and other community groups. Arroyo and Lopez (1984) suggest some alternative outreach approaches:

For example, although home visits are viewed by some agencies as being unproductive and an inappropriate use of a worker's time, such visits can be a means of intervention with Chicanos when in-office sessions are not possible. Groups sessions also may have to be scheduled outside the agency. They may be established in a school with the assistance of the principal, counselors, and teachers. These school contacts allow the development of parent education groups for parents of schoolchildren [p. 67].

Agency follow-up interviews result as people of color make informal educational and social contact with social service staff in their community clubs. Bilingual brochures and community program announcements are means of answering questions that relate to issues of family interest. The Asian Pacific Counseling and Treatment Center in Los Angeles is an excellent example of a minority agency that has preventive and outreach services, bilingual/bicultural staff, and an accessible location. Cultural Study 4-2 reports on the center.

Cultural Study 4-2

Preventive Outreach Services, Bilingual/Bicultural Staff, and Accessible Location[3]

The Asian Pacific Counseling and Treatment Center is a county- and state-funded facility near central Los Angeles. Initiated in the spring of 1977, the Center is deliberately located at a site which is accessible to but not identified with any of the ethnic communities such as Little Tokyo, Chinatown, Koreatown or Manilatown.

Since the opening of the clinic, a large number of patients have been seen from the different Asian Pacific Islander minority populations. A very high proportion of our patients are chronically psychotic and severely disordered. Approximately 50% of the patients seen at the Asian Clinic are psychotic, as contrasted with only 20% who are so diagnosed in the majority clinics.

For many Asians and Pacific Islanders, there is a persistent stigma attached to using mental health services which necessitates that efforts also be directed towards primary prevention. Therefore, in selecting staff to fill positions, a serious consideration must be their ability to relate to the community and to do outreach work.

Experience has shown that our clients are more likely to seek help from professionals who are Asian rather than non-Asian. Staff personnel are bilingual and bicultural: they all grew up in Asia or the Pacific Islands, and have been educated here in the United States.

Thus they are in an ideal position to better understand the problems of acculturation encountered by immigrants.

The generational differences among the staff are noteworthy. The overwhelming majority of the staff are first generation immigrants, all of whom received their graduate mental health training in this country. As a result, they are able to successfully bridge two cultures for our clients. One would, however, characterize the staff interaction as Asian. That is, while most identify themselves as Asian Americans, they still retain the major traits, values and attitudes of their cultural traditions (Yamamoto and Wagatsuma, 1980). The Indo-chinese staff have a somewhat different perspective on identity, having immigrated here more recently than the other immigrant staff, and also having been forced to flee their homeland as refugees.

Asian patients are mostly referred by outside agencies, with less than 20% being self-referred or referred by families, in contrast to majority patients who are mostly self-referred or referred by their families (Lam et al., 1980). Yet Asian and Pacific Islander patients are much more often still interdependent upon their families. When they come to the Asian Clinic, they often arrive with some family member. Therefore, the staff has initiated routine interviews of patients with their relatives, unless patients choose to be seen individually. That is to say, we much more often conceptualize the family as the unit to be evaluated and helped. We are aware, of course, that with some families where there is the question of high emotional involvement (Brown et al., 1972; Vaughn and Leff, 1976), we may have to see the schizophrenic patients have some relief from relatives. For instance, we may try to arrange for patients to go to Asian Rehabilitation Services, a sheltered workshop where they learn important skills and have time away from relatives who are critical, intrusive, and overinvolved.

The responsible attitudes of our patients and their families is reflected in the fact that, of all the clinics in Los Angeles County, the Asian Clinic collects the highest percentage of fees. In addition, patients very often give gifts to therapists. We have recommended that the staff accept such gifts and thank the patients and their families, despite the fact that county rules forbid the acceptance of gifts. Gift-giving is no more than a continuation of culturally syntonic behavior, that is, behavior normally responsive and adaptive to the social or interpersonal environment, and it would be insulting to reject them.

[3]From "Group Therapy for Asian American and Pacific Islanders," by J. Yamamoto and J. Yap, *P/AAMHRC Research Review*, 1984, 3, 1. Reprinted by permission.

Agency Setting

Agency setting should be conducive to the comfort of ethnic minority clients. A bilingual receptionist should be stationed to greet clients and put them at ease with refreshments. Agencies should decorate the facility with ethnic art that reflects the ethnic clientele of the area and conveys the nonverbal message to clients that the agency is sensitive to the minority community. Office staff should convey a friendly and informal atmosphere to clients. Staff should maintain their appointment schedules promptly. Clients should not be kept waiting for a long period of time. Most agencies maintain a staff member who is on call to see walk-in clients, to minimize the lag between the telephone contact and the first session.

Service Linkage

Social service agencies should establish linkage with minority organizations. They are a source of helpful suggestions for upgrading minority community services. Arroyo and Lopez (1984) suggest: "One way of maintaining community awareness is to develop and maintain linkages with other agencies serving Chicanos. These connections ensure that the agencies will have knowledge of the evolving lifestyles and patterns of immigration-migration and of mobility through a mutual sharing of information" (pp. 66–67). A directory of minority community information and referral is useful to link clients with significant others as ministers, community association leaders, and bilingual physicians and nurses. In many large cities, local and state funding has been obtained for ethnic group social service organizations composed of bilingual staff and having a governing board drawn from the various minority communities. Such organizations have targeted the needs of minority youth, immigrants, and elderly and have created a network linking program services of public and private institutions.

Planning Minority Service Delivery

The creation of a system of minority service delivery requires the willingness of social service agencies to incorporate the principles of location, staffing, community outreach, agency setting, and service linkage. The planning of service programs to meet the unique needs of minority clients is a challenge for traditional agencies. Wong, Kim, Lim, and Morishima (1983) identify ten principles for planning a minority mental health training center:

1. community-based services with strong linkages, credibility, and good reputations in the minority community and its networks;
2. a critical mass of ethnic staff and clients for a diversity of programs;
3. internship training to augment and complement existing academic training programs with special skills in working with minority populations and communities;
4. shared support and decision-making among multidisciplinary staff;
5. mutual teaching and learning environment of peers and subordinates, with staff viewed as resources for the organization;
6. a coordinated service delivery system in which staff selection and programs contribute to the total mission of the agency, (recognizing the importance of such things as the family and community networks);
7. a longitudinal perspective on programs and staff, which have positive track records based on commitment, performance, and allocation of resources;
8. outreach services for home, churches, schools, and community centers;
9. problem consultation, mental health education, community organization, and program technical assistance;
10. fluent bilingual service providers.

CASE STUDY

The Agency

A Family Service Association agency is located in a large metropolitan area with a diverse minority population consisting of 25% Black, 20% Latino, 12% Asian, and 8% Native Americans. The minority staff consists of a Black and a Chicano social worker. They are inundated with their own minority caseload and refer clients to other ethnic organizations. For several years the Family Service Association director and staff have discussed the need to increase minority services. A survey of minority social needs was conducted in the service population area. A major finding was the rapid increase in number of Mexican, Vietnamese, and Indochinese immigrants in the community.

Recently the county board of supervisors has designated block grant funds to develop minority mental health services. The director of the agency decides to apply for a grant to increase the agency's bilingual staff and minority clientele. A request for proposal (RFP) was recently sent to social service agencies in the county.

Task Recommendations

There are a number of strategic steps that can be taken to implement delivery of services to minority clients:

1. Read and discuss the first three chapters of this book as a group. Find out the participants' notions of culture, minority values, and approaches to ethnic practice.
2. Conduct a study of the needs of minority clients, service programs, and staffing. Obtain local census tract data on minority populations in your service area. Consult with minority community leaders on current social problems. Analyze present approaches to minority client contact and practice. Find out whether there is a comparable ratio between minority client populations and minority bilingual/bicultural staff.
3. Hire a case consultant in minority social work from a nearby school of social work. Initiate a consultation report on the minority mission of the agency, service needs of the minority community, and recommendations on minority programs, staffing, funding, and training. Have the minority consultant interact with staff on minority case issues and provide minority practice in-service training.
4. Chart out a step-by-step program of service delivery to minority clients: increase in qualified bilingual/bicultural staff, accessible facility location, community outreach programs, and so on.
5. Set up a steering committee composed of agency staff, minority community leaders, and minority social work practitioners and educators to oversee these developments.
6. Establish support bases for minority service delivery with the agency administrator, governing board, and minority community organizations.
7. Work out funding support for this project on a local, state, or federal level.
8. Implement a timetable for moving toward increasing minority clinical and community services to various ethnic populations.

Understanding of the Minority Community

Along with constructing a minority delivery system goes the need to establish understanding of the minority community. A social work staff should be well versed in the characteristics of local minority communities. Glasgow (1980) stresses the importance of learning about the history, problems, and demographics of a minority community. In Cultural Study 4-3 he reiterates the important facts of Watts.

Cultural Study 4-3

The Ghettoization of Watts[4]

The city of Los Angeles is a metropolis of approximately seven and a half million people spread over an area of about 454 square miles. The Human Relations Commission of Los Angeles estimated that in 1968 Blacks represented at least 17 percent of the total population. But most of these (85 percent) were compressed in an area covering about 65 square miles. Watts, a small community located ten miles south of the central city, was only one early segment of this large ghetto complex. Although Black men and women of Watts (rarely children) were seen in downtown Los Angeles, the nature of their lives and their community was unknown to most Americans, including Los Angelenos. Many Blacks commuted to jobs in the city, but in the five o'clock rush hour the vehicles headed home in color-differentiated streams: the Blacks south to Adams, Avalon, Willowbrook, and Watts; the whites north and west to the Hollywood Hills, Beverly Hills, Sherman Oaks, and the San Fernando Valley. And there they took up their separate existences, largely ignorant of one another, until the explosion of 1965 forced white America to recognize the plight of Blacks. Watts no longer remained a hidden by-way, but became a symbol of a new explosiveness among Blacks.

The ghettoization of Watts began in the early forties with the advent of the war industries boom. The development of this community as an isolated ghetto was forecast by the American Council on Race Relations as early as 1947. It noted that before World War II the population of Watts was evenly divided among Mexican Americans, Blacks, and Whites. But between 1942 and 1947 a very heavy in-migration of rural and southern Blacks was accompanied by a similar exodus of the other two groups, and by 1947 Blacks made up five sixths of the population. Although a few whites still lived there and others had moved their families but held on to their businesses, the remaining one sixth comprised Latinos, who increasingly came into conflict with Blacks. By 1949, a report noted that:

> Watts is a polygot [sic] community bothered by intercultural tensions and insecurities. By day, it is teaming [sic] with Negroes and Mexican-Americans shopping and hanging about the stores of the white merchants. One Hundred and Third Street is the half-world of Los Angeles, and the commuter passing it on his Pacific Electric car from Long Beach sees nothing outstanding about this community *except that it is Negro*. But should he walk around 103rd Street after sundown, pushing through the crowds, clustering about the bars or gathering on sidewalks to watch the wrestling matches on T.V., he would sense a difference. . . . The street lights are small and too far between to be of much help. . . . Fights and occasional killings underline the tension in this area where two minority groups are blindly pitted against each other, each group facing job discrimination, poor housing, and inadequate recreational facilities, with few attempts at intercultural education and understanding [Robinson, 1949; pp. 37–38].

[4]From *The Black Underclass*, by D. G. Glasgow, pp. 37, 38. Copyright © 1980 by Jossey-Bass. Reprinted by permission.

There are a number of suggestions for improving the worker's understanding of a minority community:

Study the demographic profile and social problems of the local minority community.
Walk through the community as a participant-observer, noting the way people live and relate to one another in their physical surroundings.
Patronize minority businesses and talk to store owners and customers about the news of the community.
Show up at social and educational community events to understand how people enjoy themselves and learn in their ethnic groups.
Become acquainted with the minority helping community to build working relationships with a wide variety of resource persons.

Brownlee (1978) suggests some common-sense principles of community understanding: look and listen before asking and acting; explore the community's attitude toward "being studied"; find out about special rules of protocol; and place human relations ahead of getting answers.

Solomon's (1983) concept of *ethnosystem* relates to community understanding. The ethnosystem is a society comprising groups that vary in modes of communication, control over material resources, and internal social structure. Involvement in the minority ethnosystem occurs in barbershops, churches, bars, and other community places. It is important for social workers to become acquainted with various parts of the ethnosystem (Solomon, 1983). Ghali (1977) argues:

Often when a poor Puerto Rican sees a professional worker he is wondering what that person thinks of the poor, of the dark-skinned, of those inarticulate in the English language. Does the professional worker understand how the ghetto has affected him? What it is like to be hungry, humiliated, powerless, and broke? Does he really want to help or just do a job? [p. 460]

Dryden (1982) reports on a community study effort that a social service department conducted with the Bengali community in England. Cultural Study 4-4 describes the practical steps that were taken in community understanding. (BWAG is the Bengali Workers Action Group, and a patch team is an area team.)

Cultural Study 4-4

Community Study and Learning Experience[5]

As the community work with the BWAG developed, so work with individual Bengali families by the social workers in the area team increased. Both heightened the awareness of the needs of this community and the failure of the traditional services to meet them. The patch team responsible for the neighbourhood where the majority of Bengali people were living undertook a patch needs and resources assessment exercise. When the area team had adopted the patch system some months before, the team had mapped out new referrals and existing cases. It became clear that there was a large area, the furthest from the office, which, though it came out high on indices of need such as overcrowding, lack of housing

(continued)

Cultural Study 4-4 (continued)

amenities, open space and facilities, and included some of the worst privately rented housing in the borough, produced very few referrals. The community work with the Bengali community centred on this area and the social worker who had taken on the original four referrals had become linked in to the network of Bengali families in the same district. The patch team struggled to make decisions about the special areas for investigation. The traditional needs of children, young people and the elderly population (which was known to be large), competed with the relatively recently identified needs of the Bengali community. Largely, I think, as a result of the alliance between the community worker (who had agreed to help the team with the exercise) and the caseworker involved with individual Bengali families, the assessment of the needs of the Bengali community was finally chosen as one of the four areas for special investigation.

Members of the team collected information in various ways including studying census material and analysing referrals. Armed with some factual information they talked to workers in the local playcentres, neighbourhood advice agencies, schools, health clinics and day care facilities about the needs they perceived in the Bengali community and the services they were providing. A walkabout headcount was done in an effort to ascertain the size of the community. This produced a conservative estimate of about 550 people, about 7 per cent of the patch's population. A by-product of this exercise was the marvellous opportunity to talk to local Bengali people about what they were doing and thinking. All the information gathered was collated in a report which looked at the community with regard to housing, health, education, employment, recreation, immigration and nationality and social services.

Collecting this information alerted the patch team to the unmet need in this community. It also gave them a basis for planning their own work and supporting their arguments for the reallocation of resources and changes in departmental policy and practice. The team decided to run a weekly advice session in a neighborhood centre in the district and a member of the BWAG is paid to attend the session as an interpreter. Team members decided also to use half a social work post to enable a worker to concentrate on developing services for the Bengali community. The needs assessment exercise was valuable both in process and product. Members of the team learned new skills in gathering and analysing information. The results they achieved enabled them to re-distribute their own resources in an informed way and contribute to departmental knowledge and thinking. In 1978 the Social Services Committee set up a race relations working party to look at the Department's services to minority communities. With the evidence from the patch assessment the team made an impressive report to the working party and presented a good case for the employment of Bengali-speaking aides in the area office.

[5]From "A Social Services Department and the Bengali Community: A New Response," by J. Dryden. In J. Cheetham (Ed.) *Social Work and Ethnicity,* pp. 157, 158. Copyright © 1982 by Allen and Unwin, Inc. Reprinted by permission.

In the process of understanding the minority community, the worker becomes known to potential minority clients. Ho (1976) believes that it is imperative for the worker to express sincerity, concern, and caring and to establish a reputation for integrity. It is also important to maintain positive working relationships and to win the support of community leaders (Ho, 1976). These achievements do not come instantly. Social distancing of the community from social service agencies reflects past neglect and institutional racism. The individual social worker must prove himself or herself over a period of time before gaining the acceptance and trust of the minority community.

CASE STUDY

The Agency

The director of the Family Service Association would like to expose staff to the living conditions of the minority community. He has visited with various ethnic community leaders and organizations of the Black, Latino, Asian, and Native American communities. He has talked with them about how his agency could effectively meet their needs. He would like to involve his staff in exposure to the minority community.

Task Recommendations

In order to establish minority community understanding, there are a number of steps that can be taken:

1. Select a geographic area of the minority community and spend a day walking the streets. Observe people at work and at home. Eat lunch in a local ethnic restaurant. Buy items in neighborhood stores. Talk with people on the street. Note the problem areas that you see.
2. Go with a staff worker or a community person who has rapport with the local minority community. Meet community leaders and visit ethnic human service agencies in the area.
3. Spend the week as the house guest of a minority family. Eat meals and spend evenings with them. During the day, "shadow" a local ethnic community worker and observe how he or she relates to minority people. Find out about local cultural customs, protocols, and the lifestyles of members of your host family.
4. Become a financial supporter of and participant in an ethnic community social service or political organization. Attend meetings and become involved in projects.
5. Establish a staff exchange program between your agency and an ethnic counterpart to cross-fertilize ideas. The results are practical on-the-job training, mutual referrals, and alternative approaches to intervention.

Relationship Protocols

Relationship protocols are observed in many minority communities. Formal expressions of respect are exchanged between the greeter and the head of household before proceeding into the main conversation. Finding out about relationship protocols is important during the initial contact with minority families. Harwood (1981) is aware of the variation among ethnic groups with respect to contact with specific relatives who may be informational resources for the clinician. He states:

> Among the Navajos, for example, matrilineally related women living in close proximity to the patient would be most appropriate; among Mexican Americans, the bilaterally extended family in general should be consulted and, for males, in particular, older male relatives; among Puerto Ricans, it might be sufficient to contact the wife/mother or, for elderly patients, their children [p. 501].

It is important for the worker to learn about the various family structures and hierarchies to discover appropriate kin persons who may provide information or serve as supportive resources. Usually the father is the acknowledged authority in the family. It is important for the social worker to acknowledge this role and to defer to the father with major questions during the initial session. An indirect way to find out about family authority is to ask how family decisions are made. This question elicits information about family rules and customs, behavior patterns, and roles. Oftentimes members of the family nonverbally acknowledge a parent with a glance when this question is posed to the family.

Ghali points out that the Puerto Rican family is patriarchal. The man is the absolute chief and sets the norms for the whole family. Family members respect and even fear the father. He is the breadwinner and decision maker. His wife is responsible for the care of the children and the housekeeping (Ghali, 1977). Other minority groups emphasize the importance of the family and define individual roles in relation to this primary unit. For Asian Americans, the family unit serves as the link between the past and future. Each family member has a specific role and function (Wong, Lu, Shon, & Gaw, 1983). The development of affective ties and family relationships is central to resolving societal problems. The family provides stability, a sense of self-esteem, and satisfaction. Close family ties, family conformity, and role structures are important to the mental health of Asians (Sue & Morishima, 1982). A similar case for Black and Native American families was made in the section on family values in Chapter 2.

The social worker should not undercut or negate the importance of the family or of the father as family authority. Rather, the worker should suggest practical ways to support and strengthen the role of the father as a good authority and the importance of family functioning. The worker should not encourage individual freedom apart from these reference points.

CASE STUDY

The Hernandez Family

A Mexican–American family, the Hernandez family, has approached the Family Services Association regarding the disruptive school behavior of ten-year-old Ricardo Hernandez. Mr. Hernandez, a 38-year-old gardener, immigrated from Mexico with his wife and has been in Los Angeles for ten years. Mrs. Hernandez, age 29, works part time in a large commercial laundry, ironing and folding linens and towels for restaurants, hospitals, and other commercial businesses. The Hernandezes have two other children: Isabella, age 8, and Eduardo, age 6. A White staff member has been assigned the case because of the Spanish-speaking worker's full caseload. The assignment was made with the understanding that the Latino social worker would serve as a consultant and support base for issues in ethnic minority practice that arise during sessions. The present caseworker has worked with minority clients in public welfare and in the present agency.

Task Recommendations

It is important to observe family protocols during the early contact stage. The worker should acknowledge family authority and harmony. Here are some practical suggestions for implementing family protocols:

Stand when the family enters the room. Greet the parents first. Speak initially to the father and take your cues for behavior and movement from him. Acknowledge his authority by asking for his insights on what has been going on.

Observe how family members interact and react to the behavior of the father. Is there respect or hostility between several members of the family and the father? What is the relationship between father and mother and between father and children? How does the perspective of the father differ from that of other family members?

When working with a single client, ask about the family to gain a sense of the role of the family in influencing the individual. Determine whether or not to involve the family with the client during later sessions.

Professional Self-Disclosure

Professional self-disclosure entails the social worker's taking the initiative to build a relationship by disclosing an area of interest common to the worker and the client. The significance attached to self-disclosure is based on the belief that minority clients come to social service agencies with reservations about social workers. Regarding self-disclosure of the professional, Lee (1982) observes:

It is not uncommon for clients to ask the therapist many personal questions about his or her family background, marital status, number of children, and so on. The therapist will need to feel comfortable about answering personal questions in order to gain clients' trust and to establish rapport. Clients, in turn, find that they can reasonably depend on the competencies of the clinician because they have been able to "evaluate" the clinician's background [p. 545].

Rather than concealing oneself behind professional policies and practices, the worker meets the client as a human being and initiates the relationship. Rather than focusing on the client's problem, the goal is to humanize the relationship by disclosing a topic common to both of their backgrounds. Professional self-disclosure lays the groundwork for the reciprocal response of self-disclosure by the client.

Among the practical suggestions for practicing professional self-disclosure are to introduce yourself; to share pertinent background about your work, family, and helping philosophy; and to find a point of common interest with the client. Revealing oneself as a human being affords the client an opportunity to assess character and form a tentative impression of the worker. It communicates the message that the worker is willing to disclose himself or herself and welcomes client response. Reciprocation on the part of the minority client may take longer than expected. An old Native American expression is: "How can I tell you about my personal life, which I share with my life-long friends, when I have met you only a half hour ago?" Mistrust and reservation are typical responses of minority clients until the social worker moves out of the category of stranger. Taking the first step of professional self-disclosure sets the stage for openness and the building of a relationship.

Research into minority practice finds that minority clients are apprehensive about professional help. Sue and Morishima (1982) cite several studies that show the anxiety-based apprehension of Asian–American university students about communication. Lewis and Ho (1975) observe that a Native American client may be reticent about disclosing sensitive or distressing topics until he or she is sure of the sincerity, interest, and trustworthiness of the worker. Solomon (1983) explains that Blacks in Southern states are distrustful of social welfare agencies because of differing benefit payment schedules for Whites and Black clients. In many welfare offices, Blacks may exhibit feelings of anger and hostility, passiveness, and dependency, reflecting their responses to frustration and powerlessness. Sue (1981) examines a number of barriers from the perspective of the minority client: mistrust of the worker, who, as an agent of society, could use information against the client; cultural barriers against intimate revelations to a culturally different person; and anxiety and confusion as a result of an unstructured relationship.

Professional self-disclosure focuses on a common link between the worker and the client. This common base personalizes the relationship and puts the client at ease. It humanizes the situation between the worker and the client. It is an extension of the social worker's use of self.

CASE STUDY

The Hernandez Family

Mr. Platt is the social worker assigned to the Hernandez family. He recognizes that minority clients have reservations about coming to an agency for assistance with family problems. Fortunately, Mr. Platt has traveled in Mexico and Central America and knows some Spanish phrases, but is unable to carry on an extended conversation in Spanish.

He begins by greeting the family and talking with the father. He shares his travel experiences in Mexico: the various cities, people, and food. He finds out about the Hernandez family and their upbringing in Mexico. He does not focus on the presenting problem. He places the family at ease with his Spanish. They laugh at his pronunciation of some Spanish words and phrases.

Mr. Platt talks about the agency's program and services. He explains the meaning of the helping process. He gives them a brochure, written in English and Spanish, that explains the services and fee schedule. Mr. Platt notices that Mr. Hernandez speaks some English and can make himself understood, although he hesitates over a few words and concepts. Mrs. Hernandez speaks Spanish fluently but has little English. The children speak English and assist in translation between the parents and the social worker. The parents speak to them in Spanish throughout the session. Mr. Platt asks each family member how they feel about coming to Family Service and his or her willingness to continue in the sessions.

Task Recommendations

Practice professional self-disclosure with a minority client in an initial session. Do not wait for the client to begin with the problem. Initiate the conversation and allow the client to get to know you as a person.

> Introduce yourself, sharing your background and some information about your work at the agency. Personalize the relationship to the extent that the client finds out about an interesting facet of your life.
> Find a common ground for conversation with the client so that it can serve as a bridge between you.
> Become a human being to your client by expressing humor or sharing a brief story about yourself. Put the client at ease by serving modest refreshments.
> Ask the client how he or she feels about coming to the first session. Support and identify with feelings of anxiety, discomfort, and uncertainty. Place yourself in the client's situation and verbalize those feelings back to him or her.

Style of Communication

The client encounters the social service agency's style of communication at the moment of contact. A bilingual and friendly receptionist, an accessible location, and an attractive facility communicate a positive message to clients. A private interviewing room, comfortable furniture, light refreshments, and a casual approach create an open and relaxed atmosphere. This setting is the basis for the positive communication style of the social worker.

Body language expresses acceptance. A posture with the body leaning slightly forward, attentive and relaxed, conveys willingness to listen with anticipation and under-standing. Sincerity and concern exhibited in facial expression, voice, and open-palm hand gestures communicate concern.

Language is the major means of communication. Bilingual social workers convey familiarity and evoke responsiveness when they are able to speak the language of the client. It is a common bond between the worker and the minority client (Ghali, 1977; Bernal, Bernal, Martinez, Olmedo, & Santisteban, 1983). Bilingual persons manifest different character traits, recall different sets of experiences, and feel a different sense of identity according to whether they are speaking English or their native language. Each language evokes a distinctive cognitive, affective, and behavioral pattern. Among disturbed Latino patients, more psychopathology is manifested when they are inter-viewed in English than when they are interviewed in Spanish. Part of the reason is that the English-speaking frame of reference is not applicable to the specific problems of the Latino patients (Marcos, Alpert, Urcuyo, & Kesselman, 1973). The implications of this research for recruiting bilingual/bicultural social workers are obvious. The case for training social workers in minority cognition, affect, and behavior is even more compelling.

Research with minority people has uncovered various culturally distinct communica-tive expressions. For instance, for a Japanese person, nodding the head does not necessarily signify agreement. Rather, it conveys attentiveness and assures the commu-nicator that he or she has been heard. Unaware of its meaning, a social worker could totally misinterpret this gesture (Kuramoto, Morales, Munoz, & Murase, 1983). Some street-wise urban Black youth relate antisocial exploits to force the worker to make value judgments. Raised eyebrows, furrowed forehead, and shifting in one's seat at sensational stories about drugs, sex, alcohol, and delinquency are nonverbal signs to these youth that the worker has made a value judgment. This tactic is employed to scare the worker off, test sincerity, and measure empathy for ghetto conditions (Franklin, 1983). The street language of Black youth employs slang words with a unique cadence, tone, and usage. The worker who is unfamiliar with these idioms should be honest about ignorance of the terms. The worker should encourage the client to educate him or her about their meanings (Franklin, 1983). Language incongruency between the worker and minority families creates a problem in communication. Pseudodialogues or parallel monologues occur when both parties attempt to communicate with each other to no avail. The worker terms this behavior "resistance," while minority family members refer to it as "social worker talk" (Minuchin, Montalvo, Guerney, Rosman, & Schumer, 1967).

The social worker should enhance his or her communication style with minority clients. In Cultural Study 4-5, Kahn et al. (1975) suggest some approaches to communi-cation when working with the Papagos.

Cultural Study 4-5

Minority Communication Styles[6]

The Papago client brings several attitudes with him which influence the mode of therapy utilized. Many of these attitudes are due to the influence of the traditional culture and, more specifically, due to the influence of the medicine man or Mai Kai. Only he possesses the knowledge to heal and only a brief diagnostic interview is required before the healing ceremony begins. Clearly, this is much different from psychotherapy, wherein the client is an active participant and has a great deal of responsibility for his improvement.

Another attitude the Papago brings to therapy is that of secrecy regarding personal matters. Most Papagos loathe discussing personal information with anyone, and doing so with strangers is certainly most uncommon.

The paucity of verbal communication (as compared to the Anglo) is another variable which has considerable influence on therapeutic methodology. Impressionistically, it seems the Papagos really aren't very verbose among themselves and certainly not with Anglo professionals or, if you will, authority figures. This brings us to another attitudinal factor of considerable importance when dealing with a Papago client.

Papagos treat age and social status with a great deal of respect. And respect within the Papago culture is often expressed by silence.

Avoiding eye contact can also be of considerable importance when dealing with Papagos in any social setting, and this includes psychotherapy. Establishing and maintaining eye contact are considered to be impolite among these desert people and may be interpreted as anger.

On the desert reservation, time is treated much differently than what urban dwellers are accustomed to. Papagos may be an hour late for a meeting and think nothing of it. This, we will discover, has a considerable influence on therapy.

These several factors then are of central importance when doing therapy with the Papagos. They include the importance of the mental health technicians, the influence of the medicine man, personal secrecy, a lack of verbosity, respect for age and social status, avoidance of eye contact, and an informal orientation to time. How these variables influence the approach to therapy is considered next.

As a group, the variables just mentioned dictate that therapy done with Papagos would involve, for the most part, at least one indigenous mental health technician and that the therapy would nearly always be of a crisis intervention nature. The need for the mental health technician is obvious. Perhaps the reliance on a crisis intervention approach has reasons which aren't so obvious. First, although a medicine man often needs only one treatment session to effect a cure, this one treatment session could last several hours. The therapist must remain flexible regarding his own time orientation. Rigid adherence to the 50-minute session is simply of no value. As one graduate student extern recently pointed out when discussing marital therapy, the therapist should be willing to spend 2–4 hours with a couple and realize that this may be the only session there will be with them.

Not only does the variable of time orientation affect what will happen in one session, it also influences the execution of other sessions. That is, the client may be several hours late and the therapist must remain flexible and try to accommodate the client whenever possible.

The fact that the Papago client has had little to do when receiving other treatments (medicine man and physician) certainly affects what will happen in therapy. Quite often the Papago will present his problems (briefly) and ask "What is wrong with me?" and "What should I do?" A Rogerian reflection or question in return from the therapist may have little meaning. The therapist must be prepared to be directive—to make suggestions.

Confrontation in the therapeutic sense could be considered taboo with the Papago client. Socially, the Papago will religiously avoid confrontation. This is simply a matter of social courtesy. The therapist who confronts a Papago client in a manner that causes intense anxiety will lose the client.

(continued)

Cultural Study 4-5 (continued)

Interviewing the Papago client has some unique features. The Anglo who attempts to establish direct eye contact with his client will make therapeutic rapport almost impossible. Similarly, an aggressive therapist with a loud voice will intimidate and perhaps anger the Papago client. The pace or tempo of the interview is also affected. That is, a longer period of time is needed to establish trust and rapport with the client. More time must be spent getting acquainted with the Papago client. Questions of a personal nature should be delayed. An opening question of "What brings you here?" could stimulate anxiety and defensiveness on the part of the client.

Because of language problems, interpretations and suggestions must be made crystal clear. A client may seem to understand but not understand at all. The pretended understanding and acquiescense [sic] are a result of trying to show respect and social timidity.

Group therapies have enjoyed considerable success in the Papago clinic. Every group has had at least one mental health technician and one university therapist. Different approaches have been used successfully, but with adaptation to the culture (Kahn, Lewis, & Galvez, 1974).

In summary, some factors which we consider to be important in providing psychotherapy for the Papago are as follows:

1. Relying on the mental health technicians
2. Using a crisis intervention approach
3. Avoiding eye contact
4. Approaching therapeutic topics slowly and cautiously
5. Avoiding confrontations
6. Making interpretations very clear
7. Utilizing directive techniques
8. Remaining flexible in regard to time
9. Talking less than usual

[6]From "The Papago Psychology Service: A Community Mental Health Program on an American Indian Reservation," M. W. Kahn, C. Williams, E. Galvez, L. Lejero, R. Conrad, and G. Goldstein, *American Journal of Community Psychology*, 1975, 3, 91–93. Reprinted by permission of Plenum Publishing Corporation.

The social worker should be aware of these cultural dimensions of communication. A knowledge of key language expressions, such as important Spanish phrases relevant to the helping process, is an advantage. A joint practice approach between bilingual and monolingual workers is preferred with non–English-speaking clients. The goal is to increase the number of bilingual social workers in proportion to the agency's caseload of non–English-speaking minority clients.

Above all, the social worker should practice fundamental skills of communication with minority clients. Lewis and Ho (1975) suggest frequent use of restatement, clarification, summarization, reflection, and empathy with Native American clients. These responses to communication are applicable to other minority groups. It is important to note that these responses amplify and enlarge on what the client has said, rather than probing for or evaluating information. Reiteration is nonthreatening and allows the minority client to set the pace. When the worker asks a series of questions, a minority client may become exasperated and defensive with extensive probing.

CASE STUDY

The Agency

As a part of the minority mental health proposal, the Family Service Association staff reviewed its intake procedure for new minority clients. For several years there have been two secretary-receptionists, one of whom could speak Spanish. The proposal asked for a Chinese–Vietnamese receptionist. Moreover, the association auxiliary was enlisted to secure local Black, Latino, Asian, and Native American artists. They were persuaded to lend some of their art work for a month to the agency for display and sales. Their paintings and ceramics not only brightened up the agency but became conversation pieces for staff and clients as they greeted each other and walked to the interview rooms.

A psychiatrist has usually met with the staff on a weekly basis to consult with them on clinical cases. This resource has been paid through state mental health consultation funds. The county mental health proposal requested funds for a minority clinical consultant. The director asked an outstanding professor of minority social work practice from a nearby school of social work to write the section on minority consultation. Various bilingual social workers were scheduled to teach the staff cultural and linguistic skills with minority clients. Three MSW positions for Latino, Chinese, and Vietnamese social workers were written into the grant proposal.

The Hernandez Family

For Mr. Platt, the goal of his first session with the Hernandez family was to get acquainted with them. He put the family at ease, acknowledged the authority of the father, and asked how the family felt about coming to the agency. The second family session is a home visit—Mr. Platt and the family meet around the kitchen table. Mr. Hernandez shows Mr. Platt his Mexican art work, while Mrs. Hernandez serves a tray of Mexican pastries. Afterwards Mr. Hernandez begins to tell the social worker about Ricardo's school problems: his poor grades, his absences without family knowledge, and his verbal abuse of his father. Mr. Platt listens and supports Mr. Hernandez. He reflects back feelings, restates thoughts, summarizes major points, and clarifies certain areas.

Task Recommendations

The social worker creates a culturally sensitive relationship with the minority client through responses to communication. The following recommendations are designed to help you and your agency increase communication with minority clients.

1. Review your agency's procedures for intake of new minority clients. Do you have a bilingual receptionist and bilingual staff for non–English-speaking minority clients? Is there an attractive and congenial waiting area for clients? Do staff convey a friendly and informal attitude to clients? Are refreshments available for staff and clients?

2. On the basis of the composition of your agency's minority clientele, establish a language program for staff to learn key phrases that are helpful in social work practice with non–English-speaking minorities. Spanish and Chinese phrases are important to learn, in view of the influx of Latino and Indochinese refugees. A fluent bilingual social worker is a resource to teach and write important questions and answers in Spanish or Chinese.

3. Try a clinical experiment. Divide your caseload into two groups: an experimental group, whose sessions are conducted in home visits, and a control group, whom you see in your agency. After a six-week period, determine the extent of relative progress of the two groups as far as communication, information disclosure, and problem resolution are concerned.

4. Using a minority case, practice the following communication responses with a partner:

> **restating**, or stating an important fact or feeling of the client again in another way;
>
> **clarifying**, or making clear the meaning of what the client has been saying or feeling;
>
> **summarizing**, or condensing the main points that the client has made at a crucial juncture in the session;
>
> **reflecting**, or mirroring or reproducing the essential thought or feeling of the client to further consideration or contemplation;
>
> **empathizing**, or conveying your own affect to the client and sharing in his or her feelings.

Communicate feelings of warmth, acceptance and concern as you engage in these response patterns. Have your partner give you feedback on your responses.

Conclusion

Contact between the client and the worker is the most crucial phase of the process of social work practice. Contact establishes relationship and ensures retention. Preparatory work involves the agency's administrator and staff in rethinking their service outreach to the local minority community. The future of ethnic minority social work practice is in the hands of public and private agencies serving the poor and the minorities. Philosophy of service delivery, bilingual/bicultural staff, minority language and culture training, a minority case consultant, and ethnic practice approaches are central ingredients for successful minority social work practice. Above all, the social worker's attitude toward minority clients pervades the entire effort. Behavioral science students, researchers, and practitioners are no more immune to racism than the average person, in spite of their training.

References

Arroyo, R., & Lopez, S. A. (1984). Being responsive to the Chicano community: A model for service delivery. In B. W. White (Ed.), *Color in a white society* (pp. 63–73). Silver Spring, Md.: National Association of Social Workers.

Bernal, G., Bernal M. E., Martinez, A. C., Olmedo, E. L., & Santisteban, D. (1983). Hispanic mental health curriculum for psychology. In J. C. Chunn II, P. J. Dunston, & F. Ross-Sheriff (Eds.), *Mental health and people of color: Curriculum development and change* (pp. 65–94). Washington, D.C.: Howard University Press.

Bochner, S. (1982). *Cultures in contact: Studies in cross-cultural interaction.* Oxford: Pergamon Press.

Boulette, T. R. (1980). Mass media and other mental health promotional strategies for low-income Chicano/Mexicanos. In R. Valle & W. Vega (Eds.), *Hispanic natural support systems* (pp. 97–101). Sacramento: State of California Department of Mental Health.

Brislin, R. W. (1981). *Cross-cultural encounters: Face-to-face interaction.* New York: Pergamon Press.

Brownlee, A. T. (1978). *Community, culture, and care.* St. Louis: C.V. Mosby.

Campbell, R., & Chang, T. (1973). Health care of the Chinese in America. *Nursing Outlook, 21,* 245–249.

Catell, S. H. (1962). *Health, welfare, and social organization in Chinatown, New York City.* Report prepared for Community Service Society of New York, Department of Public Affairs, Chinatown Public Health Nursing Demonstration.

Chen, P. N. (1970). The Chinese community in Los Angeles. *Social Casework, 51,* 591–598.

Devore, W., & Schlesinger, E. G. (1981). *Ethnic-sensitive social work practice.* St. Louis: C. V. Mosby.

Dryden, J. (1982). A social services department and the Bengali community: A new response. In J. Cheetham (Ed.), *Social work and ethnicity* (pp. 55–163). Winchester, Mass.: Allen and Unwin.

Franklin, A. J. (1983). Therapeutic interventions with urban black adolescents. In E. J. Jones & S. J. Korchin (Eds.), *Minority mental health* (pp. 267–295). New York: Praeger.

Fritzpatrick, J. P. (1981). The Puerto Rican family. In C. H. Mindel & R. W. Habenstein (Eds.), *Ethnic families in America: Patterns and variations* (pp. 189–214). New York: Elsevier.

Ghali, S. B. (1977). Culture sensitivity and the Puerto Rican client. *Social Casework, 58,* 459–468.

Glasgow, D. G. (1980). *The Black underclass.* San Francisco: Jossey-Bass.

Gonzales, M., & Garcia, D. (1974). *A study of extended family interactions among*

Chicanos in the East Los Angeles area. Unpublished master's thesis, University of California, Los Angeles, School of Social Welfare.

Green, J. W. (1982). *Cultural awareness in the human services.* Englewood Cliffs, N.J.: Prentice-Hall.

Harwood, A. (Ed.) (1981). *Ethnicity and medical care.* Cambridge: Harvard University Press.

Ho, M. K. (1976). Social work with Asian Americans. *Social Casework, 57,* 195–201.

Jenkins, S. (1981). *The ethnic dilemma in social services.* New York: Free Press.

Kahn, M. W., Lewis, J., & Galvez, E., (1974). An evaluation of a group therapy procedure with reservation adolescent Indians. *Psychotherapy: Theory, Research, and Practice, 11,* 241–244.

Kahn, M. W., Williams, C., Galvez, E., Lejero, L., Conrad, R., & Goldstein, G. (1975). The Papago psychology service: A community mental health program on an American Indian reservation. *American Journal of Community Psychology, 3,* 88–90.

Kuramoto, F. H., Morales, R. F., Munoz, F. U., & Murase, K. (1983). Education for social work practice in Asian and Pacific American communities. In J. C. Chunn II, P. J. Dunston, & F. Ross-Sheriff (Eds.), *Mental health and people of color: Curriculum development and change* (pp. 127–155). Washington, D.C.: Howard University Press.

Lee, E. (1982). A social systems approach to assessment and treatment for Chinese American families. In M. McGoldrick, J. K. Pearce, & J. Giordano (Eds.), *Ethnicity and family therapy* (pp. 527–551). New York: Guilford Press.

Lee, Q. T. (1981). Case illustrations of mental health problems encountered by Indochinese refugees. In *Bridging cultures: Southeast Asian refugees in America* (pp. 241–258). Los Angeles: Asian American Community Mental Health Training Center.

Lee, R. H. (1960). *The Chinese in America.* Hong Kong: University of Hong Kong Press.

Leigh, J. W. (1980). Hearing racial references in the interview. Unpublished paper, University of Washington, School of Social Work.

Leigh, J. W. (1984). Empowerment strategies for work with multi-ethnic populations. Unpublished paper presented at the annual program meeting of the Council on Social Work Education, Detroit.

Lewis, R. G., & Ho, M. K. (1975). Social work with Native Americans. *Social Work, 20,* 379–382.

Marcos, L. R., Alpert, M., Urcuyo, L., & Kesselman, M. (1973). The effect of interview language on the evaluation of psychopathology in Spanish-American schizophrenic patients. *American Journal of Psychiatry, 130,* 549–553.

Marsella, A. J. (1979). Cross-cultural studies of mental disorders. In A. J. Marsella, R. G. Tharp, & T. J. Ciborowski (Eds.), *Perspectives on cross-cultural psychology* (pp. 233–262). New York: Academic Press.

McLemore, S. D. (1983). *Racial and ethnic relations in America.* Boston: Allyn & Bacon.

Mendoza, L. (1980). Hispanic helping networks: Techniques of cultural support. In R. Valle & W. Vega (Eds.), *Hispanic natural support systems* (pp. 55–63). Sacramento: State of California Department of Mental Health.

Minuchin, S., Montalvo, B., Guerney, G., Rosman, B., & Schumer, F. (1967). *Families of the slums.* New York: Basic Books.

Solomon, B. B. (1983). Social work with Afro-Americans. In A. Morales & B. W. Sheafor, *Social work: A profession of many faces* (pp. 415–436). Boston: Allyn & Bacon.

Sue, D. W. (1981). *Counseling the culturally different: Theory and practice.* New York: Wiley.

Sue, S., & Morishima, J. K. (1982). *The mental health of Asian Americans.* San Francisco: Jossey-Bass.

Sue, S., & Wagner, N. (1973). *Asian Americans: Psychological perspectives.* Ben Lomond, California: Science and Behavior Books.

Valle, R. (1980). Social mapping techniques: A preliminary guide for locating and linking to natural networks. In R. Valle & W. Vega (Eds.), *Hispanic natural support systems* (pp. 113–121). Sacramento: State of California Department of Mental Health.

Vega, W. (1980). The Hispanic natural healer, a case study: Implications for prevention. In R. Valle & W. Vega (Eds.), *Hispanic natural support systems* (pp. 65–74). Sacramento: State of California Department of Mental Health.

Velez, C. G. (1980). Mexicano/Hispano support systems and confianza: Theoretical issues of cultural adaptation. In R. Valle & W. Vega (Eds.), *Hispanic natural support systems* (pp. 45–54). Sacramento: State of California Department of Mental Health.

Watkins, T. R., & Gonzales, R. (1982). Outreach to Mexican Americans. *Social Work, 27,* pp. 68–73.

Wong, H. Z., Kim, L. I. C., Lim, D. T., & Morishima, J. K. (1983). The training of psychologists Asian and Pacific American communities: Problems, perspectives and practices. In J. C. Chunn, P. J. Dunston & F. Ross-Sheriff (Eds.), *Mental health and people of color: Curriculum development and change.* Washington, D.C.: Howard University Press.

Wong, N., Lu, F. G., Shon, S. P., & Gaw, A. C. (1983). Asian and Pacific American patient issues in psychiatric residency training programs. In J. C. Chunn, P. J. Dunston & F. Ross-Sheriff (Eds.), *Mental health and people of color: Curriculum development and change.* Washington, D.C.: Howard University Press.

Yuen, S. (no date). *Aging and mental health in San Francisco's Chinatown.* (Available from Self Help for the Elderly, 640 Pine St., San Francisco, CA 94108.)

5

Problem Identification

Ethnic minority clients have been selected by mental health researchers for studying subjects of low socioeconomic status who have psychiatric disorders. Utilizing minority mental patients in state hospitals, they have tended to note gross and severe psycho-pathological traits among them in comparison to White subjects. As a result, a problem-prone stereotype of the person of color has arisen in psychiatric and psychological literature. Analysis traces the roots of this pathology back to the minority family, and sibling rivalry, which further exacerbates the already distorted picture of a severe matriarchial or patriarchial system. Psychotherapy with people of color consists of classical psychoanalysis, with the therapist as primary authority and the minority client as social misfit. The field of problem identification becomes distorted by the selection of severely disturbed minority patients and the generalization of findings to the entire ethnic group. Furthermore, many clinicians and practitioners utilize psychotherapeutic approaches that do not speak to the cultural milieu of minorities in their ethnic community (Meadow, 1983). As a result, ethnic minorities have avoided White clinical research and traditional psychotherapy.

Fortunately, social work practice has moved away from a psychoanalytic approach. It has adopted systems theory that recognizes natural support systems, ethnic family strengths, and normal problems of living. In our perspective on ethnic minority practice, the identification of problems begins with a nonpathological orientation. Hepworth and Larsen (1982) observe that problems involve unmet needs or wants. Translating complaints and problems into needs and wants enhances the motivation of clients to work toward behavioral change that brings satisfaction and well-being. Movement toward identifying strengths, resources, and healthy functioning and away from diag-nostic symptoms, disease, and dysfunction characterizes current social work practice.

In this chapter, our goal is to develop the themes of problem information—problems of the client, cultural and environmental factors contributing to problems, and target age groups and their needs—disclosure of problem area, and problem understanding, as well as problem orientation, levels, themes, and area detailing. We follow the already established format of presenting practice principles, case study, and task recommenda-tions. Client and worker systems practice issues of the problem identification stage are represented in Figure 5-1.

114

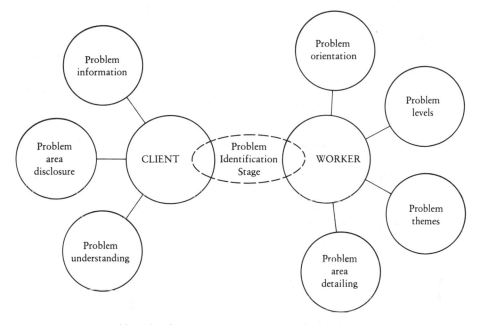

Figure 5-1.   Problem identification stage: Client system and worker system practice issues.

Client System Practice Issues

Problem Information

Problem information tends to focus on the individual characteristics of the minority client and in traditional approaches has failed to uncover vital environmental factors. This client system assumes an intrapsychic treatment approach to helping and builds a personal profile of the client. The intrapsychic model holds that the problems of clients stem from personal deficiency or disorganization rather than institutional or societal dysfunction (Bryson & Bardo, 1975). However, it is important for social work practice to evaluate relevant problem information located in the patterns of the minority client's sociocultural environment.

Recent research on minority topics has uncovered environmental issues affecting problem information. Jenkins (1981) reviewed minority literature of a ten-year period and summarized four common problem themes:

1. The lack of recognition that diverse cultural patterns exist and are factors influencing tradition and change. These variables include age, birthplace, education, recency of migration, extent of acculturation, and social class. They form a unique configuration that affects the way a helping person works with an ethnic minority client.
2. The reality of language differences and the importance of bilingualism for effective service delivery. While the dominant society does not value bilingual compe-

tency, bilingual and bicultural programs are essential services in mixed ethnic communities.

3. The existence of stereotypes that create barriers between the ethnic community and sources of help with their problems and needs. The stereotyping of ethnic groups is a reality that all races face.
4. The threat to group survival inherent in the adoption practices of child welfare agencies, which may place a child outside the group. Children are central to the survival of the ethnic group.

Vega (1980) identified a number of sociocultural issues that create service barriers. Racism and discrimination in the form of cultural insensitivity are manifested in style of service delivery, professional blindness to cultural norms, and other institutional policies. Faulty service delivery systems affect the problem information interpretation. Culturally dissonant services fail to incorporate the minority client's ways of accepting help and giving help. Cultural dimensions have not been integrated into methods of service delivery and treatment. Language and cultural values, community problems, and indigenous health practices are examples of cultural variables that require incorporation. The inaccessibility of services is exhibited in poor bilingual communication, physical location of agencies, community relations, and client management. As a result, human services have low visibility to minority populations. Community integrity is violated when human services fail to understand and utilize community cultural support networks. Human services should reinforce, initiate, educate, organize, and engage community support networks, which are vital adjunct helping resources. The process of service delivery to minorities causes problems when it does not take cultural factors into account. The social work agency's policies should be reviewed to ascertain whether they address unique ethnic behavior practices or create organizational barriers complicating current social problems.

Research on problem information has identified target age groups and their needs. Sena-Rivera's (1980) report on Latino adolescents, young adults and parents, and elderly have implications for ethnic minorities. Adolescents must struggle not only with confusion and ambivalence as a normal part of the life cycle but also with external threats to self-esteem. They are assaulted by an inferior and culturally demeaning educational system, crowded housing conditions, unemployment, cultural misunderstanding, and institutional racism. They react to the stress through drug abuse, trouble with authority, dropping out of school, early pregnancies, and parent abuse. Young adults and parents in ethnic minority groups cope with poor socioeconomic conditions compounded by unemployment or employment with a limited future; discrimination resulting in a lack of sense of self-worth, marginal self-identity, and alcohol and drug abuse; personal conflict and marital difficulties, parental confusion about children and cultural values; and for recently arrived immigrants, cultural shock. Minority elderly cope with anger and disillusionment about the behavior of the young, lack of a sense of self-worth, loneliness, and fear of family separation. The potential high-risk areas for these age groups should be taken into account when gathering problem information.

Problem information on minority clients should keep a balance between traditional personal data on the client and relevant socioenvironmental factors influencing the problem areas. Examples of the latter are cultural/ethnic variables such as number of generations removed from immigrant status, birth, (foreign-born versus American-born), language orientation, and family values. The acquisition of relevant problem information can be enhanced by the awareness of ethnic stereotyping, an adequate number of bilingual/bicultural workers, communication with the minority community, and preventive education programs for needy minority age groups.

CASE STUDY

The Hernandez Family

Problem information on the Hernandez family is enhanced by the agency's recognition of the needs of the Latino clients. Mr. and Mrs. Hernandez have migrated from Mexico and have adjusted to the local Mexican–American community. Their worker is White but has a knowledge of some Spanish phrases. A bilingual worker is available for consultation in the case. The stereotyping of minorities has been minimized by training of the agency staff in ethnic practice. Ample time is set aside for discovering the unique character of the members of the Hernandez family. Beyond learning about problem information from the family, the worker makes an effort to use ethnic community resources, such as the school, the church, and employment-related contacts, to learn more about the family.

Task Recommendations

In order to respond to the issues raised in this section on problem information, review the information intake procedure and form(s) of a social service agency. Evaluate them according to the following questions:

What ethnic minority variables do they mention?

To what extent is attention given to ethnic minority problem information such as generation and level of acculturation, language fluency, factors of racism and discrimination influencing the problem(s), and other related sociocultural areas?

What revision of existing intake procedure and form(s) might you suggest in order to raise the level of adequacy of information on ethnic minority clientele?

Problem Area Disclosure

Minority clients often feel a sense of shame and hesitation in the initial stages of the helping process. Certain cultural attitudes oppose disclosure of problems outside the immediate family. Before disclosing the problem, the client may engage the worker in a rambling conversation to find out the worker's initial reaction. A minority client may ask a series of questions intended to test out the situation. For example, the person may say, "I have a friend with a certain problem." After describing the situation, he or she may ask, "What would you suggest if this were the case?" Indirect questioning may occur under various pretenses until the client feels ready to risk disclosure and trust the worker with the problem. It is important to give the minority client enough time to acknowledge the problem. Devore and Schlesinger (1981) observe that ethnic-sensitive matters may not emerge early because of the worker's lack of knowledge, the client's reluctance to trust, a difference in ethnic backgrounds of worker and client, and lack of awareness that ethnic factors have a bearing on the problem.

These same factors that can delay disclosure may also be primary reasons why minority clients drop out after the first session. There are too many barriers obstructing the disclosure of problems. Social workers are taught the principles of direct interviewing skills, problem intervention, verbal communication, and the fifty-minute session. People of color must overcome cultural resistance and reticence about social service agencies. They have ambivalent feelings about nonminority professionals who lack their cultural background and language skills. Lewis and Ho (1975) reiterate these dynamics involved in problem area disclosure. Cultural Study 5-1 illustrates the manner in which a worker might assist a client with problem disclosure.

Cultural Study 5-1

Problem Area Disclosure[1]

The Redthunder family was brought to the school social worker's attention when teachers reported that both children had been tardy and absent frequently in the past weeks. Since the worker lived near Mr. Redthunder's neighborhood, she volunteered to transport the children back and forth to school. Through this regular but informal arrangement, the worker became acquainted with the entire family, especially with Mrs. Redthunder who expressed her gratitude to the worker by sharing her homegrown vegetables.

The worker sensed that there was much family discomfort and that a tumultuous relationship existed between Mr. and Mrs. Redthunder. Instead of probing into their personal and marital affairs, the worker let Mrs. Redthunder know that she was willing to listen should the woman need someone to talk to. After a few gifts of homegrown vegetables and Native American handicrafts, Mrs. Redthunder broke into tears one day and told the worker about her husband's problem of alcoholism and their deteriorating marital relationship.

Realizing Mr. Redthunder's position of respect in the family and his resistance to outside interference, the social worker advised Mrs. Redthunder to take her family to visit the minister, a man whom Mr. Redthunder admired. The Littleaxe family, who were mutual friends of the worker and the Redthunder family, agreed to take the initiative in visiting the Redthunders more often. Through such frequent but informal family visits, Mr. Redthunder finally obtained a job, with the recommendation of Mr. Littleaxe, as recordkeeper in a storeroom. Mr. Redthunder enjoyed his work so much that he drank less and spent more time with his family.

[1]From "Social work with Native Americans," by R. G. Lewis and M. K. Ho, *Social Work,* (September 1975), Vol. 20, No. 5, p. 381. Copyright 1975, National Association of Social Workers, Inc. Reprinted by permission.

Social workers should exercise patience, spend time in relationship building, learn culturally sensitive approaches, and allow the client to set the pace in problem disclosure. Lewis and Ho (1975) remind us:

> A Native American client will not immediately wish to discuss other members of his family or talk about topics that he finds sensitive or distressing. Before arriving at his immediate concern (the real reason he came to the worker in the first place), the client—particularly the Native American—will test the worker by bringing up peripheral matters. He does this in the hope of getting a better picture of how sincere, interested, and trustworthy the worker actually is. If the worker impatiently confronts the client with accusations, the client will be "turned off" [p. 380].

Recognizing this hesitance as an integral part of problem identification and a hurdle for the minority client to overcome is important for the social worker.

Related to studies of problem area disclosure has been research on the designation of potential minority problem areas. Based on studies regarding socioeconomic status and length of residency in the United States, recent arrivals who do not speak English or are without marketable skills are often unemployed or underemployed. They need concrete services such as information, referral, and advocacy. American-born minorities or long-term residents have greater acculturation and knowledge of the service delivery system than new immigrants. They seek counseling and related services (Kuramoto, Morales, Munoz, & Murase, 1983). Immigrants, the poor, and the elderly are minority groups under particular stress. Immigrants are exposed to tremendous life changes requiring adjustment. The incidence of physical and psychological problems increases as a result. Likewise, the poor encounter socioeconomic class conditions, and the elderly, the problems of aging (Sue, Ito, & Bradshaw, 1982). Research with potential target groups reveals the kinds of problems that each is most likely to encounter and helps the social worker anticipate the disclosures of a particular client.

CASE STUDY

The Hernandez Family

At the next session, Mr. Platt shares some of the conversation he has had with Ricardo's teacher. He mentions that the teacher, Mrs. Villa, is concerned about Mr. Hernandez's long hours. Relaying the teacher's expression of concern gives Mr. Hernandez an opening to express his feelings about the past three months. Rather than confronting the father, Mr. Platt allows him to disclose the problem area. In turn, the social worker gives Mr. Hernandez support as he tells about his two jobs, the long hours, and the economic burdens of the family. Mr. Hernandez feels obligated to help his relatives. Since the two families of in-laws arrived from Mexico, the husbands have held part-time jobs washing dishes in Mexican restaurants and harvesting tomatoes. Moreover, these three families feel that they must send money to Mexico to support their elderly parents, who are retired and living on small pensions. Mr. Hernandez feels a family obligation to support his in-laws until they can find steady employment. Mrs. Hernandez states that her family in Mexico sent money to them when they came to the United States ten years ago. Now Mr. and Mrs. Hernandez felt that it is their turn to help members of her family. However, Mr. Hernandez recognizes that he cannot spend more time with Ricardo and help him with his homework. The stress of demands on his time is too much.

Task Recommendations

Disclosure of the problem area is based on mutual trust and acceptance between the worker and client. Here are some suggestions for working on problem area disclosure:

Allow the minority client to lead you into problem area disclosure. Look for verbal and nonverbal cues from the client. Let the client state the problem area in his or her own words. Restate and clarify what the client is saying.

Discuss in a staff or student group some potential problem areas of minority immigrants, poor, and elderly.

Determine practical ways to facilitate problem disclosure without demeaning minority clients who are sensitive to revealing personal problems to social workers and other helping professionals.

Problem Understanding

The minority client needs to develop a perspective on his or her problems. When the client understands the problem he or she recognizes what has happened and owns the responsibility for coping with the problem situation. Green (1982) emphasizes the importance of finding out the client's definition and understanding of an experience as a problem. Cultures differ in their explanations of etiology, symptom recognition, treatment procedures, and desirable outcomes of problems. Members of the same culture share that cognitive map, the ability to understand and cope with a problem based on skills learned from personal, family, and community survival. There are unifying themes that bind members of a culturally distinct people to one another. Self-understanding is built on understanding one's own perception of how the world operates regarding a problem. According to Green (1982), problem understanding occurs in a cultural, social, and economic context. Normality in the world of the minority client may look like pathology from the professional point of view.

The client's interpretation of the problem is as important as the client's understanding of it. Green (1982) stresses the meaning of reality and the reaction of the client, which influence the resulting course of action. Perceiving how culture influences behavioral response gives the client an awareness of what happened and why he or she responded in a particular manner. Cultural Study 5-2 focuses on the client's understanding of the problem. The minority person in this illustration indicates that there is widespread discrimination at school. However, she is in a transitional period of adjustment. The worker wisely concentrates on identifying concrete instances of discrimination, the goal being for the client to take action. As a result, the client is encouraged to establish a social network involving a cultural support group and ethnic activities.

Cultural Study 5-2

Problem Understanding[2]

Ann is an attractive seventeen-year-old black high-school student who was referred for counseling because of her increasing depression and nervousness since she began attending a new school. She was an only child, living at home with her mother and father, who had recently moved into the new neighborhood as a consequence of the father's job transfer. The school she had attended before had been predominantly black. The new school was racially mixed, although a majority of the students were white. Ann told her counselor that there was a great amount of discrimination at the school, both within the black and white student groups as well as between them. Even though she knew that *some* black students seemed to be fairly well integrated into the social network of the white students, she personally did not feel accepted by either group. She noticed that one small group of black students congregated daily at a certain table in the cafeteria, yet she was holding herself back from introducing herself to them. Ann expressed to the counselor who was also black her feelings of isolation and confusion as to what was happening to her in the school and what she wanted for herself.

The counselor reviewed the facts as perceived and presented to her by Ann. Two hypotheses or "choice points" stood out:

Ann was being discriminated against at school, (.60), or Ann was experiencing isolation, tension, and stress from the move, complicated by her own fears and expectations of others. (.40)

The counselor decided to develop an action hypothesis based on the first hypothesis, particularly since it was highly likely that by doing so, the issues present in the second hypothesis would emerge and could be taken care of at that time. The action hypothesis was described by the counselor in this manner: "If I focused in our counseling sessions on having her specify more concretely how and by whom she was experiencing discrimination, then Ann would become more aware of what she could *do* under the circumstances."

In subsequent sessions, the action hypothesis was implemented. Ann indicated that she felt she was being discriminated against by a large number of white students, evidenced by snide remarks about her hair or body odor as she walked in the halls, being pushed and shoved while in line for nutrition and lunch, and having students get up and change seats after she sat down next to them. In the process of having her define what was happening to her, she indicated that these things might not happen to her if she were not a "loner." At first, she was not very clear about her position with the other black students. When the counselor inquired whether she felt that other black students were also being discriminated against by white students, she replied that she did not know because she was not in contact with any of the black students. She spoke about being different from them, specifically in terms of her "conservative" clothes and the fact that she did not use the "hip" jargon that the other students did. The counselor asked her to exaggerate her "differentness" and try to

(continued)

Cultural Study 5-2 (continued)

convince her (using a Gestalt technique) that she was so very different from the other black students that she could not hope to be their friend. As she tried this, Ann eventually concluded that she was not as different as she thought she was. She then spoke about the cafeteria activity and of her fear to approach the small clique of black students who gathered there daily. The counselor had her bring the cafeteria experience into the present and make it explicit by role-playing it in the office. Ann experimented with different ways to approach the group, for example by asking a question about a class assignment, or making a statement that she wanted to meet them. At this point, the counselor developed another set of choice points:

> While discrimination was a realistic issue in Ann's life, she was generalizing it to include everybody and consequently was not approaching those black students who might be interested in meeting her, (.90), or
>
> Ann's belief that everybody was discriminating against her was probably correct. (.10)

Again the counselor developed an action hypothesis: "If I suggest that Ann make contact with other black students where she could begin to establish a social network for herself through a collective identity, then I expect that Ann's feelings of isolation and being discriminated against would be significantly reduced and she would begin to feel an increased sense of her own significance and ability to handle the school situation."

The counselor followed the action prescribed and Ann agreed to try. She succeeded in making contacts with other black students and learned that many of them were also victims of racial discrimination. The students began discussing ways of actively dealing with this problem as a group. Ann also joined an ethnomusicology course on campus which taught African drumming and had both black and white students enrolled. Thus, Ann's success in establishing contacts with others, her efforts to "do something" about the issue of discrimination, resulted in reduced isolation and tension and depression. The counselor discontinued sessions upon mutual agreement but with the understanding that counseling was available at anytime Ann thought she could use it to meet a need.

[2]From *Black Empowerment: Social Work in Oppressed Communities,* by B. B. Solomon, pp. 306–308. Copyright © 1976 by Columbia University Press. Reprinted by permission.

Similarly Cultural Study 5-3 illustrates the important role of the social worker, who brought problem understanding to a minority client. Owning his responsibility for his problem behavior was the client's expression of cultural respect for his parents and family obligation.

Cultural Study 5-3

Problem Responsibility[3]

L. C., an American-born Chinese and a junior high school student, experienced a great many learning difficulties. He has habitually skipped school and, as a result, was unaware of his homework assignments. Both of his parents were passive individuals who were confused by and ashamed of their son's behavior. Also they were having severe marital problems and were striving to present a facade, pretending their marriage was on solid ground and that it had nothing to do with their son's failing in school.

L. C. was aware of his parents' problems and defensiveness, and took advantage of their vulnerability by indulging himself whenever he pleased. A family treatment team consisting of one male and one female therapist was quite successful in helping the parents to gain some insights into their problems and to communicate more openly and fully; attempts to resolve their son's school problem, however, were met with continuous resistance, especially from L. C. himself, who accused the treatment team of conspiring with his parents against him. With the permission of the family, a child worker, actually the same age as L. C. and a personal friend of the male therapist, was introduced as an additional member of the treatment team. When L. C. repeatedly blamed his parents' marital problems for his own problems, the child worker pointed out that skipping school was a sign of "copping out" and that continuation of this activity would only bring him failure. "We all have problems, but we have ourselves to blame if we do not live up to our share of responsibilities," added the child worker. The child worker's intervention gradually lessened the guilt feelings of the parents, who later were able to better assume the limiting role in dealing with their son.

[3]From "Social work with Asian Americans," by M. K. Ho, *Social Casework,* (March 1976), Vol. 57, p. 199. Copyright © 1976 by Family Service Association of America. Reprinted by permission.

CASE STUDY

The Hernandez Family

After disclosing his problem to Mr. Platt, Mr. Hernandez realizes economic conditions and family obligation have complicated the relationship with his eldest son. He is obliged to help his in-laws by virtue of the fact that they assisted him when he left Mexico for the United States. It is now his turn to assist them in their resettlement period. It seems a natural response for Mr. Hernandez, but he is overwhelmed with his work schedule and family responsibilities. Mr. Hernandez brings this cultural cognitive map—this feeling of obligation and responsibility—with him. In turn, he receives understanding of what has happened to him during the past several months.

Task Recommendations

Problem understanding is based on the assumption that there is a cultural cognitive map within the minority person. The client provides necessary information on when the problem began, how the problem has affected him or her, and what can be done to alleviate the problem. In order to increase the client's problem understanding, the following suggestions are given:

Trust the minority client who has an innate cultural understanding of the problem situation.

Facilitate a conversation that is conducive to the client's bringing out the cultural meaning of the problem.

Relate the chronology of problem events to cultural dynamics involving behavior.

Worker System Practice Issues

Problem Orientation

Reid (1978) has described a problem as an unsatisfied want. This point of view recasts the dynamics of the problem into a positive perspective. A problem becomes a motivator, the impetus toward change and the object of striving. The problem focus moves from behavior pathology and blaming the victim toward positive strivings to satisfy unfulfilled wants. The minority client expresses his or her wants and identifies barriers in his or her life situation.

Sue (1981) points out that the minority client problem tends not to be internal or inherent in origin. Traditional psychotherapy focuses on internal barriers within the person. However, the culturally sensitive social worker starts with the assumption that many minority problems are rooted in a racist society. As a result, environmental/societal conditions are responsible for unsatisfied wants of minority clients. Sue views sociotherapeutic aspects of problem identification and solving as a balance between services to individuals and social change. Extrapsychic sources of stress originate outside the person and are environmentally based. For Blacks, extrapsychic stress leads to intrapsychic maladaptive behavior: poor self-concept and feelings of hopelessness and rage (Smith, 1981). Middle-class counselors with individualistic and intrapsychic orientations tend to minimize the significance of social and cultural forces affecting Black clients (Tucker & Gunnings, 1974).

CASE STUDY

The Hernandez Family

The Hernandez family has been under increasing environmental stress since Mr. Hernandez assumed the economic responsibility of assisting his in-laws. He has been forced to support his family and relatives. Socio-economic factors and family disruption are reflected in Ricardo's school problems. Fortunately the social worker does not focus exclusively on Ricardo's behavior and parental relationship. He is aware of the family's environmental stress.

Task Recommendations

Clinical psychotherapy tends toward micro personality theories. Minority problem orientation starts with social community and environmental issues that affect individual reactions. The following are some practical suggestions for a psychosocial problem orientation:

Discuss potentially oppressive factors with which minority persons cope in their environment.

Identify human behavior and community theories that examine environmental aspects of the problem.

Discuss the external problem orientation of a minority case.

Establish procedures on how to uncover social causes of problems as you work with minority clients.

Problem Levels

Social problems have been classified along a continuum of problem levels ranging from macro (complex organizations, geographical populations) to meso (ethnic/local communities and organizations) to micro (individual, family, and small group). Social work practice has placed problems in various categories according to type. Reid (1978) catalogs these problem areas:

interpersonal conflict
dissatisfaction in social relations
problems with formal organizations
difficulty in role performance
decision problems
reactive emotional distress
inadequate resources
psychological or behavioral problems not elsewhere classified

Northen (1982) has identified a problem typology:

lack of economic and social resources
lack of knowledge and experience
emotional reactions to stress
illness and disability
loss of relationship
dissatisfactions in social relationships
interpersonal conflict
culture conflict
conflict with formal organizations
maladaptive group functioning

Problems in these areas are caused by interaction of the individual with another person, group, or institution, and situations beyond the control of the client. For people of color, problems are exacerbated by inadequate programs and service gaps, perennial problems, basic survival issues, and issues of acculturation and adjustment. Many minority individuals must cope with multiple problems beyond the limits of the average person's tolerance.

There are a number of ways to view minority problem levels. Sue and Morishima (1982) indicate at least three stress areas: culture conflict, minority group status, and social change. David (1976) illustrates these areas for the Spanish-speaking. As persons enter a new culture, they lose many reinforcing events that make life satisfying to them. Culture conflicts arise for many Spanish-speaking parents when, as heads of the family, they must rely on their children for translation and explanations of how things are done in the United States. Their sense of being a minority is heightened by absence of familiar friends, family, and institutions. Problems of social change occur when a family from a rural area experiences the smog, crime, and crowded conditions of a city or the blatant prejudice of a predominantly White society. Solomon (1983) speaks about problem levels when she states

> The presenting problems of these black clients all involve stress from external systems. If the theoretical frameworks that serve to guide social workers all relate primarily to intrapsychic functioning as the determinant of ability to cope with one's environment and not to institutional factors that might need to be changed instead or as well, the profession will have limited effectiveness in helping Afro-Americans [p. 427].

The starting point for the social worker is the stress of environmental problems and its effect on the minority client.

Oftentimes macro and meso problem stressors are manifested in a micro biopsychosocial reaction. Social work has traditionally focused on the biopsychosocial interaction between the individual and social environment. However, Ghali (1977) shares a case example (Cultural Study 5-4) of a Puerto Rican family whose problems are a mixture of macro, meso, and micro level interactions.

Cultural Study 5-4

Macro, Meso, and Micro Levels of Interaction[4]

Juan and Carmel R live in a tenement in the South Bronx. They have five children, three sons born in Puerto Rico and two daughters born in the United States. Juan was previously employed as a clerk in a New York City grocery store or *bodega*. He completed an eighth grade education in a small interior town in Puerto Rico but was unable to attend high school in the city because his parents, who had twelve children, could not afford the necessary shoes, uniforms, and transportation. Instead, Juan began working full time alongside his father in the *finca* (farm) of the wealthy L family. Juan asked God to forgive him for his envious thoughts toward his brother, Jose, who was the godson of Senor L and had his tuition paid by the wealthy farmer. Juan's own godparents were good to him and remembered all the occasions and feasts, but they were poor. When Juan was sixteen, his godfather, Pedro, got him a job on the pineapple farm of the coastal city of Arecibo. He enjoyed living with Pedro's family. At age twenty-four he fell in love with Pedro's granddaughter, Carmen, who was sixteen, in the tenth grade, and a virgin. Apart from family gatherings and Sundays in the plaza, however, he was unable to see her. Finally, he asked her father for her hand in marriage and the latter consented because he thought of Juan as a brother. The patron loaned his *finca* for the wedding and contributed a roasted pig for the occasion. Over fifty people from infancy to age ninety were there to celebrate the wedding.

Juan was very proud when his first-born was a son, but his pride as a man was hurt when Carmen had to return to work as a seamstress because of the increasing debts. Her family took care of the baby and fought over who would be the godparents. By the time a third child was born, a show of God's blessing, Juan was let go at the pineapple farm and he and his family moved to San Juan, where his brother, Jose, got him a job in a supermarket. This job did not last long and after a long period of unemployment and health problems with the youngest child, Juan moved to New York City with Carmen's brother, who obtained for him the job in the *bodega*.

Carmen was delighted with being reunited with her family, but when she became pregnant with their fourth child, the Rs moved into their own apartment. Carmen became depressed because for the first time she was not living with extended family; because of the stress of the change of culture; because of her inability to speak English; and because of the deterioration of the tenement which was impossible to keep sparkling clean. She suffered from headaches, stomach problems, and pains in her chest, but doctors told her these symptoms were due to nerves and her condition was chronic. When she felt better she would raise the volume of the *jibaro* music on the Spanish station and talk to her saints. Finally, Juan sent for Carmen's aunt to come to live with them and her arrival helped Carmen. Carmen accepted Juan's arguments that in America job, schooling, and medical facilities were better than in Puerto Rico. (In some ways the job and medical facilities in Puerto Rico were nonexistent unless one had a car.) The years passed, and Carmen consoled herself that as soon as the children finished their education they would move back to Puerto Rico where Juan could set up a business. As the children grew they adopted the ways of the neighborhood children. They no longer asked for the parents' blessings as they came and left the house; they wanted to go to parties unchaperoned; they sometimes talked back; the girls wanted to wear make-up at age fifteen and dress in nonladylike clothes. The boys had friends who belonged to gangs and smoked pot, and the parents feared the same would happen to their sons. Juan and Carmen threatened to send them back to Puerto Rico or to a *colegio* (boarding school) if they did not sever these friendships. Another important and traumatic issue that the family was faced with for the first time involved the issue of color. The youngest daughter, Yvette, age twelve, entered junior high school and found herself placed on the black side of the two camps in school. This situation affected the entire family. Carmen reminded her daughter that she was a Puerto Rican and told her to speak Spanish loudly so the schoolchildren would not confuse her with the blacks. Inside, Carmen felt guilty that her daughter's dark skin led to problems.

During this very difficult period Juan injured his back while loading merchandise and became permanently disabled. Suddenly, the family had to receive public welfare assistance, and Juan's authority was gradually becoming undermined, particularly as he was no longer the breadwinner. He began to drink. Trips to Puerto Rico, while somewhat supportive, did not provide a solution to the problems the family was undergoing. Finally, Yvette came to the attention of school authorities because of her withdrawn behavior and she was referred to a mental health center.

[4]From "Culture Sensitivity and the Puerto Rican client," by S. B. Ghali, *Social Casework*, (October 1977), Vol. 58, pp. 464, 465. Copyright © 1977 by Family Service Association of America. Reprinted by permission.

Ethnic minorities often exhibit certain biopsychosocial problems through somatic complaints and emotional disturbances. Sue and Morishima (1982) cite research on Asian Americans that associates mental disturbances with organic or somatic factors. There are reasons for that relationship. Some Asian Americans see a unity between physical and psychological states, a perception which has consequences for the mind and body. Furthermore, physical complaints express personal and interpersonal problems. Physical complaints carry less of a negative stigma than emotional/mental disturbances. Checking out physical ailments with the client's physician and being aware of the psychophysiological relationship are crucial for the ethnic-sensitive social worker. For Latino Americans, psychological factors are related to stress responses to external needs. Morales and Salcido (1983) state:

> This is *not* to say that the poor are poor because of psychological problems; rather, their impoverished status may contribute to and exacerbate their stress. Indeed, it becomes a difficult task to help someone work through separation feelings regarding the loss of a loved one when they are starving, have no place to live, or are freezing to death. In this respect, certain basic human needs related to food, clothing, and shelter are universal, and a person's emotional response to stress also has universal qualities [p. 397].

Finally, the state of the economy may have an effect on the level of funding for social programs, which in turn can have a stressful impact, especially on Black Americans in a tight financial situation. In relatively prosperous economic times, social policies tend to be liberal because the healthy economy allows all segments of society to make progress. During economic downturns, there is a trend toward conservative social policy, by which some individuals and groups gain at the expense of others and under which the most economically dependent are likely to be sacrificed (Myers, 1982).

CASE STUDY

The Hernandez Family

The Hernandez family's problems reflect the external stress encountered by minority clients who must cope with socioeconomic issues. The unemployment situation has placed undue stress on Mr. Hernandez. His relatives have been unable to find suitable employment on account of economic and transient factors. Sheer fatigue has placed Mr. Hernandez in a position of inability to sustain an adequate relationship with his family, particularly his son. Mr. Platt notes the physical, psychological, and social aspects of the problem and its effect on Ricardo. The social worker identifies some concrete indicators of environmental stress on Mr. Hernandez that are affecting his relations with his son.

Task Recommendations

Minority problem levels are general indicators to assist social workers in problem identification. Their focus is away from minority intrapsychic problems and toward external, environmental factors. In order to understand these principles, the following exercises may be useful:

In a minority case study, identify macro and meso problem stressors such as culture conflict (for example, entrance into a new culture, which sets up a conflict between ethnic traditions and White norms), minority group status (for example, the change in status from being an ethnic majority in one culture to being an ethnic minority in another), and social change (for example, impact of American metropolitan lifestyle upon ethnic provincial ways).

Continue with the same minority case. Find the biopsychosocial aspects of problems, such as micro somatic complaints, the effects of external stress upon the client's health, and socioeconomic factors having an impact on the person.

Discuss minority problem categories with an experienced clinician who has worked with people of color. Determine whether there are other relevant problem categories that have not been mentioned and which should be identified.

Problem Themes

Ideological Belief: Racism

At the basis of minority-related problem themes is the problem of racism, which is manifested attitudinally in prejudice and behaviorally in discrimination. The danger of this statement is the reduction of the analysis of ethnic minority problems to a simplistic explanation. However, there is ample evidence that racist reactions of the majority society contribute to and complicate the problems of people of color. Historically, each minority group has suffered discrimination in its interaction with the majority forces in the United States. Black Americans came to the United States predominantly as slaves, although there were some free men and women. They have, as an ethnic group, suffered racial discrimination despite civil rights legislation. Latino Americans have faced economic oppression as migrant farmworkers and cheap laborers. Asian Americans were excluded from immigration into the United States in the early part of this century. Recent Indochinese immigrants have encountered hostile racism in various parts of the United States when they have competed with their White counterparts in Gulf Coast fishing. Native Americans have been restricted to federal reservations and placed in a socioeconomically dependent role through the Bureau of Indian Affairs, Department of the Interior.

Racism has been defined as the domination of one social or ethnic group over another. It is used as an ideological system to justify the institutional discrimination of certain racial groups against others. There are a number of characteristics of racism (Hodge, 1975; Davis, 1978):

1. the belief that there are well-defined and distinctive races among human beings;
2. the belief that racial mixing lowers biological quality;

3. the belief in the mental and physical superiority of some races over others;
4. the belief that racial groups have distinct racial culture to the extent that some races are naturally prone to criminality, sexual looseness, or dishonest business practices;
5. the belief that certain races have temperamental dispositions, which is a form of stereotyping;
6. the belief that the superior races should rule and dominate the inferior races.

These beliefs may be overtly expressed or covertly felt by persons of one race concerning other races. Racism generates prejudice and discrimination.

Attitude: Prejudice

Prejudice is an attitudinal response expressing unfavorable feelings and behavioral intentions toward a group or its individual members (Davis, 1978). It primarily exhibits negative affective reactions to others. People hold certain prejudices because they can blame the out-group, do not admit uncomfortable feelings about themselves, and organize and structure their own world according to their rationale (Brislin, 1981). There have been a number of theories of prejudice, viewing it variously as cultural transmission of beliefs about certain races that result in degrees of social distance, personality manifestations of frustration and aggression leading to displacement of feelings of the in-group versus the out-group (McLemore, 1983).

From a pragmatic standpoint, there are conditions that increase and decrease prejudice. Prejudice is heightened under the following circumstances (Amir, 1969, p. 338):

1. when the contact situation produces competition between groups;
2. when the contact is unpleasant, involuntary, and tension laden;
3. when the prestige or status of a group is lowered as a result of contact;
4. when members of a group or the whole group is in a state of frustration;
5. when the groups have moral or ethnic standards objectionable to each other;
6. when the members of the minority group are of lower status or lower in any relevant characteristics than members of the majority group.

Numerous incidents illustrate these principles: the competition between Vietnamese and Gulf Coast fishermen, which produced a volatile economic and social situation; racial slurs uttered in the heat of a political campaign; the covert exclusion of ethnic groups from civil rights of voting, housing, and employment; and focusing on the alcoholism and suicidal rates of Native Americans to the exclusion of favorable cultural characteristics such as survival skills, harmony with nature and the universe, and group sharing.

Likewise, prejudice is reduced when certain conditions are present (Amir, 1969, p. 339):

1. when there is equal-status contact between members of various ethnic groups;
2. when there is contact between members of a majority group and higher-status members of a minority group;
3. when an authority or social climate favorably promotes intergroup contact;
4. when intergroup ethnic contact is pleasant or rewarding;
5. when members of both groups interact functionally in important activities,

developing common goals or superordinate goals that rank higher in importance than the individual goals of each group.

Recall various events that have lessened racial prejudice in the United States: the achievement of voting rights and political power on the local metropolitan level for Black Americans; the housing integration of middle-class professional Whites with ethnic minority counterparts; the ethnic harmony and one-world spirit exhibited at the opening ceremony of the 1984 Los Angeles Olympics; and the 1984 election's appeal to Americanism—pride of country, allegiance to God, and love of humanity—that transcends ethnic boundaries.

Behavior: Discrimination

Prior to the 1960s, social work practice was strongly influenced by minority anthropology encountered in the works of Margaret Mead and Clyde Kluckhohn. During the sixties, the focus was on the effects of discrimination which tended to impose deviant characteristics on minorities. Solomon (1983) observes that Whites felt Blacks had "concern [only] for immediate gratification, lack of interest in personal achievement, and lack of commitment to marriage and family. Moreover these supposed characteristics were viewed as deterrents to the involvement of Blacks in problem-solving relationships with social work practitioners" (pp. 423–424). Minority characteristics were magnified and differentiated from those of White society (Solomon, 1983). These examples of discrimination could be termed a discriminatory interpretation of minorities.

Discrimination refers to a behavioral response that is unfavorable to members of an ethnic or racial out-group (Brislin, 1981; McLemore, 1983). Prejudice precedes discrimination as a learned condition. A person discriminates against others because of a cognitive belief and affective attitude. There are several theories of discrimination, relating to situational pressures (a person does not associate with minority people because of peer reaction), group gains (competition for scarce resources and ethnocentrism result in ethnic domination and subordination), and institutional discrimination against minorities in employment, education, housing, and other life-sustaining areas. Discriminatory acts are likely to occur under the following conditions (Bonacich & Goodman, 1972):

1. when there are biologically, culturally, and socially distinct populations in a social system;
2. when a segment of the population is threatened by another over competition for scarce resources;
3. when a group is seen to be the common enemy of other groups, an enemy which unifies the other groups;
4. when there are unequal degrees of power in populations;
5. when institutional discriminatory actions are legitimated in social structures and cultural beliefs.

Discriminatory behavior leads to denial of equal educational, economic, and political opportunities. It holds Blacks and other people of color back and contributes to inequality of employment and income. It represents a failure in relationships between minority and majority populations who do not recognize that they are interdependent on each other's welfare. It permits injustice to fester and erupt in race riots and expressions of rebellion (Willie, 1981).

We have briefly defined and described the essential characteristics of racism, prejudice, and discrimination. These are the foundation of many of the psychosocial problems that ethnic minorities face in the United States. Racism has been viewed as an ideological belief that leads to prejudice. Prejudice is a negative social attitude against a group of people, most often experienced by ethnic minorities and other disadvantaged groups. In turn, discrimination is manifested in unfavorable behavioral actions that delegate minorities to subordinate positions. The problems confronted by ethnic minorities that can be traced back to racism, prejudice, and discrimination find expression in five forms: oppression, powerlessness, exploitation, acculturation, and stereotyping. Figure 5-2 illustrates the ethnic minority problem typology which we have described so far.

Expressions: Oppression, Powerlessness, Exploitation, Acculturation, and Stereotyping

Minority social work theorists have developed the themes of oppression, powerlessness, exploitation, acculturation, and stereotyping.

Oppression.   The source of oppression is located in social institutions that precipitate the minority client's problem. Turner, Singleton, and Musiek (1984) observe that oppression occurs when a segment of the population systematically and over a prolonged period of time prevents another segment from attaining access to scarce and valued resources. Oppression is a process and a structure. It is a process whereby specific acts are designed to place others in the lower ranks of society. It is also a structure that creates a bottom rank in a hierarchical system of ranks. Minority clients' problems are usually not due entirely to personal deficiency. They are often personal reactions to oppressive social institutions. These extrapsychic problems are oppressive environmental forces that trigger a reaction in the minority client (Leigh & Green, 1982). Group oppression is understood as the misuse of group and class to perform the labor necessary to run society and the exclusion of these people from decision making affecting the course and direction of society (Leigh, 1984).

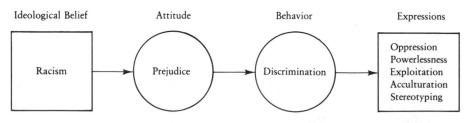

Figure 5-2 Ethnic minority problem typology.

Powerlessness.   Powerlessness is the inability to control self and others to alter problem situations or reduce environmental distress (Leigh, 1984). Solomon (1976b) explains that powerlessness arises out of a process that denies valued identities and roles, as well as valuable resources, to individuals or groups. As a result, they are unable to exercise interpersonal influence or command the social resources necessary for effective social functioning. She also argues that powerlessness is a problem for majority group members who must cope with interpersonal relationships, deficiencies in material resources, and life situations that assault their self-image.

Powerlessness stems in part from the relationship between the individual and oppressive social institutions. Solomon (1976a) has written about the Black American experience in terms of powerlessness as a state of being and the need for practical ways to experience empowerment. Minorities often feel impotent. Underrepresented, outvoted, and manipulated, minority group members—social work professionals and clients alike—both identify with similar experiences. Ethnic minority clients often feel at a loss about what to do. How does one cope with feelings of powerlessness, which are so overwhelming and devastating to a minority person? Solomon (1983) traces the vicious cycle of powerlessness, which for Blacks begins with racism, discrimination, and negative valuation. Because of White society's label of inferiority, Blacks are prevented from developing a positive self-concept or cognitive skills. In turn, Blacks are unable to develop interpersonal or technical skills and their effectiveness to perform social roles is reduced. Finally, these shortcomings confirm and reinforce feelings of inferiority and negative value, and the vicious cycle begins again.

A recent example of oppression and powerlessness was the American reaction to the influx of Vietnamese refugees into the United States during the end of the Vietnam War in the mid-seventies. Remarks by public officials and public fear of the economic competition for jobs were almost identical to the historic oppressive responses that early Asian immigrants suffered at the turn of the 20th century. Likewise, these Southeast Asian newcomers were virtually powerless politically, economically, and socially when they entered the country. They depended on the good will of churches and private sponsors. The following case analysis (Cultural Study 5-5) is an illustration of the oppression and powerless themes on the macro level.

Cultural Study 5-5

Oppression and Powerlessness[5]

The initial reaction of the American public to the admittance of the Southeast Asian refugees was essentially negative. Opinions were harsh and unfavorable. Indeed, a Gallup poll conducted in 1975 found that 54% of the American public were against admitting the refugees and only 36% were favorable. Former Representative Burt Talcott (R., Calif.) said, "Damn it, we have too many Orientals already. If they all gravitate to California, the tax and welfare rolls will get overburdened and we already have our share of illegal aliens" (Liu, 1979, p. 63). Negative reactions were not only expressed in California. Senator George McGovern was quoted as saying "Ninety percent of the Vietnamese refugees would be better off going back to their own land" (*Time*, May 19, 1975, p. 9).

In spite of all the negative reactions President Ford stood firm and reassured the public

(continued)

> **Cultural Study 5-5 (continued)**
>
> that "the people that we are welcoming today, the individuals who are in Guam or in Camp Pendleton or Eglin Air Force Base, are individuals who can contribute significantly to our society in the future" (Remark to the Advisory Committee on Refugees, May 13, 1975). President Ford was angry at widespread opposition because "we are a country built by immigrants . . . and we have always been a humanitarian nation" (*U.S. News and World Report,* May 19, 1975, p. 1). Various voluntary organizations (such as the Red Cross, International Rescue Committee), major American companies (for example, IBM), unions, (for example, AFL-CIO), newspapers and magazines (*Time, Newsweek,* etc.) all endorsed Ford's stand on resettlement.
>
> For many reasons the American public's reaction persisted even into the arrival of the second wave. The Southeast Asian refugees came at a time when the American public wanted to forget Vietnam, when interest was receding from social concern and social action efforts, and when the U.S. economy was at a low ebb (Liu, 1979).
>
> The major argument against accepting the refugees centered around the American's fear of job displacement. It was argued that resettlement en masse in certain areas such as New York, Southern California, or Texas would unduly strain the employment markets. This meant resettlement could prove to be an economic threat.
>
> [5]From "The Arrival of the Southeast Asian Refugees in America: An Overview," by T. Tayabas and T. Pok. In *Bridging Cultures: Southeast Asian Refugees in America,* pp. 7, 8. Copyright © 1981 by Special Service for Groups and the Asian American Community Mental Health Training Center. Reprinted by permission.

Exploitation.   Exploitation occurs when an ethnic minority person is manipulated or used unfairly in an economic, political, or social situation for the benefit of the majority society. Historically, people of color were exploited economically as cheap agricultural and sweat-shop laborers. Most Blacks entered the United States as forced slave laborers in the rural South. Today poor Mexicans are the farm migrant workers in agricultural fields of the western United States. Asians were imported to work on the transcontinental railroad and agricultural fields at the turn of the 20th century. Native Americans were the victims of political genocide, which forced them from their native lands across the United States and onto reservations. As a result, Native Americans have the highest rates of unemployment, illiteracy, alcoholism, and suicide of all ethnic groups in the country. Politically, Blacks and Latinos have been wooed by both major political parties as a means of gaining the minority vote and appearing as nonracists in American society.

Cultural Study 5-6 is an example of exploitation by appointing a token minority person to a social service position. This incident took place in England but is similar to those that occur regularly in the United States. Exploitation occurs when a person is caught between the agency's intent to project a favorable image of affirmative action and the compromising of his or her own integrity for the sake of maintaining the organization.

Acculturation.   Acculturation is the adoption by an ethnic minority person of the dominant culture in which he or she is immersed. There are degrees of acculturation; a person may maintain his or her own traditional cultural beliefs, values, and customs from country of origin to a greater or lesser extent. The term *Americanization* has been associated with the popular notion that persons living in the United States gave up former cultural practices and adopted the American way of life.

Cultural Study 5-6

Exploitation[6]

The black social worker who is a victim of organisational prejudice may find that he is expected to conform to the organisation's stereotype of a 'good black social worker'. As one of the few black workers employed by the organisation, he may be expected to behave in an appreciative manner, serving as a symbol of the organisation's good record in race relations. When I was appointed to my first social work job, I wondered how easily I was accepted. A few months later, I was at a cocktail party for the department where I heard the clerk to the council discussing racial prejudice in the borough. When I responded unfavourably I was promptly reminded by her that if the borough was prejudiced they would not have employed me. She was in fact one of the interviewers at my job. The 'good black social worker' is one who colludes with the organisation's view of its record in race relations.

The black social worker may also be made to feel he is different from other black people or that he is a 'superior coloured'. As a result he may feel obliged to collude with the organisation's stereotype of other blacks. Paradoxically, the 'good black social worker', though viewed differently from other black people, may also fall victim to the way his organisation categorises them. Thus he may be expected not to be assertive or selfconscious. If he is he may be labelled as pushy, aggressive and over-sensitive. In other words he must be the 'good black who knows his place'. Similarly he may be judged according to the image created by the previous black worker or other blacks at present in the organisation, and their record of satisfying its expectations. If he does not react like some of his other black colleagues who fit the role of the 'smiling nigger' he may be perceived as being anti-social, unfriendly and even anti-white. His individuality is lost.

[6]From "The Dilemmas and Contribution of Black Social Workers," by V. Liverpool. In J. Cheetham (Ed.) *Social Work and Ethnicity*, pp. 224, 225. Copyright © 1982 by Allen and Unwin, Inc. Reprinted by permission.

Stereotyping.   Stereotyping is the prejudicial attitude of a person or group that superimposes on a total race, sex, or religion a generalization about behavioral characteristics. For ethnic minorities, negative stereotyping has centered around skin color, low mentality, welfare freeloading, job competition, and pathological behavior. Stereotyping occurs in the context of racism as a means of explaining away ethnic minorities as inferior or defective. Stereotyping reflects the degree to which a dominant race views itself as superior to other ethnic groups in a pluralistic society.

We present illustrations of the problem themes of acculturation and stereotyping as they have occurred on micro and macro levels. Cultural Study 5-7 reiterates the history of forced acculturation and its effects on Native American groups. Yet the traditional values of metaphysical and cosmological principles expressed in spiritual rituals persisted throughout this process. These transcendent values of nature offer an alternative to modern society. The rediscovery by minorities of traditional cultural values has

Cultural Study 5-7

Macro Level Acculturation[7]

It has been suggested, with reason, that policies of forced or "directed" acculturation to which all Indian groups have been subjected, may lead to violent reactions which reject change and reaffirm traditionalism. A converse possibility which has been neglected by the specialists has been the role of the half informed, usually sentimental, "Indian lovers," the "do gooders," who would preserve certain of the "more noble" Indian values, albeit they should be incorporated with those "logical" modern innovations in such things as housing and hygiene. Paradoxically, such seemingly sympathetic approaches to Indian traditions may be far more corrosive to traditional values than the uncompromising ethnocentric attitudes of those agents of civilization who insist on total assimilation achieved through force if necessary.

Among the vast array of forces which may work for the persistence of traditional values is the often neglected psychological factor of the inherent stability of the basic personality structure which acts as a selective screen in processes of change. A dimension central to this complex question, but which is inaccessible to the quantitative experiential tools of either cultural anthropology or psychology, is the qualitative power of metaphysical, or cosmological, principles and the degree to which these become virtual or effective within the individual substance through participation in traditional rites and spiritual methods. Related to this entire question of the quality of personality is the fact that where Indians are still able to live within a world of as yet unspoiled Nature, potentially they have access to a vast array of transcendent values. It is essential to add, however, that for this potential source to become virtual for the Indian he must still possess, to a certain degree at least, the Indian's traditional metaphysic of nature. Where this metaphysic is still understood, and can be directly related to the supporting forms of the natural world, here the Indian has perhaps his strongest ally for the persistence of essential values; it is also in this metaphysic of nature that we find the Indian's most valuable message for the contemporary world.

A final factor relating to the persistence of values must be mentioned since it is crucial today to a multitude of problems deriving from attitudes in America towards minority groups of various ethnic backgrounds. White-American racial attitudes have historically so tended to devaluate physical types of other cultural traditions that these peoples generally have been relegated to positions of inferior status in the larger society. With the possibility of social or cultural mobility thus being denied, many of these groups have tended to seek retention of cohesion and identity through reaffirmation of their own traditional values. The resulting low index of intermarriage between these minority groups and the dominant majority has in addition tended to slow acculturation. This is a situation, incidentally, which has not occurred in Mexico where positive valuation has been given to the Indian heritage. Among the ramifications of negative racist attitudes is the fact that many Indians who do attempt to assimilate into segments of White-American culture tend to undergo a cycle of progressive disenchantment, a process often hastened by the slum conditions of cities, or by participation in foreign wars. When such persons then attempt to reintegrate back into their own traditional patterns they often serve as powerful agents for the preservation of traditional values.

[7]From "The Persistence of Essential Values among North American Plains Indians," by J. E. Brown, *Studies in Comparative Religion, 3,* 216–225. Copyright © 1969 by Perennial Books, Ltd. Reprinted by permission.

resulted from acculturation to the majority society. Cultural Study 5-8 touches on the theme of stereotyping Native Americans on the macro level. There are positive images of natural harmony and admiration for Native American culture. However, there are negative stereotypes of Native Americans in the media and in mental health treatment. On the micro level, the utilization of cultural rituals and support on the reservation helped to alleviate the hopelessness of a stereotypical attitude toward mental illness in a Native American.

Cultural Study 5-8

Macro Level Stereotyping[8]

Tribal affiliation is the Native American's most basic identification. The tribal teachings and experiences determine to a great extent the personality, values, and life goals of the individual, including the meaning of death and customs surrounding the burial of the dead. Because of extreme forms of discrimination toward Indians in certain parts of the country, many Indians have denied their tribal affiliation in fear of losing their lives or suffering physical harm.

The attitude of American society towards Native Americans is a strangely ambivalent one. The popular holistic health movement with its emphasis on the harmony of body, mind, and spirit embraces to a great extent the world view of Native Americans with their emphasis on the natural harmony of all living things. Native American speakers have been invited to holistic health seminars to share their philosophy on many occasions. Native American art and jewelry have never been more popular. People everywhere seem to be wearing turquoise rings, bracelets, and necklaces handcrafted by Indian silversmiths. Indian symbols and designs are found on the wallpaper, bedspreads, and rugs of plush Fifth Avenue apartments. Indian-designed sweaters are seen from coast to coast. It would appear that the Indian culture is to be admired and embraced.

On the other hand, social scientists, television, and the film industry portray a drunken Indian, suicidal and hopeless. Native Americans are either to be glorified and idealized as having mystical wisdom or ridiculed and stigmatized as being the shame of society. Mental health practitioners need to understand the self-image predicament Native Americans find themselves in when reacting to these extremely positive or negative stereotypes. The Indian client desires to be seen as a human being, with feelings of pride in his heritage and a desire for others to respect his beliefs and cultural traditions.

Negative stereotypes of Native Americans contribute to false impressions of behavioral adjustment (Shore, 1974). One commonly held assumption is that Indians as a group have many psychiatric problems and there is no hope for them (Beiser, 1974). After working with Native Americans of over a hundred tribes in the San Francisco Bay Area, I can recall a dramatic example of a young Hopi man experiencing auditory hallucinations after a family death. The local psychiatric emergency ward erroneously interpreted the hallucination as a psychotic symptom rather than part of the symptom complex associated with unresolved grief. Our agency intervened and this man was returned to the reservation to participate in a series of rituals and tribal ceremonies appropriate for the burial of the dead. Shortly after the ceremony he was free from the hallucinations. This man could have been hospitalized in a state mental hospital as a psychotic patient if Native American mental health personnel had not intervened on his behalf. In most instances practices that are difficult to understand

(continued)

This emphasis on external forces is not an excuse for individual responsibility and self-assertiveness. Rather, it is an opportunity to challenge and change the nature of oppressive social institutions (Solomon, 1983). The minority client cannot blame the system for his or her problems. To do so would be to surrender his or her responsibility for mobilization and action. To focus on the root causes of the problem is an opportunity for the minority client as the consumer and the social worker as the professional advocate to correct discrimination.

CASE STUDY

The Hernandez Family

The minority-related problem facing the Hernandez family revolves around the socioeconomic situation of poor and minority people. Struggling to survive in a metropolitan city with immigrant relatives and family obligations affects the entire family. High unemployment compounds the existing stressful situation. Myers (1982) observes that current economic conditions influence the degree to which the factors of race and social class are a source of stress for minorities. Stress is magnified under conditions of poverty with recession and limited social supports. Race becomes the determining factor in the struggle. It is mediated by economics and social conditions that determine relative group status and power.

Poor and minority people, particularly new immigrants, have suffered under the present economic recession. At the same time, White blue-collar and middle-class workers have lost their jobs and are unemployed. The powerless minority family struggles to survive in an oppressive system that discriminates between the needy and the truly needy. In cases such as that of the Hernandez family, Carrillo (1982) states that socioeconomic changes affect family structure. The Latino family in this country has its roots in migration. One of the reasons for geographic migration is pursuit of educational achievements, job opportunities, and personal relationships. These changes require the family to restructure, reintegrate, and realign itself systematically to meet the needs of its members. The Hernandez family is an example of those whose transition process following migration has been complicated by socioeconomic conditions.

Task Recommendations

In this section on problem themes, we have discussed oppression, powerlessness, exploitation, acculturation, and stereotyping. These issues have been developed from the perspective that external, oppressive social institutions affect the existence of the minority client in an adverse manner.

Identify current examples of oppression, powerlessness, exploitation, acculturation, and stereotyping affecting ethnic minorities on macro, messo, and micro levels. In the boxes of Table 5-1, write examples of these themes as they occur on all three levels. Brainstorm to bring as many incidents as possible to mind.

Discuss present social, economic, and political conditions that are adverse to ethnic minorities.

Outline positive strategies to cope with present forms of oppression, powerlessness, exploitation, acculturation, and stereotyping affecting minority clients

TABLE 5-1. Problem Levels and Themes

	Oppression	Powerlessness	Exploitation	Acculturation	Stereotyping
Macro Level (complex organizations, geographical populations)					
Meso Level (ethnic/local communities and organizations)					
Micro Level (individual, family, small group)					

Problem Area Detailing

Problem area detailing focuses on particular aspects of the client's problem. Bloom and Fischer (1982) discuss problem specification. The first step is to conduct a survey of relevant problems or people with which or with whom the client—whether an individual or a group—is having the most difficulty. Next comes selecting a specific problem about which the client is concerned. Once problem selection has been achieved, a problem is defined in observable, clear, and countable terms. However, there are covert problem details that surface under culturally understood conditions. Social workers should be aware of cultural dynamics that influence problem detailing.

During the seventies and eighties, there has been an influx of minority refugees and immigrants into the United States. The majority of these people of color have arrived from Cuba, Southeast Asia (Vietnam, Cambodia, and Laos), Korea, Philippines, Thailand, India, and Pakistan. These patterns of immigration have produced reactions among several groups: the refugees themselves, who have experienced cultural readjustment; governmental and social service agencies, who have geared up for the transition; and the American public, who have expressed mixed feelings. Brown (1982) has identified numerous problems facing Indochinese refugees: emotional responses to separation, such as guilt and a sense of obligation, as well as the problem of misapprehension; symptoms of vocational transition, such as frustration and violence; and intergenerational conflict, including acculturation of the young. Brown states:

> The loss of reference group, the destruction of vocational and social roles, and the drastic reorganization of family roles necessitated by survival considerations combine to create a threatening new world within which the refugees must begin the painful process of defending and redefining the self. Immersed in a foreign culture and language, refugees are deprived of the feedback processes that normally help to guide role performance [1982, p. 159].

Timberlake and Cook (1984) suggest that Vietnamese refugees are likely to experience psychosocial dysfunction if they are unable to make sense of the contradictions between habits and beliefs of their old, familiar culture and those of the new culture of pluralistic America. Problems become manifest in confusion of thought, affect, and behavior, as well as in somatic and affective symptoms of depression.

Kitano (1969) reports that Japanese–American clients cite parent-child difficulties, marital problems, intergenerational stresses, and problems of ethnic identity as central concerns. Yet Kitano asserts that mental health professionals are not meeting the needs of minority clients in those areas. Some of the reasons for that lack of congruity between the minority client and the helping professional are culturally motivated attempts to hide problem behavior, cultural styles of expressing problems, inappropriate service delivery, and lack of relevant connections to the therapeutic community. Human-service helpers must be sensitive to how minority clients indirectly express problem details. With some Asian Americans, obtaining details of a problem may be difficult. Admitting a problem is seen as a lack of self-control, determination, and will power and a family defect (Ho, 1976). For Black Americans, problem details may be expressed by analogy. Solomon (1983) explains:

> Thus, feelings of depression may be described as "I feel like I do not have a real friend in the world" rather than "I have feelings of intense loneliness." This tendency of a client to give examples of his or her experience of a problem rather than to isolate and analyze specific factors is often considered reflective of a lack of insight or ability to abstract when it may be a style of communication instead [p. 419].

Social workers should be ready to piece together and interpret details or cues that are interwoven in a conversation.

Boyd (1982) suggests that many minority families present a variety of socioeconomic problems that relate to the welfare system, housing, child welfare, schools, courts, churches, police departments, and other institutions. From the multiplicity of problems, it is important to pick out a problem that can be solved within a reasonable time frame. Problem detailing involves determining who is involved, what the major issues are and when and where the problem dynamics take place. Cultural dimensions of the problem are included among the facts of problem details.

CASE STUDY

The Hernandez Family

For the Hernandez family, problem details consist of three interrelated issues: first, the recent arrival from Mexico of two immigrant families and the inability of the heads of those households to find steady employment; second, the physical fatigue and emotional stress experienced by Mr. Hernandez, who feels obligated to help these families and works at two jobs for extra income; and third, the academic and social problems of Ricardo, the eldest child, which have prompted referral by the school to the Family Service Association. The social casework task is to decide which problems could be broken down into specific components that are amenable to solution. Making adequate resources for job finding available to the two immigrant families would eliminate the necessity of Mr. Hernandez's working at two jobs. He would have time to spend with his son Ricardo. Which problem has a workable solution with reasonable closure? How can the social worker assist the family? How can Mr. Hernandez facilitate employment for his in-laws? What are the natural ethnic community support systems available to alleviate the problems of the Hernandez family?

Task Recommendations

For the purposes of problem detailing, it is important to obtain sufficient information about the problem(s) and to identify a specific problem whose solution is feasible. Some of the minority-related aspects of problem detailing deal with facilitating problem information and understanding language analogies, selecting the problems to be solved, and encouraging the client to make decisions.

Discuss whether there are sufficient details of the Hernandez family's problems. What information is missing from the case study? Are there sufficient details to identify a workable solution to the problem?

Select a focal problem area: unemployment problems of recent immigrant families, Mr. Hernandez's job stress, Ricardo's school problems. What is your rationale for selecting one of these areas? How can the social worker assist the Hernandez family and allow Mr. Hernandez to carry the momentum?

Conclusion

Relationship building is a prerequisite to problem formulation. Problem identification focuses on environmental/societal conditions that affect the minority client. Problem disclosure may be delayed as the minority client evaluates the character and style of the social worker. Problem themes are racism, prejudice, and discrimination, which are expressed through oppression, powerlessness, exploitation, acculturation, and stereotyping. Problem detailing may be expressed by analogy or other indirect means. Social workers should be attuned to styles of communicating problems and piece together details interwoven in the conversation. It is important to reiterate and confirm the problem details with the minority client. Social work educators and practitioners must examine how they conceptualize, teach, and implement problem formulation with students and clients. Minority clients' problems must be seen in terms of an alternative set of problem identification principles.

References

Amir, Y. (1969). Contact hypothesis in ethnic relations. *Psychological Bulletin, 71,* 319–342.

Bloom, M., & Fischer, J. (1982). *Evaluating practice: Guidelines for the accountable professional.* Englewood Cliffs, N.J.: Prentice-Hall.

Bonacich, E., & Goodman, R. F. (1972). *Deadlock in school desegregation: A case study of Inglewood, California.* New York: Praeger.

Boyd, N. (1982). Family therapy with Black families. In E. E. Jones & S. J. Korchin (Eds.), *Minority mental health* (pp. 227–249). New York: Praeger.

Brislin, R. W. (1981). *Cross-cultural encounters: Face-to-face interaction.* New York: Pergamon Press.

Brown, G. (1982). Issues in the resettlement of Indochinese refugees. *Social Casework, 63,* 155–159.

Brown, J. E. (1969). The persistence of essential values among North American Plains Indians. *Studies in Comparative Religion, 3,* 216–225.

Bryson, S., & Bardo, H. (1975). Race and the counseling process: An overview. *Journal of Non-White Concerns in Personnel and Guidance, 4,* 5–15.

Carrillo, C. (1982). Changing norms of Hispanic families: Implications for treatment. In E. E. Jones & S. J. Korchin (Eds.), *Minority mental health* (pp. 250–266). New York: Praeger.

David, K. H. (1976). The use of social learning theory in preventing intercultural adjustment problems. In P. Pedersen, W. J. Lonner, & J. G. Draguns (Eds.), *Counseling across cultures* (pp. 123–138). Honolulu: University Press of Hawaii.

Davis, F. J. (1978). *Minority-dominant relations: A sociological analysis*. Arlington Heights, Ill.: AHM Publishing Corporation.

Devore, W., & Schlesinger, E. G. (1981). *Ethnic-sensitive social work practice*. St. Louis; C.V. Mosby.

Ghali, S. B. (1977). Culture sensitivity and the Puerto Rican client. *Social Casework, 58,* 459–468.

Green, J. W. (1982). *Cultural awareness in the human services*. Englewood Cliffs, N.J.: Prentice-Hall.

Hepworth, D. H., & Larsen, J. A. (1982). *Direct social work practice: Theory and skills*. Homewood, Ill.: Dorsey Press.

Ho, M. K. (1976). Social work with Asian Americans. *Social Casework, 57,* 195–201.

Hodge, J. L. (1975). Domination and the will in Western thought and culture. In J. L. Hodge, D. K. Struckmann, & L. D. Trost, *Cultural Bases of Racism and Group Oppression* (pp. 9–48). Berkeley: Two Riders Press.

Jenkins, S. (1981). *The ethnic dilemma in social services*. New York: Free Press.

Kitano, H. (1969). Japanese-American mental illness. In S. Plog & R. Edgarton (Eds.), *Changing perspectives in mental illness* (pp. 257–284). New York; Holt, Rinehart & Winston.

Kuramoto, F. H., Morales, R. F., Munoz, F. U., & Murase, K. (1983). Education for social work practice in Asian and Pacific American communities. In J. C. Chunn II, P. J. Dunston, & F. Ross-Sheriff (Eds.), *Mental health and people of color: Curriculum development and change* (pp. 127–155). Washington, D.C.: Howard University Press.

Leigh, J. W. (1984). Empowerment strategies for work with multi-ethnic populations. Unpublished paper presented at the annual program meeting of the Council on Social Work Education, Detroit.

Leigh, J. W., & Green, J. W. (1982). The structure of the Black community: The knowledge base for social services. In J. W. Green (Ed.), *Cultural awareness in the human services* (pp. 94–121). Englewood Cliffs, N.J.: Prentice-Hall.

Lewis, R. G., & Ho, M. K. (1975). Social work with Native Americans. *Social Work, 20,* 379–382.

McLemore, S. D. (1983). *Racial and ethnic relations in America*. Boston: Allyn & Bacon.

Meadow, A. (1983). Psychopathology, psychotherapy and the Mexican-American patient. In E. E. Jones & S. J. Korchin (Eds.), *Minority mental health* (pp. 331–361). New York: Praeger.

Morales, A., & Salcido, R. (1983). Social work with Mexican Americans. In A. Morales & B. W. Sheafor, *Social work: A profession of many faces* (pp. 389–413). Boston: Allyn & Bacon.

Myers, H. F. (1982). Stress, ethnicity and social class: A model for research with Black populations. In E. E. Jones & S. J. Korchin (Eds.), *Minority mental health* (pp. 118–148). New York: Praeger.

Northen, H. (1982). *Clinical social work*. New York: Columbia University Press.

Reid, W. J. (1978). *The task-centered system*. New York: Columbia University Press.

Sena-Rivera, J. (1980). La Familia Hispana as a natural support system: Strategies for prevention in mental health. In R. Valle & W. Vega (Eds.), *Hispanic natural support systems: Mental Health promotion perspectives* (pp. 75–81). Sacramento: State of California Department of Mental Health.

Smith, E. J. (1981). Cultural and historical perspectives in counseling Blacks. In D. W. Sue, *Counseling the culturally different: Theory and practice* (pp. 141–185). New York: Wiley.

Solomon, B. B. (1976a). *Black empowerment: Social work in oppressed communities*. New York: Columbia University Press.

Solomon, B. B. (1976b). Social work in a multiethnic society. In M. Sotomayor (Ed.), *Cross-cultural perspectives in social work practice and education* (pp. 165–177). Houston: University of Houston Graduate School of Social Work.

Solomon, B. B. (1983). Social work with Afro-Americans. In A. Morales & B. W. Sheafor, *Social work: A profession of many faces* (pp. 415–436). Boston: Allyn & Bacon.

Sue, D. W. (1981). *Counseling the culturally different: Theory and practice.* New York: Wiley.

Sue, S., Ito, J., & Bradshaw, C. (1982). Ethnic minority research: Trends and directions. In E. E. Jones & S. J. Korchin (Eds.), *Minority mental health* (pp. 37–58). New York: Praeger.

Sue, S., & Morishima, J. K. (1982). *The mental health of Asian Americans.* San Francisco: Jossey-Bass.

Timberlake, E. M., & Cook, K. O. (1984). Social work and the Vietnamese refugee. *Social Work, 29,* 108–113.

Tucker, R. N., & Gunnings, T. S. (1974). Counseling Black youth: A quest for legitimacy. *Journal of Non-White Concerns, 2,* 208–217.

Turner, J. H., Singleton, R., Jr., & Musiek, D. (1984). *Oppression: A socio-history of Black-White relations in America.* Chicago: Nelson-Hall.

Vega, W. (1980). Mental health research and North American Hispanic populations: A review and critique of the literature and a proposed research strategy. In R. Valle & W. Vega (Eds.), *Hispanic natural support systems: Mental health promotion perspectives* (pp. 3–14). Sacramento: State of California Department of Mental Health.

Willie, C. V. (1981). *A new look at Black families.* Bayside, N.Y.: General Hall Publishers.

6

Assessment

Assessment, in social work practice, is an in-depth investigation of psychosocial dynamics affecting the client and the client's environment. It analyzes the forces interacting between the client and the situational configuration, with particular focus on the environmental impact on the client and the resources available for responding to the problem. Assessment of ethnic minority clients identifies positive cultural strengths available in the client's ethnic background. It moves away from a pathological investigation, which tends to evaluate internal and external liabilities. Dieppa (1983) raises an interesting point regarding a pathological stance toward ethnic minorities:

> In addition, knowledge from sociology, psychology, and social work has been used to explicate the ethos of ethnic and racial minorities within an ethnopathological framework. Socio-cultural and psychological theoretical analyses have frequently placed causative factors and solutions within the context of the individual and familial psyche. Why has a profession that views life, behavior, and social problems within the context of an ecological or systems theory (which should include culture as a significant element) focused its goals, priorities, and resources on a "mental health solution" to the problems of oppressed populations [p. 120]?

Ethnic-oriented assessment should strive for a psychosocial balance between objective, external factors of the community and subjective, internal reactions. Ethnic beliefs, family solidarity, community support networks, and other cultural assets are intervening variables.

The social work profession should take into account that certain environmental stressors are examples of institutionally caused powerlessness. Deep federal budget cuts, which have an impact on social service programs for the poor and minorities, and the lack of national commitment to the civil rights and social well-being of Black, Latino, Asian, and Native Americans are examples of institutional policies that have negative societal results for people of color. Furthermore, social work should recognize that cultural assets are implicit in ethnic community support systems. It must incorporate knowledge of collective cultural strengths in its assessment base.

This chapter focuses on the psychosocial aspects of socioenvironmental impacts on clients' psycho-individual—internal cognitive, affective, and behavioral—reactions. It asserts that the client interacts with and reacts to the social environment within an ethnic context. There are unique environmental forces interacting with societal and ethnic factors. Likewise, the minority client draws upon familiar ethnic coping mechanisms when confronted with these forces. In turn, the social worker should be aware of client's unique psychosocial action and reaction. Our task is to identify the assessment factors that influence the client and the worker, who must frame the psychosocial situation, note unique assessment dynamics, and formulate an assessment evaluation.

As Figure 6-1 illustrates, the client system practice issues are understood in terms of socioenvironmental impacts that result in psycho-individual reactions. The worker system practice issues are related to the analysis of assessment dynamics and the formulation of assessment evaluation.

Client System Practice Issues

Socioenvironmental Impacts

In the previous chapter, we sought to identify a particular set of problems affecting the person of color. In assessment we investigate the scope of socioenvironmental impacts and their effect on the minority client. Romero (1983) discusses the etiology of minority groups' social problems:

> It is the belief of this author that the majority of mental health problems exhibited by Chicanos are not pathological. Rather, they result from a combination of socioeconomic stresses that are compounded by poverty, racism, oppression, lack of access to educational and legal systems and institutions as well as to health care, and the experience of acculturation and culture shock [p. 91].

Harwood (1981) makes the point that among ethnic groups, there is a psychosocial

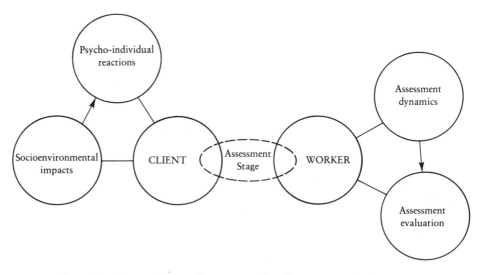

Figure 6-1.   Assessment stage: client system and worker system practice issues.

perspective on illness that includes emphasis on interpersonal and environmental conditions:

> The cultural traditions of most ethnic groups tend to view illness episodes in both a psychosomatic and an ecological framework. That is, in many ethnic subcultures both psychological stresses, worry, and strained interpersonal relations, on the one hand, and unfavorable environmental and living conditions, on the other, figure importantly among the multiple etiological factors that are used to interpret and understand illness [p. 23].

Moreover, ethnic minority groups view psychological states, such as stress, worry, and grief, and situational factors, such as poor housing, loss of work, and family disputes, as causing or contributing to disease. Likewise, the ethnic minority's perception of illness is based on the duration, location, and intensity of symptoms and the extent to which the symptoms interfere with valued social activities or the fulfillment of role responsibilities (Harwood, 1981). It follows naturally that social work should focus on the removal of specific symptoms and assist the client with the gradual resumption of normal social activities and roles.

Socioenvironmental impacts measure the influence of problem areas. Kim (1981) has given us an assessment that encompasses issues of newcomer survival, psychosomatic illness, psychological identity, mental illness, and problems of the elderly. Kim has then grouped a number of related problem clusters under each heading. The model is geared toward mental health assessment with Asian–American clients. However, it is applicable to other ethnic minority groups whose psycho-social-cultural problems are affected by time factors (that is, length of stay and generational differences) and acculturation (that is, movement from native culture to Americanization). These factors account for some of the socioenvironmental impacts that affect the minority client in various ways. For example, after only a brief length of stay, a newcomer may be struggling with such survival problems as culture shock, language barriers, and unemployment. Acculturation in this initial critical period is exacerbated by these factors. For second-generation minorities, one might anticipate psychological identity problems such as ethnic identity confusion, value conflict, and issues raised by women's liberation. Temporal (time-related) factors may involve first-generation parents and second-generation children. Acculturation tends to move the children toward Western mentality and behavior, while parents have opposed total acculturation. Kim's (1981) model uses a chart on which two of the three dimensions are temporal factors and acculturation. The remaining dimension consists of the following five problem clusters:[1]

Newcomer syndrome (basic survival issues)
    food, housing
    job/welfare
    culture shock/culture dislocation
    language barrier
    transportation
    legal/immigration problems
    school for children

[1] Adapted from lecture on "Minority Assessment," by Dr. Luke Kim, presented at California State University, Sacramento, Division of Social Work, Spring, 1981. Used with permission.

Psychosomatic syndromes
  anxiety/depression
  headache/back pain/shoulder pain
  hypertension/gastrointestinal disturbance
  loneliness/isolation/alienation
  insomnia/weight loss/no energy
Psychological/identity issues (second and third generations)
  ethnic identity confusion, conflict, ambivalence
  self-hatred/negative identification/rebellion
  cultural value conflict
  family role conflict/husband-wife role conflict
  women's liberation/emancipation/sexuality/divorce
  dating/mate selection/intermarriage
  parent-child conflict
  youth delinquency/gang/rebellion
Major mental illness (acute, chronic psychosis, affective disorder)
  inadequate treatment in public, private facilities (few bilingual staff members)
  stigma of mental illness
  family rejection
  lack of support system
Elderly problems
  isolation/despair
  confusion
  disorientation

In the following sections, selected issues are examined in terms of assessment.

Survival

Socioeconomic survival means maintaining basic necessities: food, shelter, clothing, and financial resources. These concrete survival needs may force the minority client to seek social services. Among the crucial needs are adequate nutrition, housing, child care, health care, recreational activities, clean air, and police and fire protection. Myers (1982) identifies three factors that influence survival stress and that relate to the fluctuating environment:

1. the present social and economic conditions;
2. the operating racial and social class dynamics that influence both exposure to stress and the contingencies governing options for coping with stress;
3. the availability and accessibility of resources and supports.

These variables are particularly critical for minority immigrants. Although immigrants must have a sponsor who ensures employment and housing, minority newcomers are confronted with basic survival needs. American society and lifestyle are a different experience from what minority immigrants have known, especially those who come from a non-English speaking country and are accustomed to a rural environment. There is an initial period, commonly called culture shock, of stressful adjustment to unfamiliar culture. The minority person must overcome the language barrier and learn alternative cognitive expressions. Finding reasonable housing, adequate employment, transportation, and school for the children are hurdles of the transition period. Language plays an important part in socioeconomic achievement. Monolingual minority clients without command of English may be restricted to their own ethnic neighborhoods (such as Chinatowns or *barrios*). These people are able to express themselves in their native language. However, they communicate in faulty and halting English. Language restrictions curb mobility, produce social uncertainty, and limit employment opportunities. As a result, there may be role and socioeconomic reversal for the minority person who cannot attain the social prestige and economic status he or she had formerly enjoyed. The Vietnamese physician, the Pilipino lawyer, and the Mexican school teacher must work toward state licensure and educational standards in this country. Because of language difficulty, professional requirements, and field practicum, they may require several years to meet American credentials. Basic survival needs are a central reality for newcomers who have been economically displaced through loss of status, differences in professional credentials, and language problems.

To a large extent, socioeconomic survival depends on the state of the economy and public policy. With an economic recession, a tight federal budget, and a politically conservative administration, there have been cutbacks in human services, political rhetoric about the truly needy, and subtle racial discrimination. The locus of problem assessment should be shifted from the individual to social recognition that minorities are placed in disadvantaged situations (Jackson, 1973). Jones and Seagull (1977) speak about survival:

> The therapist owes it to the client to deal with these more immediate real-life problems, either directly or through referral, before dealing with intrapsychic issues. In the statement, "I'll talk about my father if you want me to, but you have to know that there's no food to feed my kids tonight," lies a real dilemma [p. 854].

Socioeconomic survival is a primary area of impact for minority assessment.

Environmental Conflict

Another area of socioenvironmental impact is issues of environmental conflict, which have influence on identity ambivalence and resolution. To what extent has a minority client resolved ethnic identity conflicts? Atkinson, Morten, and Sue (1979) offer a model of minority development that traces the stages of conformity (preference for dominant cultural values), dissonance (cultural confusion and conflict), resistance and immersion (endorsement of minority views and rejection of dominant society and culture), introspection (individual autonomy), and synergetic articulation and awareness (cultural self-fulfillment). Cultural conflict is expressed in ethnic religious values, family roles, loss of face, self-hatred, negative identity, and marginality. It is important to assess the points of conflict, the degree to which internal skills and knowledge have been acquired to achieve a well-balanced minority identity, and the resources of family and kinship group patterns.

Issues of environmental conflict tend to surface in second and third generations of minorities who rediscover their ethnic roots and heritage in the midst of life crisis. They experience the tension of living in two cultures: American individuality, freedom of choice, and self-determinism, on the one hand, and collective decision making, family obligation, and self-restraint on the other. These two polarities produce a unique identity conflict matching the personalities of parents and children, peers, and social-cultural values.

Cultural Study 6-1 illustrates the dilemmas of minority identity conflict and their effects on a young Spanish–American woman in her late adolescence who is struggling with an identity crisis. Geographic readjustment, the beginning of college, and the need for a support group have caused the client to begin to question her past upbringing in light of a new situation confronting her.

Cultural Case Study 6-1

Family Helping System[2]

This client identifies herself as "Spanish-American." Her ancestors have resided in North-ern New Mexico under conditions of relative sociocultural isolation for generations. She is fluent in both Spanish and English, but her Spanish retains regional archaicisms unfamiliar to other Latinos and her English is slightly accented. Her politics are conservative. She was educated in a Roman Catholic school system, is committed to the dicta of her faith, and was reared in the large extended family structure that is traditional in that region.

Maria's life adjustment was uneventful until she left home for the first time and enrolled in a California college. There she was shocked by her encounters with Chicanos and Chicanas who were personally assertive, less inhibited in personal decorum, and more liberal politically. She could not deal with the rejection and disdain she experienced when she identified herself as "Spanish," rather than Chicana. This is her opening statement when she sought counseling.

> Moving away from home had a great psychological impact on me and my ideals. I had some difficulty adjusting myself to a completely new and independent form of life. Being Spanish-American, I was always closely bound to the family. When I tried to deviate from the norm, I was reprimanded and reminded of the obligation I had to the family. Living away from home taught me to appreciate them (family) and their conservative values more than I had before . . . but we sure are different from the people in California.

The brief history and presenting complaint identify Maria as a Latina whose subcultural identification is Hispano. Our comments on Latino ethnohistory, as well as the client's own opening comments, confirm the contention of differences across Latino subculture groups. Maria voices awareness that she is "different from the people (Chicanos) in California." and we agree. Furthermore, we argue that Maria would become aware of other subculture group differences if her encounter had been with Puerto Ricans (or Cubans, or other Latinos), rather than California Chicanos.

With regard to degree of acculturation, Maria seems basically bicultural. Available history indicates she is a bilingual who is equally familiar with the values and traditions of both the majority culture and the Latino culture. Examining her personal value system stemming from identification with her Hispano subculture, she seems less assimilated into the Chicano subculture attending California colleges, than to the majority culture in some ways. This is an important point, expanded further in our discussion of sources of stress and recommendations for counseling.

Examining intrapsychic sources of stress first, Maria's major problem seems to be she is a college freshman away from home for the first time. Like other young people in a similar situation (regardless of ethnicity), Maria is almost certainly homesick and lonely. She probably misses friends, relatives, and familiar places. Her opening statement refers to problems in "adjusting." Her ability to tolerate and lessen distress is lowered because of her absence from familiar support systems (home, family, and church), while in a new, taxing, demanding, different, and frightening environment. At a less obvious level of analysis, there are hints that Maria is experiencing an identity crisis. She is clearly uncertain of subculture group identification as reflected by questions such as, "Am I Spanish as we call ourselves within the family, or Chicana as my new friends insist?" Maria has noted that fellow students are more assertive, striving, and goal-oriented; now she is beginning to wonder if perhaps she would get more of what she wanted out of life if she were less passive. For example, feminism and the Chicano movement intrigue Maria, but the people involved seem "pushy" to her in many ways. And at a more personal and intimate level, Maria is beginning to question her traditional conservatism and her decorous sexual mores.

With regard to extrapsychic sources of stress, Maria denies any major hassles with the dominant culture. While she is subjected to the same general level of prejudice and discrimination that other Latinos are, it seems neither personal or [sic] excessive at this time. Note, however, the anomalous situation with regard to her treatment by Chicanos and Chicanas. The Chicano student community rejects Maria because her self-designated "Spanishness" is misperceived as an attempt to deny her "Mexicanness."

How does the counselor respond to this complex of problems, and in what priority? We shall outline a culturally relevant treatment program but encourage the reader to anticipate our recommendations and to amplify upon them as he or she goes along. First, it seems to us the problem of priority is Maria's sense of personal isolation. We would recommend a supportive approach to minimize this intrapsychic source of stress. Although unstated, Maria is almost certainly experiencing dysphoric affect, probably depression ranging somewhere between mild to moderate degrees of severity. An initial approach that works well with problems of this sort is to minimize any tendencies toward apathy and social withdrawal by encouraging interpersonal interaction. Specifically, Maria, like any young person with depressive tendencies, should be encouraged to date, to go to parties, to mix with people her own age and so on. Simultaneously, Maria's major assets should be identified and reflected back to her, repeatedly if necessary, to enhance self-esteem. For example, if she is doing well academically she should be reminded of her intellectual assets: her bright mind, her good study habits, her perseverance, and so on. This supportive approach of confronting Maria with positive aspects of her life adjustment will tend to retard movement in the direction of increased depression.

A problem of second-order priority for Maria is her estrangement from the local Chicano student community. This is particularly lamentable for Maria because this group represents a "natural" but underutilized resource to combat what has been termed Maria's "first problem": her combined sense of low self-esteem, loneliness, mild depression, and isolation. Maria is a Chicana in more ways than she is not; and mutual realization of this aspect of her identity will facilitate Maria's admission into the Chicano group; in turn, it can provide her with much needed emotional support.

One reason Maria and the Chicano group have failed to achieve harmonious rapprochement may be a mutual misjudgment of how each perceives the other. It is conceivable that Maria is unaware that Chicanos perceive Mexican Americans who call themselves "Spanish" as denying their heritage; and some of the Chicanos may not know that

(continued)

Cultural Study 6-1 (continued)

Mexican Americans from Northern New Mexico refer to themselves in that manner with no connotation of deliberate efforts to "pass" from one ethnic group to another. Reconciliation may be achieved if both parties become more familiar with their own ethnohistory. While this goal could be attained by the counselor bringing this issue to the attention of the ethnic studies department, if one exists, and having them plan a course or lecture on ethnohistory, we propose an alternative course. We recommend Maria be informed of the possible source of the mutual misunderstanding discussed here, and that she be encouraged to confront those Chicanos who have been scornful. This approach has several advantages; Maria will be required to become more assertive; her approach behavior toward others will counteract her withdrawal tendencies; and everyone involved examines the problem from a fresh perspective.

The third problem for Maria is her blurred, changing, and developing sense of personal identity. She seems to be going through a psychological growth phase that involves questioning life values, but this process is evaluated by us as "normal" or "healthy" (Wrenn & Ruiz, 1970). She is not exactly certain "who she is" as yet, but continued self-exploration should be encouraged by her counselor because enhanced self-awareness will minimize subjective discomfort and expediate [*sic*] self-actualization. The counselor maintains the responsibility, of course, for determining whether this third general recommendation is appropriate for Maria; and if so, of selecting the techniques and methods thought to be maximally growth-inducing for this client.

²From "Counseling Latinos," by R. A. Ruiz and A. M. Padilla, *Personnel and Guidance Journal, 55,* 405, 406. Copyright © 1977 by American Association for Counseling and Development. Reprinted by permission.

Psycho-Individual Reactions

Coping Skills

Individuals react to environmental impacts in various ways. Myers (1982) identifies a number of cultural and psychological impacts. Individual temperament and disposition determine the degree of stress tolerance. Previous problem-solving success or failure influences present coping efforts to analyze situations and to determine the best course of action. Successful coping with problems engenders efficiency and competence, whereas failure to handle difficulties results in impotence and helplessness. The minority client should be able to differentiate failure for which he or she is responsible from that which is due to external factors. People of color may experience failure and frustration because of institutional systemic barriers. When they are able to recognize failure that is externally controlled, they reduce the amount of subjective stress, blame, and sense of worthlessness. The perceptive ability distinguishes personal responsibility from oppression by the system.

Negative discrimination has also stimulated the development of a strong collective identity, an extended family network, creative coping strategies, personal and collective resilience, and even physiological and genetic resistance to disease. Hobbs (1962) observes that persons have cognitive houses to protect themselves from the incomprehensibilities of existence and to provide some architecture for daily experiencing. These built-in forms of cultural protection often form the basis for minority coping skills. Are there coping skills that contribute to survival? How has the client withstood the pressures, stresses, and strains of meeting life's needs? What resources have been available or are potentially present for assistance? These questions are relevant to our discussion of assessment dynamics.

Psychosomatic Reactions

Psychosomatic symptoms represent a reaction to environmental stress. Many minority cultures teach individual self-control as a method of dealing with the problems of life. Negative feelings are held within. Sue (1981) reports that restraint of strong feelings and the shame and disgrace of having psychological problems cause many Asian Americans to express their difficulties through physical complaints, which represent an acceptable means of manifesting problems. Chinese tend to somaticize their depressive reactions (Marsella, Kinzie, & Gordon, 1973); Chinese and Japanese students in a psychiatric population exhibited more somatic complaints than their control counterparts (Sue & Sue, 1971). Psychosomatic illness is socially acceptable because a physician is sought rather than a mental health professional. In Native American culture, physical, mental, and social illness is understood as a disharmony with other forces. Physical, psychological, and cultural realities are interrelated. Finding the forces of disharmony that pervade life is the assessment task (Lewis & Ho, 1975; Stuckey, 1975).

In many minority settings there are acceptable ways of expressing psychosomatic symptoms that are related to life disharmony, interpersonal stress, and other malfunctions. For example, amont the Latinos the *ataques* reaction is a form of hysteria characterized by hyperkinetic seizures as a response to acute tension and anxiety. It is a culturally expected expression of extreme displeasure over a negative act. Its purpose is to control other family members, such as a teenage son who gets out of hand or a husband who is going out to drink. Physical symptoms include vomiting spells, convulsions, and extreme fatigue, which lead to medical intervention and hospitalization (Ghali, 1977). Among Asian Americans, a mother expresses her extreme displeasure over a son's stealing or a daughter's promiscuous behavior by lying on the floor and going into a hysterical fit of crying and irrational shouting. It is a maternal expression of suffering and anger over the misbehavior of a child. In turn, the members of the family impose sanctions against the guilty member for upsetting the mother. Rather than making the assessment that the minority client or family member has gone into an acute schizophrenic reaction, the social worker should recognize that this psychosomatic expression is a cultural behavior reaction.

Green (1982) describes categories of disease among Latinos as an imbalance between physical and social well-being. Three disruptions of balance are *empacho, mal ojo,* and *susto. Empacho* (indigestion) is a physiological condition in which food lodged on the side of the stomach causes stomach pains. The food is in the form of a ball that can be broken up and eliminated by back rubbing and the use of purgatives. *Mal ojo* (evil eye) is the result of imbalance in social relationships; the sufferer exhibits headaches, sleeplessness, drowsiness, restlessness, fever, and vomiting. *Mal ojo* is precipitated by the covetous glances, admiring attention, or interest of another person. The eyes of another initiate the condition. It is treated by prayers, gently rubbing the body with a whole egg, or having the perpetrator touch the head of the afflicted, drawing off the threatening power of the relationship. *Susto,* (fright) is the loss of spiritual essence through an upsetting experience. Symptoms include depression, lack of interest in living, introversion, and eating disruption. The cure is to coax the lost spirit back into the individual's body. Treatment consists of prayers, body massages, spilling cold water over the patient, and sweeping the body with small branches while talking the spirit back into the body. The ethnic community recognizes this cultural means of dealing with stress.

CASE STUDY

The Hernandez Family

The Hernandez family can be seen as a case example of socioenvironmental impacts and psycho-individual reactions. Social work family assessment reveals socioeconomic survival issues. The arrival of in-laws from Mexico as recent immigrants to an uncertain economy has shifted the burden to Mr. Hernandez. He is approaching a point of inability to cope with the demands of extra work. His family obligation is to assure adequate support for the other two families until his two brothers-in-law can find steady employment. However, he complains about fatigue and long hours on two jobs.

A major task for the social worker is to assess the community resources potentially available for employment finding, school tutoring, English classes, and newcomer services. At the same time there are relevant assessment areas, such as role identity and stress tolerance, affecting the family.

Task Recommendations

In order to investigate the socioenvironmental impacts and psycho-individual reactions, conduct a detailed assessment of the Hernandez family. Answer the following questions that are related to this case.

What are the family's practical needs pertaining to food and shelter, employment, finances, and other problems of living?

Is there a sense of powerlessness due to lack of adequate resources?

What are the institutional barriers obstructing socioeconomic survival and coping abilities?

What is the client's level of stress tolerance?

Does the client possess any problem-solving skills that may be applied to the present situation?

Can the minority client differentiate between failures for which he or she is responsible and those due to institutional barriers?

Have there been any somatic symptoms accompanying the personal or family problems?

Has the minority client seen a physician or ethnic healer in the past
three to six months?
What are the natural family and community support systems available
for the minority client?

Worker System Practice Issues

Assessment Dynamics and Evaluation

Assessment dynamics and evaluation merge together to form the worker system practice tasks. We intend to cover a number of crucial areas related to the minority client, family, and community which are factors to determine significant information to formulate an assessment evaluation. For the worker's purposes, the word *assessment* means the estimation or determination of the significance, importance, or value of resources. Weaver (1982) declares:

> Search for strength relates to the social worker's emphasis on positive aspects of individual and family systems. It is crucial to begin with strengths of the family system: families move on strengths, not weaknesses. There are inherent strengths in the design of every family; the social worker must help the family use their own strengths in making choices and decisions that will enable them to achieve their desired goal. This skill, as it relates to the search for and use of strength within the family system, has the potential for being very empowering [p. 103].

Lee (1982) identifies several assets that underscore the creative use of the client's cultural strengths:

> Strengths such as support from extended family members and siblings, the strong sense of obligation, the strong focus on educational achievement, the work ethic, the high tolerance for loneliness and separation, and the loyalties of friends or between employer and employee should be respected and used effectively in the therapeutic process [p. 547].

Clinical psychotherapy has misused assessment as an evaluation of pathological defects, particularly with people of color. However, applying the root meaning of the word to clinical practice, assessment connotes the investigation of positive strengths, healthy functioning, and support systems that can be mobilized for goal planning and problem solving. Assessment is the link between problem identification and intervention strategy.

Characteristics of the Client

Psychosocial assessment of people of color begins with identifying significant characteristics of the minority person and the ethnic environment. The physical characteristics and appearance of the minority client consist of skin color, hair texture, and body type. Discussing racial background and family history offers clues on ethnic awareness and identity, self-concept, and significant others. Dress may reveal personal values, lifestyle, and ethnic orientation. Behavioral mannerisms may reveal traditional etiquette of respect for authority. In many ethnic cultures, prolonged eye contact signifies rude staring or casting an evil eye on a person. Avoidance of eye contact expresses respect, humility, and shyness. The worker should follow the lead of the client in interpreting these nuances of manner. Nonverbal cues such as a smiling face, humor, eye avoidance. silence, and other mannerisms may be culture-bound to the client. Rather than constru- ing them as signs of depression, avoidance, detachment, and inappropriate affect, the worker should explore the cultural dimension with an ethnic colleague or consultant before formulating an assessment.

State of Health

An important area for minority assessment is physical and mental health. For some people of color, asking detailed questions about their history of physical and mental illness is a social taboo. For example, Chinese do not like to talk about sickness, mental illness, or death. The mere thought of these tragedies may become a reality, as if one wished misfortune or bad luck on another. Moreover, the whole Chinese community may learn about mental illness in a family, and the family could be ostracized as a result. Many are afraid that their children will marry into such families and have abnormal offspring. It is best to ask about general health and to have the client sign a medical waiver for consultation with the family physician. Avoid explicit questions about sexual behavior, such as frequency of intercourse, menstrual cycle, masturbation, and homo- sexual relations. Minority clients hesitate to answer these private questions, particularly when they have no bearing on the problem. The social worker should be discreet in sensitive areas and allow the client to bring up those matters.

The assessment of state of health should emphasize the positive. Sena-Rivera (1980) asserts that the Latino family is a vital cultural and societal force that enhances the mental health of its members. The focus is on family wellness and strengths rather than the identification of pathology. Social work assessment should reflect these assets.

Level of Motivation

Motivation and resistance belong to another area of assessment. Motivation refers to the momentum toward change, and resistance suggests an unwillingness to cooperate or participate in the process of growth. People of color may be involuntary clients who have been ordered by the court system or the social service agency to go for counseling. It is important for the worker to acknowledge the unwillingness and anger of the client or the family who is forced to attend sessions. The task of the worker is to offer assistance and deal with the barrier. Asking open-ended questions that lead to acknowledging the uneasiness of both parties, triggering negative feelings from the client, and agreeing on a reasonable course of action are important points to cover in the relationship.

Prolonged silence may be culturally based. It may simply allow the client time to think through and to meditate on the words of the worker. Or it may signal resistance, confusion, and uncertainty as to what the worker means or wants from the client. Silence is productive and helpful at crucial turning points when the client is able to select a course of action. It is important to verbalize what is happening during long periods of silence. Many Black Americans are not willing to disclose problems and feelings until significant rapport and trust have been established. In the meantime, they remain silent, become placid, and answer briefly. Likewise, Asian Americans may remain silent, briefly verbalize the problem, and wait for the social worker to take the initiative in the relationship. This use of silence is not an example of a defense mechanism. Rather, it is a culturally distinct way of relating and responding.

Cultural Assets

Minority clinicians have been critical of a traditional assessment orientation on deviancy. Kuramoto, Morales, Munoz, and Murase (1983) observe that the majority society defines cultural differences as deviant or abnormal by first imposing behavioral expectations and then penalizing those unable to meet such levels. A negative value judgment is superimposed on cultural resources, rather than viewing the unique strengths of cultural differences as minority assets. Foreign traits are immediately cast in a negative light.

Furthermore, many human service workers tend to impose American value assumptions on ethnic minorities. Bernal, Bernal, Martinez, Olmedo, and Santisteban (1983) differentiate the culture-specific values of Latinos from those of White Americans. There is a discrepancy between the American value of individualism, which fosters independence, and the Latino family concept of the individual who is a member of a close-knit family. Assessed in the independence/dependence relations, the minority client may appear too dependent on the family. In actuality the minority client is participating in a functional family hierarchy that maintains family harmony and collective decision-making. It is important to understand the cultural dynamics and tap into the positive family assets rather than superimposing the values of individuality and independence.

Both behavioral and social sciences have stereotyped Black intelligence and family structure. Bell, Bland, Houston, and Jones (1983) cite theoretical assumptions about the mental status of Blacks in American society. For example, the genetic fallacy theme holds that races differ in inherited mental qualities. Blacks are inferior to Whites in intellectual potential and achievement. Although social work rejects that theory, the thinking has supported beliefs about Black inferiority in American scientific circles and has led to a focus on cultural liabilities. Sociological analysis of the Black family has propagated the idea of a pathological Black matriarchy. Black women are unfeminine, promiscuous, and dependent on welfare, while Black men are inadequate fathers who have deserted their families, are unemployed, and are unable to provide for their children. Accordingly, Black Americans have suffered irreversible psychological damage that has left them with low self-esteem and self-hatred.

These examples provide evidence that behavioral and social science perpetuate a notion of deviance with respect to ethnic minorities. Human service workers may be prone to making certain assumptions in their assessment on the basis of these stereotypes. An alternative to this approach is to focus on cultural assets and strengths of the minority client, such as the ability to cope with stress, to implement survival skills, and to utilize extended family and community support systems.

Cultural assets are found in the ethnic community. The term *ethnosystem* has been coined for use in describing the extent to which the minority client is related to various ethnic systems. Solomon (1976) has defined the ethnosystem as a collective of interdependent ethnic groups sharing unique historical and/or cultural ties and bound together by a single political system. The task of assessment is to discover the assets of the ethnic individual, family, and community. The minority client may be related to an ethnosystem that has values, knowledge, and skills embedded in the person, family, and community. The client is the best teacher to inform the social worker about his or her own ethnosystem. Discovering the positive assets of the client's ethnosystem is a major aspect of minority assessment. Kuramoto, et al. (1983) state:

> Theory development is also needed in relation to the role of informal and natural support networks in the help-seeking behavior of Asian and Pacific Americans. What is the potential for such networks to serve as mechanisms for identifying persons requiring services and for facilitating access to and utilization of services? Theory development is needed to comprehend the functions of informal support networks within each Asian and Pacific American community, to suggest ways in which they can be strengthened as resources and to provide the basis for promoting more effective communication between the informal and formal service networks [pp. 143–144].

This statement has universal application for ethnic minorities and differentiates categories of an ethnosystem. Assessment of positive cultural strengths of minority clients is essential to incorporate into practice process.

Natural Support Systems

Psycho-individual reactions rely on indigenous community patterns. Minority literature has highlighted the importance of natural community support systems (friends, neighbors, church relationships) that provide support and opportunities for personal development (Rappaport, 1981). These natural settings "work to provide niches for people that enhance their ability to control their lives and allow them both affirmation and the opportunity to learn and experience growth and development" (Rappaport, 1981, p. 19). It is important to assess the significant components of the support system that already exists in the ethnic community for the minority client. Zuniga (1983) reminds us:

> Recognition must be given to the fact that culturally based supports providing nurturance act as a buffer to hostile institutions such as unresponsive welfare departments, discriminatory housing authorities, or other negatively perceived institutions that are supposed to foster social well-being. . . . Thus, attention must be given to the natural support systems that have been developed within one's cultural base [p. 260].

Ethnic minority social networks have been the focal point for assessing potential resources and for intervention strategies. These natural support systems help people of color to master their environment, retain or increase their self-esteem, participate in their communities (Kelly, 1977), and maintain individuals in relative health and comfort (Caplan, 1972).

There are a number of major network components. Central to this discussion are the kinship patterns among minority families. Boyd (1982) observes that Blacks have strong ties of kinship with extended families, which include blood relatives, friends, and acquaintances who are forged into a coherent network of mutual emotional and economic support. Members of the extended family interchange roles, jobs, and family functions such as child-rearing and household chores. Stack (1975) describes these patterns as "coresidence, kinship-based exchange networks linking multiple domestic units, elastic household boundaries, and lifelong bonds to three generation households" (p. 124). Among Black families, informal adoption and child-raising form the basis for joint assistance. This network extends to the care of the elderly, who are often absorbed into the homes of family members and who care for children (Hill, 1972).

In the Latino family there is a bond of loyalty and unity in nuclear and extended families and a social network of friends, neighbors, and community. The Latino family has obligations of loyalty. The children express *respeto* to the parents, to whom the child owes its existence. The debt of obligation can never be repaid. The father is the decision maker and disciplinarian who is concerned about the economic welfare and well-being of the family. The mother oversees the upbringing of the children and provides emotional support. Extended family members supplement parental roles and form a network of reliance (Bernal et al., 1983).

Among Native Americans, most tribal groups function in extended family roles. Tribe, clan, family, and heritage are means of cultural system identity. Within the Native American extended family system are traditional child-rearing practices, generational roles, and sex role identity development (Trimble, Mackey, LaFromboise, & France, 1983). Likewise, Asian Americans have a social network consisting of nuclear and extended family and family associations in major cities. Relatives, friends, and neighbors are called "uncle" and "aunt," which are terms of endearment. This system functions for mutual support and assists with financial need, social activities, joint projects, and other ventures. Ethnic churches, food stores, and language/cultural schools are sources of communication and informational assistance.

Two case studies underscore the importance of the family, particularly the extended network, when working with ethnic minority clients. Red Horse, Lewis, Feit, and Decker (1981) present an example in which the public welfare system ignored the natural family helping network. In Cultural Study 6-2, traditional social service policy dictated the normal procedure of a foster home placement and rejected the resource of grandparents in the family network.

Cultural Study 6-2

Minority Identity Crisis[3]

Nancy, for example, was an eighteen-year-old mother identified as mentally retarded and epileptic by the department of welfare officials. Although retardation was subsequently disproved, the department assumed control and custody of Nancy's infant child.

Nancy's parents insisted that the family network was available for assistance, if necessary. The welfare staff, however, considered this offer untenable. The grandparents were deemed senile and unable to care for an infant. They were in their early fifties.

The staff ignored the fact that the grandparents had just finished caring for three other young and active grandchildren without dependence on institutional social intervention.

(continued)

Cultural Study 6-2 (continued)

Moreover, these children appeared to be well-adjusted. The officials simply insisted in this case that standard placement procedures be followed; a foster home was obtained for Nancy's child.

[3]From "Family Behavior of Urban American Indians" by J. G. Red Horse, R. Lewis, M. Feit, and J. Decker, *Social Casework,* (February 1978), Vol. 59. Copyright © 1978 by Family Service Association of America. Reprinted by permission.

Cultural Study 6-3 highlights the use of the family network by the worker, who recognizes the natural helping system, preparing the client for reentry. Family symbols of welcoming marked the reentry and restoration of the client. Attneave (1969) offers this case in support of tribal network intervention.

Cultural Study 6-3

Family Network[4]

Maria and the therapist arrived on a sunny afternoon a couple of weeks later, carefully prepared for Maria's reentry into the network. She had purchased a bag of candy and gum with the pennies she had "earned" in the foster home, and during the 40-mile drive she counted over and over one piece of candy and one piece of gum for each half sib and adult she knew, and a reassuring surplus for any others who might come. This time Maria was bringing the bag of sweets, and her anxiety was as high as if someone had explained that by doing so she could make amends for her past behavior and henceforth participate in the family ritual of sharing. Symbolically it was her bid for induction into the family.

This was indeed accomplished, but in even more dramatic and comprehensive fashion than the therapist had foreseen. As the car pulled up under a tree and the family came out to greet Maria, she suddenly gave a cry of recognition and thrust one of her offerings into the hands of a strange woman standing on the porch. The network, mulling over the therapist's remark, had stretched its links across two states and brought the absent grandmother to spend two weeks.

During the next 24 hours the bestowing of a tribal name at dawn and the eating of a very American birthday cake at the noon feast completed Maria's restoration to the family and network. During the ceremonial meeting of adults, the grandmother and her new husband sat as honored guests and had many things explained to them. Included were elements that had not been explicitly comprehended by Maria's mother, but which she now learned without embarrassment or loss of status. She was also able to fulfill an important ceremonial role, with her mother present, and thus symbolize the new integration of self and identity she had acquired without having to deny or bury her past. The husband also gained some sense of unsuspected dimensions of her as a person. Mr. T. was able to express his appreciation of his wife publicly as well as to secure the network's expressions of supportive interest and pleasure in her and in Maria.

The next afternoon sitting on the hillside the therapist observed Maria and her half siblings and cousins playing around a tire swing. Around an outdoor fire, Mrs. T. and some of the other women were showing the grandmother how to make "fry bread" and over further under the trees a group of men, including step-grandfather, were drumming softly, practicing songs, and shaving kindling.

Grandfather T., the eldest member of the network-clan, stopped beside the therapist and watched the same scene. After a few minutes he observed "Hum—a good idea to know that grandmother. . . . " Then with a piercing glance and the suspicion of a twinkle he gathered himself up to walk off. Turning, he raised an arm that embraced the group below in a majestic sweeping gesture—"*That* is much better than a lot of noisy talk."

[4]From "Therapy in Tribal Settings and Urban Network Intervention" by C. L. Attneave, *Family Process*, 8, 201, 202. Copyright © 1969 by Family Process, Inc. Reprinted by permission.

These ethnic social networks practice understood codes governing behavioral standards and values. Any action taken by a family member is a reflection on the entire group. Social family and community systems are sources of aid and support and boundaries for ethical actions. Community leaders reinforce behavioral protocols in the ethnic community. Several questions in assessment evaluation involve an understanding of the kinship and social network. Are there supportive resources available for the client in the social network? Which particular significant other(s) seems most helpful? Are there available persons, services, or institutions that can be mobilized on behalf of the client? Focusing on these positive aspects of ethnic behavior and social networks is important for both the social worker and the minority client.

Criteria for Assessment Evaluation

The social worker is ready to formulate an assessment evaluation based on socioenvironmental impacts, psycho-individual reactions, and categories of assessment dynamics. Cheetham (1982) offers a number of practical suggestions and specific questions related to assessment evaluation:

In making your assessment/decision consider the influence of your client's ethnic background on his/her behaviour and its implications for your decisions.

Do not confuse long-standing cultural/religious traditions with responses to current social, political and economic pressures. Compare any traditional ways of solving the problem with the intervention of a public agency.

Open your eyes to strengths: do not be blind to need.

Now ask your client and yourself these questions:

1. Is the problem connected with cultural/ethnic conflict *or* with socio-economic factors *or* with both *or* with neither?
2. Do you think the problem is common with people from this ethnic background? If so why? (Ask your colleagues and your clients too.)
3. If cultural/ethnic considerations seem important is the conflict
   - within the family/individual?
   - between the family/individual and the local community?
   - between the family/individual and public agencies?
   - between any combination of the above?
4. Could/should the expectations/behaviour of any party be modified? If so, with what costs and gains?
5. What local support systems are there for people from this ethnic background?
6. Would/could your client use them? If so, with what costs and gains?

7. What experience has your client had of public welfare services?
8. How does she/he want to solve the problem? Is this possible? If so, with what costs and gains?
9. How do you want to solve the problem? Is this possible? If so, with what costs and gains?

PAUSE: Picture your client's world
       Imagine yourself as your client
Make a tentative assessment/decision
Share it with your client
Share it with your colleagues
Reconsider/modify your assessment/decision
Act upon it
...If your client is hostile, do not turn away [pp. 145–146].[5]

She has summarized a number of themes related to this chapter: ethnic background and behavior, traditionalism, ethnic strengths, cultural conflict, support systems, agency contact, and mutual problem solving.

From our perspective, we would set forth the following criteria for assessment evaluation of the minority client:

1. What are the significant socioenvironmental impacts upon the minority client?
    a. issues of survival
    b. issues of environmental conflict
    c. psychosomatic issues
    d. mental illness
    e. problems of the elderly
2. What are the psycho-individual reactions of the minority client?
3. What are the predominant assessment dynamics that involve the minority client and are pertinent to formulating an assessment evaluation?
    a. characteristics of client
    b. state of health
    c. level of motivation
    d. cultural assets
    e. natural support system
4. What are the predominant problems emerging from socioenvironmental impacts, psycho-individual reactions, and assessment dynamics?
5. What are the significant resources and supports that are available for planning an intervention strategy?
6. What problems or needs occur that are not addressed in this assessment perspective?

We now apply these criteria for assessment evaluation to the situation of the Hernandez family in order to present various aspects of the case and integrate the six evaluative questions.

[5]From *Social Work and Ethnicity* by J. Cheetham, pp. 145,146. Copyright © 1982 by Allen and Unwin, Inc. Reprinted by permission.

CASE STUDY

The Hernandez Family

There are positive strengths emerging from this family. Mr. Platt notices the determination and energy of the husband and wife to work overtime and provide for the needs of the two other families who have recently moved to the city. There is a sense of family obligation that pervades the relationship. A clinical worker could easily have focused on the neglect of the father for his family due to his two jobs or on the poor academic performance of Ricardo. Instead Mr. Platt assesses the strengths available from the support network in the ethnosystem of the local Latino community.

The Hernandez family has been a part of the local Latino community for several years. However, they are unfamiliar with community helping resources available for their particular problems. A major resource for the Hernandez family is the newcomer services sponsored by Catholic Social Services. Mr. Platt has often worked with Latino social workers who provide job finding, tutoring, and housing services for families newly arrived in the city. This resource seems appropriate to the needs of the Hernandez family. Rather than clinically assessing the relationship between the father and son, Mr. Platt evaluates how external ethnic services can be marshaled and implemented to realign the family and reduce family stress.

Task Recommendations

Conduct a practice assessment on this minority family case from two perspectives. First, focus on the problem aspect of the case, having to do with a malfunctioning of the client. Investigate and uncover the aspects of the intrapsychic problem that contribute to the problem configuration. Assess the ego coping mechanisms of the client to determine the level of functioning. Find out the dynamics of the particular problem and their effects on the client, family, and community. Use the data to determine a clinical diagnosis from the **Diagnostic and Statistical Manual of Psychiatric and Mental Disorders** (DSM-III) of the American Psychiatric Association.

Second, conduct an assessment of the positive resources and strengths emerging from the client and his environment. What are the personal, family, and community strengths available to the family? What are the existing healthy functions that can be increased for the client's benefit? What are the informal and formal community support networks available to the client? What are the cultural customs, beliefs, and traditions that are useful in the change process? How can family support and ethnic pride become an assessment resource? These basic questions lead toward positive assessment areas.

Which approach would you employ in a minority client assessment? Is there merit in blending both perspectives? Are you inclined toward an assessment that uncovers client and community resources and strengths?

Conclusion

This chapter asserts that minority social work assessment should focus on positive resources of the minority client and community. There are cultural elements that support the survival of peoples of color. Seidman and Rappaport (1974) have argued for the need to build on the existing cultural values and strengths in a minority community. They emphasize supporting programs that provide cultural amplifiers, or ways of expanding the community's resources into the agency's programs. This approach offers an alternative to the ideological environment of blaming the victims. In a sense, the approach of this book has been to uncover helping principles embedded in the various ethnic minority communities and to apply those cultural elements to social work practice.

Minority assessment focuses on understanding the competencies and strengths of the minority person. Its fundamental assumption is that people of color are competent, adequate, and different. They are not automatically deficient or maladjusted. Social workers should identify resources in the minority system that can operate to the benefit of the client and determine practical ways to obtain and use them. We have asserted that assessment means the evaluation of assets rather than dysfunctional defects of the minority client. Among such assets are coping abilities, natural support systems, problem-solving abilities, and tolerance of stress.

The assessment procedure involves an ecosystem perspective allowing the exploration of an ethnic social ecology. Rappaport (1977) states:

> The principle could be translated into an apparently simple imperative—"know the system before you try to change it." The problem from an action point of view is that it is not always clear when one does really "know" the system. It therefore could serve as a rationalization for inaction. There are some guidelines for assessment which suggest that key questions involve actual and potential roles of members, the resources and rules for their distribution, as well as the relationship of the setting to its surrounding environments [p. 154].

In one sense, the foregoing discussion on ethnic minority assessment covers basic information about minority family roles, community resources, ethnic rules, and setting. The practice framework section covering assessment included discussion of ethnic family history, behavioral protocols, physical and mental illness as a social taboo, the meaning of prolonged silence, and other nuances of working with minority clients.

Social workers should select psychosocial assessment issues that are appropriate to each minority client. In the final analysis, we must study and understand the social ecology of the particular ethnic community as it pertains to the minority client, who is a part of the cultural community and the assessment process.

References

Atkinson, D. R., Morten, G., & Sue, D. W. (1979). *Counseling American minorities: A cross-cultural perspective.* Dubuque, Iowa: William C. Brown.

Attneave, C. L. (1969). Therapy in tribal settings and urban network intervention. *Family Process, 8,* 192–210.

Bell, C. C., Bland, I. J., Houston, F., & Jones, B. E. (1983). Enhancement of knowledge and skills for the psychiatric treatment of Black populations. In J. C. Chunn II, P. J. Dunston, & F. Ross-Sheriff (Eds.), *Mental health and people of color: Curriculum development and change* (pp. 205–238). Washington, D.C.: Howard University Press.

Bernal, G., Bernal, M. E., Martinez, A. C., Olmedo, E. L., & Santisteban, D. (1983). Hispanic mental health curriculum for psychology. In J. C. Chunn II, P. J. Dunston, & F. Ross-Sheriff (Eds.), *Mental health and people of color: Curriculum development and change* (pp. 65–94). Washington, D.C.: Howard University Press.

Boyd, N. (1982). Family therapy with Black families. In E. E. Jones & S. J. Korchin (Eds.), *Minority mental health* (pp. 227–249). New York: Praeger.

Caplan, G. (1972). Support systems. Keynote address to the conference of the Department of Psychiatry, Rutgers Medical School, and the New Jersey Mental Health Association, Newark, New Jersey.

Cheetham, J. (1982). *Social work and ethnicity.* Winchester, Mass.: Allen and Unwin.

Dieppa, I. (1983). A state of the art analysis. In G. Gibson (Ed.), *Our kingdom stands on brittle glass* (pp. 115–128). Silver Spring, Md.: National Association of Social Workers.

Ghali, S. B. (1977). Culture sensitivity and the Puerto Rican client. *Social Casework, 58,* 459–468.

Green, J. W. (1982). *Cultural awareness in the human services.* Englewood Cliffs, N.J.: Prentice-Hall.

Harwood, A. (Ed.) (1981). *Ethnicity and medical care.* Cambridge: Harvard University Press.

Hill, R. (1972). *The strengths of Black families.* Washington, D.C.: National Urban League, Research Department.

Hobbs, N. (1962). Sources of gain in psychotherapy. *American Psychologist, 17,* 741–747.

Jackson, J. J. (1973). Black women in a racist society. In C. Willie, B. Kramer, & B. Brown (Eds.), *Racism and mental health* (pp. 185–268). Pittsburgh: University of Pittsburgh Press.

Jones, A., & Seagull, A. (1977). Dimensions of the relationship between the Black client and the White therapist. *American Psychologist, 32,* 850–855.

Kelly, J. G. (1977). The ecology of social support systems: Footnotes to a theory. Paper presented at the American Psychological Association convention, San Francisco.

Kim, L. I. C. (1981). Lecture on minority assessment. Presented at California State University, Sacramento, Division of Social Work, Spring 1981.

Kuramoto, F. H., Morales, R. F., Munoz, F. U., & Murase, K. (1983). Education for social work practice in Asian and Pacific American communities. In J. C. Chunn II, P. J. Dunston, & F. Ross-Sheriff (Eds.), *Mental health and people of color: Curriculum development and change* (pp. 127–155). Washington, D.C.: Howard University Press.

Lee, E. (1982). A social systems approach to assessment and treatment for Chinese American families. In M. McGoldrick, J. K. Pearce, & J. Giordano (Eds.), *Ethnicity and family therapy* (pp. 527–551). New York: Guilford Press.

Lewis, R. G., & Ho, M. K. (1975). Social work with Native Americans. *Social Work, 20,* 379–382.

Marsella, A. J., Kinzie, D., & Gordon, P. (1973). Ethnocultural variations in the expression of depression. *Journal of Cross-Cultural Psychology, 4,* 435–458.

Myers, H. F. (1982). Stress, ethnicity, and social class: A model for research with Black populations. In E. E. Jones & S. J. Korchin (Eds.), *Minority mental health* (pp. 118–148). New York: Praeger.

Rappaport, J. (1977). *Community psychology: Values, research, and action.* New York: Holt, Rinehart & Winston.

Rappaport, J. (1981). In praise of paradox: A social policy of empowerment over protection. *American Journal of Community Psychology, 9,* 1–25.

Red Horse, J. G., Lewis, R., Feit, M., & Decker, J. (1981). Family behavior of urban American Indians. *Social Casework, 59,* 67–72.

Romero, J. T. (1983). The therapist as social change agent. In G. Gibson (Ed.), *Our kingdom stands on brittle glass* (pp. 86–95). Silver Spring, Md.: National Association of Social Workers.

Seidman, E., & Rappaport, J. (1974). The educational pyramid: A paradigm for research, training, and manpower utilization in community psychology. *American Journal of Community Psychology, 2,* 119–130.

Sena-Rivera, J. (1980). La Familia Hispana as a natural support system: Strategies for prevention in mental health. In R. Valle & W. Vega (Eds.), *Hispanic natural support systems: Mental health promotion perspectives* (pp. 75–81). Sacramento: State of California Department of Mental Health.

Solomon, B. B. (1976). *Black empowerment: Social work in oppressed communities:* New York: Columbia University Press.

Stack, C. (1975). *All our kin: Strategies for survival in a Black community.* New York: Harper & Row.

Stuckey, W. (1975). Navajo medicine men. *Science Digest, 78,* 34–41.

Sue, D. W. (1981). *Counseling the culturally different: Theory and practice.* New York: Wiley.

Sue, S., & Sue, D. W. (1971). Chinese American personality and mental health. *Amerasia Journal, 1,* 36–49.

Trimble, J. E., Mackey, D. H., LaFromboise, T. D., & France, G. A. (1983). American Indians, psychology, and curriculum development. In J. C. Chunn II, P. J. Dunston, & F. Ross-Sheriff (Eds.), *Mental health and people of color: Curriculum development and change* (pp. 43–64). Washington, D.C.: Howard University Press.

Weaver, D. R. (1982). Empowering treatment skills for helping Black families. *Social Casework, 63,* 100–105.

Zuniga, M. (1983). Social treatment with the minority elderly. In R. L. McNeely & J. L. Colen (Eds.), *Aging in minority groups* (pp. 260–269). Beverly Hills, Calif.: Sage Publications.

7

Intervention

Intervention is derived from the verb *intervene,* which means "to come between" and connotes "an influencing force to modify or resolve." In the context of practice, intervention is a change strategy that alters the interaction between the client and the problem environment. As indicated in the framework chapter (Chapter 3), intervention occurs when the biopsychosocial needs of the client are met through individual, family, group, and community resources. In social work practice, intervention has been associated with a number of casework schools of thought (namely, psychodiagnostic, functional, problem-solving, crisis intervention, task centered, and behavioral). The theories behind them offer a range of alternatives for various case situations. However, recent research into mental health of people of color has questioned the adequacy of traditional methods of psychotherapy for minorities. Weems (1974) holds that because of important cultural differences, the concepts, institutions, and practices of mental health are ill adapted to ethnic problems and needs. Moreover, Jones and Korchin (1982) assert that traditional interventional therapies lack sensitivity to the ethnic *Weltanschauung* and lifestyle and misunderstand minority ways.

Clearly there is a need in minority social work to develop approaches to intervention that are compatible with the needs of minority clients and their ethnosystems. Rather than adapting a particular casework school of thought to the minority experience or vice versa, we contend that there are indigenous principles of intervention in the minority culture that require identification and integration. Because the effectiveness of existing mental health therapies for minority clients has been questioned, there is a need to redefine and reinterpret social casework emphases that are appropriate for the minority situation.

The purpose of this chapter is to present interventional strategies and levels that are compatible with the minority experience. It draws from a range of practice theories. Figure 7-1 portrays the intervention stage, showing the interaction between the worker and client around joint goals and agreement, joint interventional strategies, and micro, meso, and macro levels of intervention. While we are sympathetic to the criticism that traditional psychotherapy approaches may not be suitable for minorities, we are convinced that there are applicable practice principles which can be used in an ethnic setting. Ethnic minority social work practice is a new field which is undergoing the development of knowledge theory and practical application. To this end our task is to formulate intervention based on previous stages and current minority practice trends.

Client and Worker Systems Practice Issues

Joint Goals and Agreement

How does one formulate appropriate goals, objectives, and a contract? Social work intervention begins with the establishment of goals for intervention from which a contract can be drawn between the worker and the client. Goals are terminal outcomes to be achieved at the completion of the intervention stage. Objectives are intermediate subgoals or a series of connecting steps that accomplish outcome goals. Goals and objectives should be tailored to the specific situation confronting the client and the worker.

Solomon (1976) identifies ethnic-related goals of intervention that enlist the mutual involvement of the minority client and the worker:

1. to help the client perceive himself or herself as causal agent in achieving a solution to his or her problem or problems;
2. to help the client perceive the social worker as having knowledge and skills that he or she can use;
3. to help the client perceive the social worker as peer collaborator or partner in the problem-solving effort;
4. to help the social worker perceive the oppressive social institutions (schools, welfare department, courts) as open to influence to reduce negative impact [p. 26].

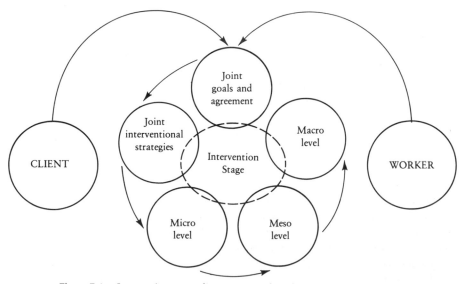

Figure 7-1. Intervention stage: client system and worker system practice issues.

These goals of intervention are general guidelines that affirm the minority client as a problem solver along with the social worker who is also a source of knowledge and skill and agent of institutional change. Both clinical and community intervention are implied in these goal statements. Furthermore, these broad goals are landmarks for articulating more specific goals based on unique patterns of the problem situation emphases of assessment. For example, specific statements of intervention goals can be drawn up relating to problem solving, peer collaboration, use of social work knowledge and skills, and institutional change, according to the particular problem-client-worker situation.

For new minority immigrants, Fujiki, Hansen, Cheng, and Lee (1983) suggest the following intervention goals:

1. to clarify role expectations in therapy and in the client's personal life;
2. to avoid situations in which parents act out their personal problems before their children (separate talks might work better since intense feelings of anger might be countercultural);
3. to assist families in creating more successful problem solving approaches;
4. to assist children in their development in both cultures with minimal conflict;
5. to assist families in learning how to establish an equilibrium as they live in two cultures;
6. to provide programs that are community supported endeavors with ethnic client participation;
7. to recognize and provide help for clients with psychopathology regardless of symptom severity;
8. to utilize ethnic and cultural communities, experts, and programs in assisting minority clients

Statements of outcome goals should be specific in detailing what is to be accomplished, clear as to what responsibilities each party will undertake, limited to a time period of from four to six weeks, and conditional in designating situations in which behavioral change will occur. Whenever possible, the minority client should define the outcome goals in his or her own words. The worker should write down the exact words in which the client states what he or she wants to change and accomplish. Consultation with the client's significant others are useful in sharpening goal statements based on cultural and personal preference. By this method, goal statements are established that are both acceptable and culturally relevant to the minority client. Once goals have been stated, the worker and client must formulate specific tasks to implement the goals. These subgoals or intermediate steps are listed under each goal to specify a step-by-step strategy of change. Once the goal outcomes and subgoals have been defined, a contract is formulated, designating areas of agreement and delineating responsibilities of the client, worker, and community resources. It should also specify the intervention(s) to be employed, the time frame (expressed in number and frequency of sessions), mechanisms for monitoring progress, and practical activities for problem-solving.

How do worker and client agree on an appropriate intervention strategy? There are at least five criteria for agreeing on a particular intervention:

1. *The intervention should examine and resolve the problem behavior in a manner*

relevant to the minority client. The social worker and minority client should agree on an intervention that addresses and resolves the problem behavior and situation.

2. *The intervention should focus on immediate past, present, and future time sequences related to the problem.* It is important for the intervention to deal with the recent history of the problem (within the last three to six months) and to affect changes that influence and redirect the course of events in the near future. We are concerned with moderate and significant interventive changes that can occur in the present and alter the series of problems that have been mounting in the recent past.

3. *The intervention should address the psychosocial dimensions of the problem.* We have indicated that there are biological-physical, psychological-emotional, and social-cultural dimensions of the person and the environment that must be addressed and changed in the intervention stage. For people of color, changes in the external environment have an effect on cognitive, affective, and behavioral perspectives of the client. Community helping services, surrogate helpers, and natural family systems have tangible impacts on psychosocial problem areas.

4. *The intervention should initiate behavioral tasks to mobilize the client toward positive action.* In social work intervention, change lies with the client, who implements a series of positive behavioral tasks to effect it. These interventive tasks are based on intervention goals, which are translated through practical activities performed by the client.

5. *The intervention should demonstrate that change has occurred through a decrease of the problem behavior following clinical contact and during the successive stages of problem identification, assessment, intervention, and termination.*

CASE STUDY

The Hernandez Family

On the basis of what they have learned through contact, problem identification, and assessment, the Hernandez family and Mr. Platt are ready to devise an intervention strategy for coping with the job situation confronting the three families as well as the academic performance of the oldest child. From extensive discussion between the family and the social worker, a number of goals have emerged. Members of the family are now able to state what they would like to accomplish as a result of meeting with the worker. Mr. Platt writes down the exact words in a series of goal statements.

Goal Outcomes

1. **Job finding.** To assist the two families of new arrivals from Mexico in finding full-time employment.
2. **Father at home.** To enable Mr. Hernandez to work at his regular job and be home in the evenings with his family.

3. **Tutoring for the son.** To provide Ricardo with tutoring assistance with his classroom assignments.
4. **English classes for mother.** To teach Mrs. Hernandez how to speak, read, and write English.
5. **Resettlement.** To help the two families of in-laws with adjustment problems due to their recent migration from Mexico into an urban American setting.

It is agreed that Mr. Platt will serve as a case manager who will coordinate various resources of the ethnic community in implementing these goal outcomes. It will be the responsibility of each family member to follow through on a number of appointments that will be made for job finding, tutoring assistance, classes in English as a second language (ESL), and newcomers' services. The family and Mr. Platt agree that within the next two weeks, contact and appointments will be made with Catholic Social Services, located in the neighborhood Mexican–American church. Follow-up on the effects of these services will be made with the family in the third and fourth weeks. A number of behavioral changes will be expected during the four-week process.

Behavioral Changes

1. **Job finding.** The securing of full-time jobs for the two brothers-in-law.
2. **Father at home.** Adequate time in the evenings for Mr. Hernandez to spend with his family, particularly helping Ricardo and the other children with their homework.
3. **Tutoring for the son.** Improved academic performance of Ricardo: homework turned in on time and classroom work accomplished within the time frame established by the teacher.
4. **English classes for mother.** Free time two evenings a week for Mrs. Hernandez to attend an ESL class in her neighborhood.
5. **Resettlement.** Periodic progress reports on social adjustments made to urban American life (driving a car, shopping in grocery and clothing stores, paying bills) by the two newly arrived families.

It is also decided that before the intervention strategy is initiated, all three families will have a joint session with Mr. Platt to review these goal outcomes, responsibilities, time limits, and behavioral changes, giving them the opportunity for comments, suggestions, and revisions.

A brief session is subsequently held with all three families to review the intervention plan and to permit Mr. Platt to become acquainted with the two other families who have lately migrated from Mexico. Rather than having the conference at the Family Service Association and causing "a misunderstanding" among the three families, the Hernandezes hold a dinner in their home. Mr. Platt is invited and brings wine for the occasion. After dinner, Mr. Hernandez mentions to the men that Mr. Platt will be making some job contacts for them. He will also ask the newcomers' center to assist the wives with adjusting to American life. Catholic Social Services will be the organization to help in these areas. The families seem agreeable to this plan, and the rest of the evening is spent in establishing rapport and finding out about each other.

A number of task objectives are suggested by Mr. Platt and agreed upon by the persons involved.

Task Objectives

1. **Job finding.** The brothers-in-law will go to initial interviews with Catholic Social Services to find out about available jobs. They prefer to work for a Mexican–American employer who owns a business in the city. If job placement is secured, they will check back with Mr. Platt after a two-week interval to tell him how they feel about their work.

2. **Father at home.** During this period, Mr. Hernandez will gradually taper off his second job and return home for dinner and the evening with the family. He will begin particularly to relate to Ricardo, assisting him with difficulties in homework assignments. During this two-week transition period, he will also let Mr. Platt know what is happening as far as his time and activities with the family are concerned.

3. **Tutoring for the son.** Mr. Platt will refer Ricardo for school tutoring service with the teen-age tutoring unit of Catholic Social Services. Mexican–American high school teenagers volunteer their time to assist elementary school children with school subjects. They receive credit from their high school and work closely with the classroom teacher and the tutoring coordinator who assigns tutor-student pairs. The tutors focus on specific subject areas and skill problems, and in many cases, they tutor in both English and Spanish for children who are bilingual. Mr. Platt plans to monitor the tutoring experience with Ricardo in weekly family sessions and with the tutoring coordinator and assigned student-helper.

4. **English classes for mother.** Mr. Platt will also check into ESL classes for Mrs. Hernandez. He will investigate an evening class that meets in her neighborhood at the Catholic Social Services community center. Mrs. Hernandez will attend classes after coming home from work and cooking dinner. Mr. Hernandez will watch the children while she is at class. The sessions are twelve in number, and students have an opportunity to join an intermediate class the following semester. Mrs. Hernandez will begin her class after Mr. Hernandez resumes his regular hours. She will practice her English at home, with her husband and children supporting and reinforcing her conversations. She will report on her progress at weekly sessions with Mr. Platt.

5. **Resettlement.** Mr. Platt will ask the coordinator of the newcomers' center unit to get in touch with the two newly arrived families and to help them with shopping, paying bills, school, driving, and other adjustments. Although Mr. and Mrs. Hernandez have taken the families around the

community, they still need assistance in some areas of adjustment, such as registering for Social Security, buying a car, and reading advertisements in the newspaper.

Contracting

There is no formal, written contract drawn up between Mr. Platt and the Hernandez family with their relatives. Rather, a verbal agreement delineating goal outcomes and task objectives is communicated at the session with the Hernandez family and the follow-up dinner meeting with the three families. Verbal consent is the substance of the contracting arranged between the parties involved.

The intervention strategy plan seems to examine and resolve the problems of the Hernandez family, particularly the collective responsibility for the welfare of the two newcomer families, the work stress of the father, and the academic performance of the son. It focuses on the relevant past and present events having an impact on the family. It addresses the psychosocial dimensions of the problem by designating environmental resources in the ethnic community. It initiates a series of behavioral tasks to implement the goal outcomes devised by the social worker and the families involved. It fulfills the assumption that well-being of minority individuals depends on membership in an ethnic community by tapping indigenous ethnic social services provided by bilingual/bicultural workers who are familiar with the people and problems of the neighborhood. The services of the Catholic Social Services center located in the church are a symbol of the positive community assets that are available to Latino families under stress of social adjustment. In a real sense, the intervention strategy uses the collective human services program of the ethnic community and reunites these three families with their local Latino American community.

Task Recommendations

We have sought to set forth a strategy for intervention with minority clients that is clinical and community oriented and that relies on structure (goal outcomes, behavioral changes, and task objectives) as well as community (ethnic services, collective membership). In order to implement these guidelines, select a current or past minority case and apply a minority intervention approach:

1. Review the several sets of goal statements listed in the section on joint goals and agreement. Devise appropriate goal outcomes, behavioral changes, and task objectives for your case.
2. Explain how the intervention
   a. examines and resolves the problem behavior in a manner relevant to the minority client;

b. focuses on immediate past and present time sequences related to the problem;
c. addresses the psychosocial dimensions of the person and the environment;
d. initiates behavioral tasks to mobilize the client toward focused positive action;
e. demonstrates that intervention has occurred through a decrease of problem behavior during the social work practice process.

Joint Interventional Strategies

There are at least five interventional strategies related to the minority experience. These themes of intervention must be seen as polarities paired with minority problem situations. Elsewhere (Lum, 1982) we have described a structure of problem situations and interventional strategies using the following themes:

oppression versus liberation
powerlessness versus empowerment
exploitation versus parity
acculturation versus maintenance of culture
stereotyping versus unique personhood

The chapter on problem identification dealt with these problem themes in depth. This section applies each solution to its corresponding problem.

We make the assumption that the person of color may encounter a number of problem situations (oppression, powerlessness, exploitation, acculturation, and stereotyping) in his or her relationship with the dominant society. For each problematic state, there are corresponding interventional strategies (liberation, empowerment, parity, maintenance of culture, and unique personhood). These five pairs of problem situations and interventional strategies are Eriksonian polarities and are a means of explaining how a minority client can move from a problem situation to an intervention solution. In many minority cases, there are multiple problem situations and intervention strategies. Since the introduction of the powerlessness/empowerment theme, minority social work practice has needed to address related problems and strategies. Identification of these five themes is an attempt to move minority practitioners beyond a single thematic problem and solution. At the same time, minority social workers should scrutinize the field to recognize emerging problem areas and devise interventive strategies that are not discussed in this section.

Liberation

Liberation involves the minority client's experiencing of release and freedom from oppressive restraints through psychosocial change. It is based on growth and decision making that occur when the client exercises choices in the face of oppressive conditions. Cultural Study 7-1 illustrates a person's movement from oppression to liberation in a teaching situation.

Cultural Study 7-1

Oppression versus Liberation[1]

George Chin, a 28-year-old Chinese American, came to a Family Service Association agency with signs of despondency. He was in his second year as a junior college instructor in mathematics and held a master of science degree in his field from a nearby state university. During his year-and-a-half of teaching, Mr. Chin was the subject of subtle discrimination and felt excluded from the decision-making power of his department. He heard through the department grapevine that two faculty members were critical of him. In the face of this, Mr. Chin was polite and reserved—his Asian background taught him to respond to threats in this manner. Because he had not yet received tenure, he was unable to confront those colleagues who were oppressive.

The worker helped Mr. Chin to establish a network of support and trust with those among his colleagues who were friendly and who were aware of the irritating personality characteristics of the two who had criticized him. He was also invited to join an assertiveness training group. After doing this, he discovered the assertive side of his personality. He learned how to be assertive when receiving teaching assignments from administrators and how to be more effective at faculty meetings and with the two faculty members who had criticized him. Finally, the social worker and the client decided to investigate the possiblity of the client leaving the junior college position so that he could apply for a Ph.D. program in mathematics.

[1]From "Toward a Framework for Social Work Practice with Minorities," by D. Lum, *Social Work,* (May 1982), Vol. 27, No. 3, pp. 246–248. Copyright 1982, National Association of Social Workers, Inc. Reprinted by permission.

Empowerment

Empowerment refers to the development of skills enabling the person of color to implement interpersonal influence, improve role performance, and develop an effective support system (Leigh, 1982). Among the helping interventions relevant to empowerment are educating the person to the effects of the oppressing system, mobilizing material and interpersonal resources, building support systems, informing people about their societal entitlements and rights, and strengthening a positive self-image (Leigh, 1984). Cultural Study 7-2 illustrates the themes of powerlessness and empowerment in a public housing project.

Cultural Study 7-2

Powerlessness versus Empowerment[2]

Charles Washington, a 58-year-old black American, lived in a public housing project. After he complained to the local housing authority about the need for repairs on his apartment, a construction firm finally "fixed" his roof, windows, and doors, but the work was shoddy and only half finished. Yet a surcharge of $350 was billed to him. Numerous complaints to the manager of the housing complex and to the building inspector of the repair unit did no good. Mr. Washington felt powerless and unable to obtain satisfaction for the wrongdoing that he had suffered. Other tenants had similar grievances about the same construction company, which routinely received repair contracts from the housing authority.

(continued)

Cultural Study 7-2 (continued)

Fortunately, a concerned second-year MSW student was working in a nearby elementary school and began to develop a relationship with several families in the public housing project. Eventually, a tenant committee was organized to deal with several issues. A letter detailing the incidents of faulty repairs and illegitimate billings was sent to the housing authority director, which resulted in a meeting between the tenant committee and the director and his staff. The leading newspaper of the city ran a series of articles exposing the contractor's corruption and the lack of response of the housing officials. At the next meeting, members of the city council requested a full report from the housing director. It was then revealed that two of the repair inspectors from the housing authority had accepted favors from the contractor in question. Both inspectors were suspended without pay until a full hearing could be held.

[2]From "Toward a Framework for Social Work Practice with Minorities," by D. Lum, *Social Work*, (May 1982), Vol. 27, No. 3, pp. 246–248. Copyright 1982, National Association of Social Workers, Inc. Reprinted by permission.

Parity

Parity is the achievement of equality in power, value, and rank. It is fairness and rightful access to services, compensations, and resources. It is the minority client's response to exploitation by manipulators in the dominant society. Cultural Study 7-3 portrays exploitation versus parity in an employment situation.

Cultural Study 7-3

Exploitation versus Parity[3]

Marie Redthunder was a paraprofessional child care worker who was responsible for coordinating transportation and community affairs between American Indian families in a Northwest semirural community and the agency in which she worked. Although she enjoyed her work, her bottom-of-the-ladder job had her locked in. Other employees who had college degrees had been able to obtain higher positions at the center, but Mrs. Redthunder had been kept at the same salary for several years. She had been put off in her requests for advancement by the director of the center, although the American Indian parents utilizing the day care services had a strong rapport with her. In short, she felt exploited by her employment situation because no provisions had been made for her to develop her abilities via continuing education and a career ladder.

Recently, an American Indian social worker was hired by her tribe to offer casework and social advocacy to individual tribe members. Mrs. Redthunder approached the social worker about her problem, and after several problem-solving sessions, Mrs. Redthunder decided to resign from her position. She obtained a scholarship from a private foundation and enrolled in an undergraduate human services program at a four-year university that is thirty miles from her home. She now works part time in a family service agency as a paraprofessional community outreach worker. Her ultimate goal is to complete her undergraduate degree in human services and move her family to a metropolitan area so that she can work toward an MSW.

[3]From "Toward a Framework for Social Work Practice with Minorities," by D. Lum, *Social Work*, (May 1982), Vol. 27, No. 3, pp. 246–248. Copyright 1982, National Association of Social Workers, Inc. Reprinted by permission.

Maintenance of Culture

Maintenance of culture is a minority intervention theme that employs the use of cultural beliefs, customs, celebrations, and rituals as means of overcoming social problems. Culture is a source of strength and renewal. Ethnic minority people rediscover their past heritage and utilize it in their coping with present and future life problems. Cultural Study 7-4 emphasizes the value of culture in the theme of acculturation versus maintenance of culture.

Cultural Study 7-4

Acculturation versus Maintenance of Culture[4]

Ben Dancewell is a thirty-four-year-old full-blooded Cheyenne-Arapahoe who was medically diagnosed as an alcoholic. He is married and has four children. He is an excellent dancer and has won several contests. The timing of the therapy was unique in that it was held after the ceremonial dances.

The ceremonial dances served Ben in many therapeutic ways such as 1) helping him to ventilate his feelings; 2) helping him possess a unique sense of identity and pride in his culture; 3) giving him a great sense of belonging through being with other Native Americans. 4) As he danced, one could see other Indians giving him support; therefore, he gained a unique support system. 5) This experience enhanced his altruistic feelings and made him uniquely ready for therapy.

In attendance was his entire primary family, as well as his parents. Each week, he began to ventilate, for example, about his pride at being an Indian but how he felt inferior when he was in the majority culture. After several sessions of ventilating and using the extended family as support, drinking diminished and he was able to hold a job.

[4]From "Cultural Perspective on Treatment Modalities with Native Americans," by R. Lewis. An unpublished paper presented at the National Association of Social Workers Professional Symposium, San Diego. Copyright © 1977 by Ronald Lewis. Reprinted by permission.

Unique Personhood

The theme of unique personhood recognizes the individuality of each person and seeks to discover personal and corporate ethnic worth. It is the opposite of stereotyping, which prejudges an individual by a negative generalization about the group. Bochner (1982) cites numerous studies that indicate that persons who are deindividuated are likely to behave less responsibly and be treated less favorably than individuated persons. Similarly, discrimination against out-group members could be reduced by individuating them. Cultural Study 7-5 shows the shift from stereotyping to unique personhood during the counseling process.

Cultural Study 7-5

Stereotyping versus Unique Personhood[5]

Robert Collins, a 40-year-old black man, was an imposing figure when he and his wife entered the Family Service Association for marriage counseling. He was six feet tall and weighed two hundred pounds. The predominate [sic] features that struck the social

(continued)

Cultural Study 7-5 (continued)

caseworker were Mr. Collins's beard and masculine facial structure. Although Mr. Collins was dressed in a conservative three-piece suit, complete with a custom-made ring, his carriage was that of a majestic ruler ready to wage effective combat. One felt intimidated by his presence. Perhaps this reaction to Mr. Collins as a powerful and potentially volatile black American was stereotypical. Yet, during the marital counseling, he was revealed as a unique person who was searching for direction in the middle years of his life. Because of his smile, his sensitivity, and his insight into his marital problems, he became an individual to the caseworker. Consequently, the caseworker gradually was able to work through his own stereotypical hangups about blacks. Both client and worker discovered each other's humanity in the practice process.

[5]From "Toward a Framework for Social Work Practice with Minorities," by D. Lum, *Social Work,* (May 1982), Vol. 27, No. 3, pp. 246–248. Copyright 1982, National Association of Social Workers, Inc. Reprinted by permission.

Levels of Intervention

Social work practitioners have described practice in terms of intervention in the microsystem, mesosystem, and macrosystem (Mullen, Dumpson, & associates, 1972). The microsystem involves the unit systems of the individual, family, and small group (Meyer, 1972). Examples of micro level interventions with minority clients include friendly neighborhood sharing (Blackwell & Hart, 1982) and support services linking clients to schools, churches, and other organizations (Weil, 1981). Leigh (1982) suggests that we begin with immediate micro level change that can be accomplished in the short range.

Intervention means mesosystem study and analysis of the conditions and problems of the local community. It makes use of helping agencies and local organizations (Turner, 1972). Meso intervention among minorities has included group-based services involving immigrant children, adolescents, and parents in transitional adjustment to the United States (Weil, 1981) and practical action in the community, such as improvement of street lighting, garbage collection, police protection, and neighborhood stores (Blackwell & Hart, 1982).

The macrosystem involves complex large-scale entities affecting large geographical populations. It has a bearing on poverty, racial and social class discrimination, substandard housing, drug abuse, mental illness, and other national problems related to minorities. Macrosystem practice occurs in large organizations between population aggregates and social situations. Planning, policy, and administrative action are the modalities of intervention (Webb, 1972). Macro level change often requires changing power relations, which is a long-range aim (Leigh, 1984). Macro intervention for minorities includes social welfare programs and services for refugees that encourage individual productivity, responsibility, and sense of self-worth (Weil, 1981), better quality education, and improvement of the economic condition (Blackwell & Hart, 1982).

In the following section, micro, meso, and macro intervention levels are described in depth. The social work practitioner and minority client should collaborate on the selection of appropriate intervention strategies and levels according to the nature of the social problem. There is wide latitude for orchestrating an interventional approach based on the given criteria for selection, strategies, and levels. Both the worker and the client might ask: Are we dealing with a psychosocial problem that focuses on minority empowerment and cultural maintenance that affect the individual and family micro level? Or are we struggling to formulate an intervention that calls for liberation and parity strategies at the local community and complex organizational levels? To begin discussion, Table 7-1 is a chart with spaces for writing case problem situations in the appropriate categories in order to identify relevant intervention levels and strategies.

Micro Level

Micro level intervention has traditionally focused on psychosocial change affecting the individual, family, and small group. Social casework, family casework, and group work have been formulated around offering interventional approaches to these target groups. Historically, clinical social work practice has been oriented to at least five theories: psychodiagnosis, which has combined Freudian psychoanalysis and systems theory; functionalism, which has been influenced by Rankian psychology and has reemerged in existential psychology; crisis intervention, which is oriented to ego psychology and the Eriksonian life crisis stages; problem solving, which has its base in cognitive theory and was popularized by Perlman (task-centered casework of Reid and Epstein is an effort to combine problem solving with an empirical behavioral approach); and behavioral therapy, which has its base in learning theory and has been adapted to social work by Thomas, Fischer, and others. Social work practitioners have been oriented to one or more of these theories of clinical practice by their academic and professional education. We take the position that there are a number of appropriate theories of social work intervention that are applicable to minority clients under various situations. An under-

TABLE 7-1. Intervention Levels and Strategies

	Liberation	Empowerment	Parity	Maintenance of culture	Unique personhood
Micro Level (individual, family, small group)					
Meso Level (ethnic/local communities and organizations)					
Macro Level (complex organizations, geographical populations)					

pinning of intervention with ethnic minority clients is to apply selected social casework emphases to the particular problem.

Clinical approaches.   For example, *psychodiagnostic intervention* may be useful for exploring past role relationships involving grandparents, parents, and children across generational lines. It may also be helpful in probing for significant instances of racism and prejudice, cultural adjustment, and other related events. *Crisis intervention* may be applicable when there are cultural conflicts requiring the use of ethnic values to restore coping mechanisms. It is relevant when the minority client is in the midst of life transition and experiencing temporary immobilization due to overwhelming stress factors of moving to a strange environment and encountering difficulties in employment and housing. *Existential intervention* may be employed with a minority person who is in the midst of an ethnic identity crisis and the process of growth. This person requires self-affirmation drawn out of resolving a commitment to cultural heritage in relation to the contemporary demands of society. Discovering ethnic expressions of self-actualization and fulfillment of human potential are unique ways that a worker and client can work together in the midst of a growth crisis. *Problem-solving intervention* may be helpful when working on practical life adjustment and survival decision making. In the struggle between ethnic minority and dominant majority cultures, a client has built up a rational way of working out everyday dilemmas. Problem solving offers a helpful way to reinforce what he or she knows on a cognitive/intuitive level. *Behavioral intervention* may be effective when focusing on specific, identifiable problems such as misbehavior at home or school due to difficulties in acculturation, which require reeducation and change. The ethnic culture's natural practices of reward and punishment could be useful reinforcers to facilitate learning and relearning ways of changing behavior. All in all, the social worker and minority client should determine together which interventional modalities are applicable and suitable to the unique problem situation that confronts both of them.

Treating symptoms.   There has been an emphasis, in working with ethnic minority clients, on the interventional objective of resolving symptomatic problem behavior. Bell, Bland, Houston, and Jones (1983) suggest an ethnically oriented short-term approach:

> There is a need for training in therapies utilizing a systematic approach to treatment, where the emphasis is on rapid change in symptomatic behavior accomplished through alteration of the social context as agreed upon by the therapist and the family. Such an approach is in congruence with the holistic tradition of African folk healers and is more effective in crisis intervention than a lengthy investigation of causes of behavior [p. 226].

Among the basic principles for brief treatment of minority clients are the following (Bell, Bland, Houston, & Jones, 1983; Brown, 1975):

1. focus on the interactional processes of the group or family as the force that maintains symptomatic behavior;
2. direct and rapid attention to the symptomatic behavior rather than to investigating the cause of the symptom through the use of insight;

3. an immediate approach designed for quick relief of symptoms;
4. alteration of the social context;
5. attention to practical problems;
6. application of immediate measures to handle perceived problems.

Several social casework interventions are adaptable to a short-term approach that centers on resolving specific symptom behavior. Problem-solving intervention sets forth a rational step-by-step procedure (Perlman, 1970):

1. problem definition;
2. immediate problem history;
3. a range of problem-solving alternatives;
4. selection and implementation of a particular solution;
5. feedback and evaluation.

Another approach involves attention to the present problem, enumeration of the client's assets, involvement of significant others, education of the client in helpful skills, recognition of environmental and interpersonal factors, rehearsal of new behavior in real life settings, and new understanding of the way behavior may be maintained (Gambrill, 1983). The task-centered approach to intervention is an outgrowth of the problem-solving school. It emphasizes formulating target problems and implementing behavioral tasks to accomplish interventive goals and resolve problem behaviors (Reid, 1978). This intervention highlights agreement on goal outcomes and client assignments, a brief series of contacts, focus on behavior change, and evaluation of results (Gambrill, 1983). Behavioral intervention identifies clear objectives, describes the association between behavior and internal/external factors, measures observable problem behavior and overt behavioral change, and determines and rearranges current factors related to desired change. It stresses learning and relearning of behavior, pursuing outcomes important to clients and significant others, evaluation of progress, planning for maintenance of change, and identification of the client's assets (Gambrill, 1983). Although these interventions have distinct characteristics and diverse assumptions, they fit the preceding description of brief treatment with minorities.

However, it would be ill advised to confine a micro level intervention with minority clients to symptomatic behavior and the initiation of immediate relief of symptoms. One suspects that this is a response to the effectiveness of short-term treatment and a reaction to the usefulness of long-term psychotherapy. Whereas it would be pragmatic to resolve the immediate problem situation, it would be helpful to utilize the range of interventional approaches available to the social worker and the minority client.

Existing approaches to helping minority clients can and should be supplemented, but they cannot be altogether replaced. For some they are necessary. Jones and Korchin (1982) observe:

There remains the problem of treating ethnic individuals who are in psychological distress now, and existing forms of mental health care can clearly contribute here. It must be kept in mind, too, that even in a more ideal society there are likely to be psychological casualties, for whom the treatment of choice would seem to be some form of psychotherapy [p. 16].

Selection of a particular interventional approach must be based on the specific behav-

ioral issue, the cultural background of the minority client, and the professional evaluation of the worker and supervisor.

Example of application.   The Inter-Tribal Council of Arizona, Inc., combines a
micro existential approach to intervention with the interventional strategy of empowerment. It makes the following suggestions for working with Native American
communities:

1. a non-directional approach eliminates imposition and emphasizes cooperation
   and participation instead of competition between people;
2. the maximum utilization of all local resources, specifically the extended family
   system, which is representative of tribal culture and lifestyle;
3. the involvement of all community people in decision making, thus reinforcing the
   old traditions of respect for all in community collaboration for community
   problem solving (Inter-Tribal Council of Arizona, Inc., no date).

This existential intervention stresses the attitude of "I–Thou," or a spiritual relationship with people. There is also the element of collective community empowerment,
which brings together the extended family, the tribe, and the total community.

Meso Level

Meso level intervention is increasing as a means of working with minority clients in the
context of extended family and community network resources. Minority family and
community intervention has been developed. Jones and Korchin (1982) introduce
commitment therapy as a Third World alternative to existing helping models. Commitment therapy is based on the assumption that the well-being of a minority client
depends on membership in a community (Reiff, 1968; Sarason, 1972). A positive
community is necessary. It offers meaning and hope to its members through their
participation, and the individual can merge himself or herself with it. Cultures likewise
serve this function as systems of religious, philosophical, or ideological integration.

Recently there has been renewed interest among minority communities in historical
roots and ethnic culture, identification and affinity with the group of origin and other
minority group members, and an emphasis on community solidarity and group action.
At the same time, ethnic group psychology has developed. For example, according to
African psychology, the Black American retains a sense of being a communal person who
subordinates personal goals to the survival and well-being of the historically African
group. Similarly, among Latinos there has been a movement toward dissimilation,
return to cultural roots, assertion of ethnicity, and the active politicization and pride of
cultural differences. Commitment therapy emphasizes returning the individual to an
ethnic community, membership which results in an effective pattern of symbolic
integration (Jones & Korchin, 1982).

The community.   This collective use of the ethnic community and the reuniting of
the minority individual to that minority entity have implications for ethnic support
systems and social work practice. Cultural Study 7-6 emphasizes the use of the full range
of family and community social supports for meso level intervention. Meso intervention

focuses on the importance of the minority collective community as a primary modality. Its goal is to rejoin the minority client with his or her own ethnic community, which provides the basis for identity, support, and cultural resources. Osborne, Carter, Pinkleton, and Richards (1983) stress that an understanding of the ethnic community and cultural supports is essential to treatment interventions. Among the components of the African–American community are knowledge of personal groups, family, and community supports. There are also cultural elements such as philosophy of life, music, patterns of behavior, religion, morals, habits, rules, knowledge, art, language, beliefs, customs, and ways of living. The minority client experiences linkage with these collaborative networks as part of the treatment.

Cultural Study 7-6

Family and Community Social Supports[6]

In this model of practice, intervention begins at the level of community social structure. The support has to be deliberately designed to support the family structures as they exist; observing functions as a measure of adequacy rather than design. Those aspects of family function that provide biological needs, emotional needs, and support for acceptable values and goals, rather than the process by which they are achieved.

For example, the father role may be played by a grandfather, who enjoys, accepts, and is enhanced by the role. The child loves, accepts guidance, and turns to him for protection and help. The record should reflect this, rather than a long social monologue on illegitimacy, loose morals, absentee father, and weak parental involvement. The state of the family functioning must be reflected and supported.

The role of the black church and its influences must be recognized, accepted, and worked with to broaden its social structural involvement. Its institutional posture has historically evaded overt colonial interference to the degree that it has survived as a perpetuated institution over time. Since the interference with it is more pronounced and reacted to, it stands as a monument in the black community. Community mental health efforts must be tied to the spiritual and moral needs of the black community.

For example, the space available in black churches should be made use of when and on whatever conditions possible. They should be generously reimbursed for lending their community relations, moral sanction, and facilities to mental health services. The role of the minister in the leadership of the local congregation should entail a concentrated financially supported training program for black ministers in mental health leadership and a total congregational participation in a carefully designed, well-delivered membership training in community mental health and counseling knowledge. This is critical to insure the survival of mental health practice when the mental health funds are no longer available.

A deliberate program with local schools, businesses, and absentee vested interest to identify and plan their responsibility in local community mental health is necessary.

For example, the local movie theater owner who builds his business on the showing of "X"-rated movies in local neighborhoods might consider a matinee for the children as well as local residents on a continuous basis of human relations, community development, and black-oriented films on weekend afternoons. This is by no means a limit to local community support structures accessible to the community mental health practitioner.

[6]From "Minority Issues in Community Mental Health" by S. Tucker. In B. R. Compton and B. Galaway (Eds.), *Social Work Processes*, pp. 122, 123. Copyright © 1979 by Dorsey Press. Reprinted by permission.

Sue and Morishima (1982) discuss the use of indigenous community workers and natural community caretakers such as ministers, relatives, prominent community members, and family physicians. They also differentiate various natural resources in terms of individual skills and strategies, interpersonal support systems such as family and friends, and institutional systems such as churches, herbalists, family doctors, and folk healers. For Chinese Americans, family associations were historically responsible for community governance, financial support, and political ideology. Later, Chinese Christian churches functioned as learning and social service institutions offering teaching of English and the Bible, provisions for the poor, assistance with immigration, socialization, and counseling. More recently, Asian–American professional workers and young activists have organized the poor and powerless into grass-roots organizations that offer social service and politicization.

The extended family.   Morales and Salcido (1983) explain social network intervention in terms of formal and informal systems involved in Mexican–American family life. The goal of social network intervention is to deal with the individual and family structure by rendering the network visible and viable and by restoring its function. The social network includes extended kin, *compadres* (coparents), friends, *curanderos* (folk healers), and other concerned individuals. These subsystems provide emotional strength, support, and practical assistance to the family. The Latino extended family system is tightly knit and includes the nuclear family, relatives, and close friends in *compadrazgo* (coparenthood). There are emotional displays of affection, hierarchical roles, and distinctive child-rearing practices. Family members seek advice and support from each other before going for professional help. *Compadre* and *comadre* are godfather and godmother of a child who is baptized. They have important family roles and perform parental duties in case anything happens to the natural parents (Carrillo, 1982). The Puerto Rican family in particular maintains good relationships with extended family, friends, and people with connections in order to receive help with job or educational opportunities. In some extended networks, children are raised by families other than their own who offer opportunities for education, employment, and marriage. The extended family and friends of the family go out together for recreational and social purposes. In some small communities, storekeepers, teachers, and neighbors are all concerned about and watch out for each other's children. Ghali (1977) states:

> It should be borne in mind that the family has within it the resources and strengths to restore the homeostasis. The therapist and other sensitive professional workers simply help the family to release the energy needed to meet their proper tasks so that the individuals can be free to grow. The family capacity to love, to share, and to be generous and hospitable is the foundation to build on [p. 468].

For the minority client, the family and community are potent forces for intervention and support.

The church.   Another influential institution for minorities is the ethnic church. Solomon (1983) emphasizes the role of the church in Black community life in the areas of civil rights and job discrimination. In addition to human rights, the church advocates prayer, Black unity, and the collection and distribution of funds on behalf of needy people. The church provides social leadership, mutual assistance, and spiritual strength. Solomon (1983) explains:

> God is never an abstraction not linked to the here-and-now. He is personalized and included in daily life situations. It is not uncommon to hear Afro-Americans relate a conversation they have had with God or with His son, Jesus Christ. Prayer is a frequent response to everyday crisis, even by those who do not profess to any deep religious convictions [p. 422].

For Black Americans, the church is intricately involved in personal, family, and social needs. It has a bonding effect on the Black community.

Latino Americans are also spiritual people. Ghali (1977) observes that Puerto Ricans turn to spiritualism and mysticism. Traditionally Catholic, they may not be regular churchgoers. Some may attend special services only on Christmas, Palm Sunday, and Easter and for weddings and funerals. They love processions, rituals, and pageantry and make promises to God and the saints in return for favors. For other Latinos, the church represents a place of worship, ethnic socialization, strengthening of family moral values, and provisions of community services.

Patterns of helping.   Extended family and community support systems play a vital role in minority meso intervention with people of color. However, research on informal support systems has placed qualifications on meso interventions involving family, friends, and neighborhood resources. Siegel (1984) has reported that among neighbors, friends, and family of the elderly there are distinct patterns of helping under varying situations. Kin are best for functions involving long-term commitment to the elderly that require time, energy, or money. This point is particularly relevant when the elderly are helpless and require prolonged care in illness. Friends with whom the elderly have something in common are important for companionship and leisure time activities. Neighbors are useful for tasks that require speed of reaction, such as emergencies, continuous observation and knowledge of the neighborhood, and granting a favor such as picking up an item at the store. Among informal support networks, there are clear differences among the functions of subgroups: friends for socialization, neighbors for short-term assistance, and nuclear and kinship family for long-term crisis. Moreover, Cantor (1970) found the following patterns among elderly Blacks, Latinos, and Whites in New York City:

1. Blacks were most likely to have a wide-ranging support network made up of kin and nonkin members.
2. Latinos were equally divided between having functional support systems composed of family (spouse, children, and relatives) and nonfamily.
3. Latinos were most likely to have a living spouse and a greater number of functional children who saw them on a frequent basis.
4. Latinos have the greatest amount of help given by their children.

Meso level intervention involves a reuniting or joining together of two entities, the minority client and his or her minority community, which offers a rich heritage and tradition of customs, beliefs, and person-oriented resources. Bringing together the minority community's strengths for change intervention and the minority client's problem set is the objective of this intervention. The dramatic case study of the healing effect of a family network on a Native American client (Cultural Study 7-7) underscores the meso level intervention approach.

Cultural Study 7-7

Family Network Intervention[7]

The . . . example . . . involves a network-clan with a single extended family at its core. At the time the therapist entered the picture, it was composed of a grandmother, several adult sons' and daughters' families, and their close or significant friends. This network was deteriorating rapidly. There had been two murders, a suicide, a crippling assault, and the death from a heart attack of the grandfather who had headed the group.

The man upon whom the network then depended for survival was acutely and suicidally depressed. He was ambivalent about assuming the leadership role. He was not only concerned about his ability to cope with the task, but he was overwhelmed with a feeling of guilt and loss of face about a dishonorable Army discharge, after 15 years of honorable military service. This element assumed real importance because of the cultural importance of honor in battle as an Indian tradition, which might not have parallel importance in another culture. In addition to suicidal ruminations, his symptoms included an inflammation of shrapnel induced arthritis sufficient to render him unemployable, at a time when many of his kin were also facing financial crisis.

Clinical judgment indicated that this man required inpatient hospitalization. Rather than arrange a quick admission to the United States Public Health Service Indian Hospital, the network-clan and the patient were invited to participate in finding a solution. This seemed imperative since it had appeared to the therapist even before this man presented himself as a patient, that the network-clan itself was sick.

The first stage was a rapid gathering of the network-clan at the grandmother's home. This permitted introducing two elements that had been lost: First, an element of hope in getting treatment for the potential leader and second, some success experiences in reaching short-term reachable goals. These quick success experiences actually consisted of raising $20.00 via a bingo game and finding temporary employment for one son. It was also possible for the clan to offer support and help for the therapist in treating the depressed patient, which could be received gratefully.

The network-clan, reeling from a series of disasters, had been unable to exchange positive experiences in this fashion between its members for some time and consequently had been resonating and amplifying pathology. Once this pathology was dampened, it was possible to discover that admission to a VA Hospital would symbolically expunge the dishonorable discharge. This was arranged through the therapist's liaison with the professional agencies and was ceremonially validated in a formal meeting.

As a result of the opportunities for interaction with individual network members during these activities, the therapist was able to share the grief with the grandmother and other individuals in such a way that they found a release in tears and could get about the work of mourning, which eliminated another source of pathology within the network.

Supportive contacts between the network-clan and the depressed man began within hours of his brief hospitalization. Although the VA psychiatry department found him "unsuitable" for psychotherapy, his somatic and suicidal symptoms disappeared and his arthritis was brought under medical control. The network worked through the patient's practical problems by helping him find a job, transportation, and so on, as well as providing the therapeutic relationships needed. He was able to show his own resilience three months later when he handled the details of a terminal illness and funeral of another of the network members. That event would probably have triggered another wave of suicidal-murder catastrophies [sic] had not pathology been halted within the group.

Within 12 months the destructive processes had been reversed and the reciprocal healing strengths of network and ex-patient network-clan leader were such that he and one or two others were visibly assuming interlocking leadership roles as tribal representatives at pow wows and in the elected tribal business organization.

Evidence that real changes in network pathology had occurred is deduced from the fate of one family unit which for a variety of reasons (mainly job opportunities) moved several hundred miles away at the height of pathological period. This family was not present during the period of therapeutic intervention and was out of touch with the network in an unusual fashion. Before contact was reestablished, the state newspapers headlined that this family had another "unexplained" murder and suicide incident which left only one surviving child. In an institution for delinquents at the time of the parents' deaths, the child continues to be both "incorrigible" and "isolated."

This continued antisocial experience of that one surviving delinquent is in contrast to the other children of the network-clan who survived similar family destruction during the pathological period. They have now faded into public anonymity. Local authorities ignore them since they are in school, not delinquent, and not in need of "public assistance" as they have been scattered among network-clan families. While clinicians might predict some psychic scar tissue, they probably could not write a better therapeutic prescription than the network's cooperative distribution of nurturing responsibilities. It is probable that a professional clinic or agency could not deliver these services as efficiently as the restored network-clan.

7From "Therapy in Tribal Settings and Urban Network Intervention," by C. L. Attneave, *Family Process*, 8, 204–206. Copyright © 1969 by Family Process, Inc. Reprinted by permission.

In social work intervention, the social worker serves as an intermediary between a minority client and a helping resource of the minority community to ensure the appropriate referral and delivery of services. It involves helping the client to select a suitable ethnic service organization or helping person, arranging a referral, and establishing a working relationship for follow-up community intervention. At the core of intervention is a strategy for change that involves a joint decision by the worker and client to follow a course of action. It engages the worker and the client in problem solving within the context of the minority community. Action is taken in consultation and concert with the spirit and values of the minority community. It is within the community's realm of influence that problem-solving action takes place. Problem solutions are not independent of the ethnic community. They have a point of reference from which they are formulated, agreed upon, and implemented. At this interventional level, the change-effecting decision ultimately involves a transaction whereby the ethnic community influences the outcome of action. For example, the minority client who is coping with a specific problem may need the support of or feeling of belonging to the caring and nurturing part of the minority community. In this sense, the feeling of oneness with the ethnic community, or finding one's place in it, involves identifying with a particular group of people having a history and tradition, beliefs and values, customs and practices, and family and collective cohesion. Resolving a specific problem is an overt act of coping with stress or conflict and a symbolic way of finding one's ethnic lifeline.

Example of application.   The meso level of intervention focuses on the use of the extended family and community network resources in working with minority clients. Among the interventional strategies relevant to the meso level is maintenance of culture. A prime example is the creation of an approach of cultural corporate intervention to working with a local ethnic community. Red Horse (1982) suggests an ethnic collective interventional approach for Native Americans involving an age-integrated developmental day-care service. It would be organized as a model of a cultural network, bringing families at risk together for collective therapeutic support and incorporating individuals from allied community programs to serve as cultural and social role models. It replicates a cultural community designed to meet the social and emotional needs of children, youth, adults, and elders and reaffirms Native American extended kin systems. There would be daily social contact between families at risk and professional staff who could keep abreast of emerging family crises. Staff of allied programs could meet the developmental needs of children through natural informal relationships. The result would be a true ethos of family development. Red Horse outlines a multigenerational therapeutic community that draws on cultural and ethnic perspectives.

Macro Level

Macro level intervention poses the challenge of formulating new approaches to change in the realm of perennial large-scale social issues that affect minority populations in a changing political and economic situation. Macro intervention emphasizes both individual betterment and social change in the direction of social equality, social justice, new institutional structures, and distribution of wealth and resources (Washington, 1982).

Social policy, planning, and administration have been macro interventional tools for affecting social change in major problem areas. *Social policy* is the body of stated goals, directions, and guidelines that govern the implementation of programs, activities, and efforts related to public and private human services organizations. Presidential and congressional leadership, public and private interest groups, and the political and economic situation influence and affect social policy. In turn, social policy is translated into a rational formulation of program goals and objectives, design, implementation, and evaluative components involving social planning. *Social planning* sets forth a systemic formulation that embodies goal priorities, program policies, and regulations. Accompanying funding incentives usually induce the participation of the public and private sectors and their compliance with the terms of the legislative program. *Social administration* oversees the funding of programs, the monitoring of program intent, and the implementation of program activities on behalf of the public legislation. Application proposals are written on the local level and submitted for review, approval, and funding on the state, regional, and national levels. Local city, county, and state departments are liaisons between federal officials and local participants and assist with the implementation of national social programs.

Changing social, economic, and political situation. Since the beginning of the Reagan administration, there have been major changes in social policy
affecting macro intervention. Together with ethnic minority groups, social workers
having policy, planning, and administrative skills are in the process of devising alternative policies, program designs, and strategies based on this changing context.

With the rise of a conservative political philosophy, social attitudes toward poverty
and minorities have changed. Hopps (1982) observes that the new conservative philosophy has dismantled policies and programs that have worked for people of color and
other vulnerable groups. This political conservatism has altered the funding of federal
programs, which have been the most consistent source of social assistance for ethnic
minorities. It has shifted the federal government's role from the public promotion of
social welfare to the provision of incentives for the private sector to increase productivity
and economic growth, create jobs for the able-bodied, and lessen public reliance on
government. At the same time, social assistance programs have been cut, producing a
devastating effect on the resources of minority communities because of their dispropor-
tionate reliance on these programs (Walters, 1982).

The prime impetus behind these moves has been inflation, declining public social
resources, shifts in national priorities, and majority power tactics. Rivera and Erlich
(1981) point out that due to inflation, social work has sought to respond to rapidly
expanding needs with ever-declining resources. National defense, energy supplies, and
inflation have replaced minority issues as top priorities and have shifted program
resources away from ethnic communities. Competition for resources has taken place
among minorities, who are in conflict over the meager remaining funds available to
them. Latinos claim that they will soon surpass the Black population in size and become
the largest minority group in the United States. Latin American and Asian immigrants
have gained access to public services and compete for employment with Blacks, who have
been denied or have made minimal gains for generations (Walters, 1982).

As a result, the majority power tactics toward ethnic minorities have been overtly
expressed in the control of distribution of benefits. Walters (1982) states:

> To maintain this control, they use a variety of tactics in dealing with subordinated groups,
> such as suffocating minority demands by avoiding decisions, manipulating the bias of the
> demands by reinterpreting issues, developing manipulative actions that anticipate the
> reaction of the subordinate groups, co-opting subordinate groups' demands and denying
> their legitimacy, and denying minority groups entrance into the bargaining arena [p. 27].

Institutional racism affecting the social responsibility of delivering resources to minorities is expressed through declining affirmative action, barriers in housing, and school
segregation (Walters, 1982). These trends in public policy influence the social environment by limiting opportunities and resources available to people of color and reducing
self-worth and behavioral security among minority people (Longres, 1982).

Alternative formulations and strategies for macro intervention.
Ethnic minorities have reinterpreted the changing nature of the social, economic, and
political situation confronting them. As a result, macro intervention for the 1980s has
assumed directions that address the conservatism and racism of this period.

Community network intervention is a natural response to program cutbacks, reduced services, and restrictive eligibility requirement tests. There has been an inward turn toward survival resources of the indigenous social network. Rivera and Erlich (1981) describe neo-*Gemeinschaft* communities in which primary cultural, social, political and economic interrelationships have been developed by new immigrants or ethnic groups occupying a geographic area. A support structure has been developed along horizontal lines in the face of an antagonistic environment and dwindling resources. For example, members of the Cuban immigrant community in the Miami, Florida area employ bartering as a form of service sharing. Lacking money, many have turned to craft skills learned in their country of origin as a medium of exchange for necessary goods and services. Churches have been a primary source of help to newcomers through fund raising, housing, English classes, training in basic survival skills, and emergency food and clothing.

Intervention through the networks of the minority community requires funding for the community's grassroots service organizations and churches. Delgado and Humm-Delgado (1982) suggest that community mental health funding should be directed to local churches to assist with minority youth programs. A national policy of family assistance payment would alleviate the burden of minority families with elderly and disabled at home. Moreover, the Department of Health and Human Services and its counterparts at the state level should establish strong minority bureaus to coordinate minority health care, housing, and services to children, youth, and the elderly. Local county revenue sharing and state block grants should give high priority to funding minority human services sponsored by indigenous bilingual/bicultural organizations.

Political impact intervention is another alternative strategy for influencing politicians and highlighting macro problem issues affecting minorities. The Democratic party's 1984 presidential primaries witnessed the campaign of the articulate Rev. Jesse Jackson, who raised minority and social issues and sought to form a Rainbow Coalition of disenfranchised groups. As a result, minority voter registration increased, particularly among Blacks across the country. One political impact strategy is the encouragement of minority candidates to run for local, state, and national offices to maintain political visibility and leverage for minority influence and social change. Hopps (1982) believes that as a primary agenda, people of color must return to political activism and organization at the grassroots level and speak out for necessary policies and programs. Coalitions must be formed with other groups who are affected by conservative policy cutbacks and human and civil rights retrenchment. Ethnic minorities must register and vote for candidates who are willing to champion their cause. In short, the effectiveness of political impact intervention is dependent on the development of local political intra-structures of minorities around issues and candidates who are able to affect relevant social change.

Legal advocacy intervention is a long-term means of achieving social change through far-reaching landmark decisions in the courts. Morales (1981) asserts that we need advocates who plead the cause of clients before organizations and who represent the interests of an aggrieved class. For Third World communities, Morales is particularly concerned about the need to continue class action suits on behalf of people of color. He cites the work of John Serrano, a social worker, who initiated the now-famous case of

Serrano v. *Priest.* In this class action suit before the California State Supreme Court, it was argued that the quality of a child's education should not be dependent on the wealth of a school district. The ruling issued was that the financing scheme of public education in California, which relied heavily on local property taxes, violated the equal protection clause of the Fourteenth Amendment to the United States Constitution. Wealthier school districts were favored, to the detriment of poorer districts. As a result, a financial plan must assure equal funding for each child throughout the public school system of the state. Morales' point is that this argument could be extended to equal protection under the law in areas such as welfare, health, and mental health services. In light of government cutbacks, legal class action advocacy of a range of governmental services could be initiated on behalf of minorities. The distribution and quality of human services could be standardized under the equal protection clause in a class action suit.

Example of application.   Macro level intervention addresses national and regional social problems that affect minority populations. Dealing with those problems involves large-scale change with respect to entire minority communities and social classes. The above examples of macro level intervention allude to various minority strategy themes. Community network intervention relies on the support structure of the minority community and emphasizes the corporate nature of strategies of empowerment and cultural maintenance. Political impact intervention calls forth the interventional strategies of liberation and empowerment through the use of minority bloc voting and visible minority candidates who achieve local, state, and national political offices. Legal advocacy intervention strives to incorporate the interventional strategy of parity through class action judicial decisions.

A case example is the design of macro intervention to address the issue of minority unemployment. High unemployment among Black youth and adults looms as a continuing social and economic problem. The majority society's perception is that Blacks have an aversion to work and exhibit personal and cultural defects. The minority view of unemployment is that systemic racial discrimination has been excluding Blacks from the job force. In addition, educational inequality, technological/industrial innovation, and the use of alien labor for the production of domestic goods have excluded minority Americans from employment (Moss, 1982). It is estimated that in 1973 Blacks lost $19 billion in national income due to job discrimination and $5.9 billion in property due to illicit activities (Thurow, 1975).

Moss (1982) recommends the following policy objectives for employment of youth:

1. ensure the accessibility of the labor market to all young people, regardless of race, sex, and national origin;
2. provide means of identifying gaps in employment among minority youth and design programs to meet the needs of the hard-core unemployed;
3. develop a monitoring and working procedure with employers who resist changes in discriminatory employment practices.

A means of implementing these objectives is a subsidized on-the-job experience through direct federal grants to private employers. The subsidy would consist of a graduated wage increase over a five-year period, to a maximum of $5000. Employers would receive bonuses for hiring hard-core groups (Thurow, 1975). Much of the bleak outlook on unemployment for people in general and minority youth in particular depends on the economic growth, federal funding, and presidential and congressional leadership. At the present time, these factors translate into a conservative leaning toward tax credit incentives for private industry for hiring minority youth.

Certainly a major interventional initiative in social policy is to devise a clear and effective program for employment training and placement of people of color. Implementation of such a program might include the following guidelines for minority intervention strategy:

1. an employment training and placement program that liberates the person to select a career field from an open range of choices;
2. an employment training and placement program that empowers the person with relevant training experience to compete with marketable skills;
3. an employment training and placement program that selects those who are most in need of economic stability and security;
4. an employment training and placement program that fosters cultural maintenance by creating industrial work zones in the minority community;
5. an employment training and placement program that recognizes the unique personhood of the minority person by providing jobs in which individual creativity can be demonstrated.

The task of the minority-oriented social work practitioner is to design appropriate ethnic intervention strategies (liberation, empowerment, parity, culture maintenance, and unique personhood) on micro, meso, and macro levels. Depending on the scope of the problem theme and level, there are multiple interventional levels and strategies that can be devised by the worker and the client.

CASE STUDY

The Hernandez Family

Having established a plan for an interventional strategy Mr. Platt begins to implement various aspects with service resources and family members. Indispensable to the success of the plan is Father Carlos, a Catholic priest who directs the local satellite center for Catholic Social Services. He commands the respect of the community both as a Latino clergyman and as a competent, warm administrator of ethnic social service programs. He is aware of the community's social needs and has been able to obtain program and funding resources and establish an indigenous program staffed with bilingual/bicultural service workers. It was natural for Mr. Platt to turn to this person and his organization, with their positive reputation and track record in the community, to provide assistance for the Hernandez family. Over the years, Father Carlos has brought together job-finding, tutoring, child care, and newcomers' services under one roof and identified the church as a practical instrument for helping with the problems of the Latino community. His staff has also cultivated excellent relationships with the county welfare departments, general hospital, and housing authority and is able to refer clients to ethnic-sensitive and sympathetic workers in those agencies.

At the next session, members of the Hernandez family report that initial contact has been made with the various unit workers. The two brothers-in-law were interviewed by a Spanish-speaking worker who had a number of job openings available with a local Latino contractor. Although they are not skilled trade workers, they have a promise of steady employment with apprentice class status. They have been working on a local construction site for the past several days and seem to be adjusting to the work procedure. As a result, Mr. Hernandez has taken a leave of absence from his second job as a night machine operator in a food processing plant and begun to spend evenings with his family. Ricardo has been assigned a high school senior to tutor him in math, spelling, and social studies. Mrs. Hernandez is scheduled to register for her ESL class through the adult education program of the local school district. A Mexican-American woman who works as a volunteer at the newcomers' center has already made contact with the wives of the two immigrant families and has been helpful with practical problems of adjustment. All three women came from the same part of Mexico. Parts of the intervention plan are in motion and appear to be running smoothly.

Task Recommendations

Principles of micro and meso intervention advocate the use of indigenous helping activities, programs, and persons in the ethnic community that are available to minority clients and ethnically aware human service workers. The following suggestions are designed to enhance your awareness and utilization of these resources:

1. Identify and use appropriate ethnic community resources, such as a family system network, a community leader, minister, or service organization, to meet your particular problem need and further your interventional plan.

2. Serve as an intermediary advocate-broker coordinator between the minority client and the minority helping resource. Support the relationship between the minority client and the community entity.

3. If your community has a lack of ethnic community service organizations, conduct a preliminary study identifying ethnic social needs, key ethnic community leaders, funding sources, and specific services that can be initiated with seed money.

Conclusion

At the core of minority social work practice is intervention, which affects social change for the ethnic minority client. This chapter has detailed the elements of goals and agreement, interventional strategies, and interventional levels from a unique minority perspective. The social worker has a variety of strategy themes (liberation, empowerment, parity, maintenance of culture, and unique personhood), along with micro, meso, and macro levels, with which to create an appropriate intervention for each minority client's situation. Of particular concern are the relevance of micro casework theories that speak to the minority individual, family, and small group; meso level extended family and community resources; and macro level interventional responses to socioeconomic-political dimensions of society. A wide range of minority-oriented interventions is given, enabling the social worker to select pertinent combinations that fit the problem needs and assessment requirements of the client.

References

Bell, C. C., Bland, I. J., Houston, E., & Jones, B. E. (1983). Enhancement of knowledge and skills for the psychiatric treatment of Black populations. In J. C. Chunn II, P. J. Dunston, & F. Ross-Sheriff (Eds.), *Mental health and people of color: Curriculum development and change* (pp. 205–238). Washington, D.C.: Howard University Press.

Blackwell, J. E., & Hart, P. S. (1982). *Cities, suburbs, and Blacks: A study of concerns, distrust and alienation.* Bayside, N.Y.: General Hall.

Bochner, S. (1982). The social psychology of cross-cultural relations. In S. Bochner (Ed.), *Cultures in contact: Studies in cross-cultural interaction* (pp. 5–44). Oxford: Pergamon Press.

Brown, B. S. (1975). The life of psychiatry. *American Journal of Psychiatry, 133,* 489–495.

Cantor, M. H. (1970). The configuration and intensity of the informal support system in a New York City elderly population. Unpublished paper. New York: New York City Department for the Aging.

Carrillo, C. (1982). Changing norms of Hispanic families: Implications for treatment. In E. E. Jones & S. J. Korchin (Eds.), *Minority mental health* (pp. 250–266). New York: Praeger.

Delgado, M., & Humm-Delgado, D. (1982). Natural support systems: Source of strength in Hispanic communities. *Social Work, 27,* 83–89.

Fujiki, S., Hansen, J. C., Cheng, A., & Lee, Y. M. (1983). Psychiatric mental health nursing of Asian and Pacific Americans. In J. C. Chunn II, P. J. Dunston, & F. Ross-Sheriff (Eds.), *Mental health and people of color: Curriculum development and change* (pp. 377–403). Washington, D.C.: Howard University Press.

Gambrill, E. (1983). *Casework: A competency-based approach.* Englewood Cliffs, N.J.: Prentice-Hall.

Ghali, S. B. (1977). Culture sensitivity and the Puerto Rican client. *Social Casework, 57,* 459–468.

Hopps, J. G. (1982). Oppression based on color. *Social Work, 27,* 3–5.

Inter-Tribal Council of Arizona, Inc. (no date). Community resources for American Indians. In E. F. Brown & T. F. Shaughnessy (Eds.), *Introductory text: Education for social work practice with American Indian families* (pp. 201–230). Tempe, Ariz.: Arizona State University School of Social Work, American Indian Projects for Community Development, Training and Research.

Jones, E. E., & Korchin, S. J. (1982). Introduction. In E. E. Jones & S. J. Korchin (Eds.), *Minority mental health* (pp. 3–36). New York: Praeger.

Leigh, J. W. (1982). Empowerment as a process. Unpublished paper. Seattle: University of Washington School of Social Work.

Leigh, J. W. (1984). Empowerment strategies for work with multi-ethnic populations. Paper presented at the Council on Social Work Education Annual Program Meeting. Detroit.

Longres, J. F. (1982). Minority groups: An interest-group perspective. *Social Work, 27,* 7–14.

Lum, D. (1982). Toward a framework for social work practice with minorities. *Social Work, 27,* 244–249.

Meyer, C. H. (1972). Practice on microsystem level. In E. J. Mullen, J. R. Dumpson, & associates (Eds.), *Evaluation of social intervention* (pp. 158–190). San Francisco: Jossey-Bass.

Morales, A. (1981). Social work with third-world people. *Social Work, 26,* 45–51.

Morales, A., & Salcido, R. (1983). Social work with Mexican Americans. In A. Morales & B. W. Sheafor, *Social work: A profession of many faces* (pp. 389–413). Boston: Allyn & Bacon.

Moss, J. A. (1982). Unemployment among Black youths: A policy dilemma. *Social Work, 27,* 47–52.

Mullen, E. J., Dumpson, J. R., & associates (Eds.). (1972). *Evaluation of social intervention.* San Francisco: Jossey-Bass.

Osborne, O., Carter, C., Pinkleton, N., & Richards, H. (1983). Development of African American curriculum content in psychiatric and mental health nursing. In J. C. Chunn II, P. J. Dunston, & F. Ross-Sheriff (Eds.), *Mental health and people of color: Curriculum development and change* (pp. 335–375). Washington, D.C.: Howard University Press.

Perlman, H. H. (1970). The problem-solving model in social casework. In R. W. Roberts & R. H. Nee (Eds.), *Theories of social casework* (pp. 129–179). Chicago: University of Chicago Press.

Red Horse, J. (1982). Clinical strategies for American Indian families in crisis. *The Urban and Social Change Review, 15,* 17–19.

Reid, W. J. (1978). *The task-centered system.* New York: Columbia University Press.

Reiff, R. R. (1968). Social intervention and the problem of psychological analysis. *American Psychologist, 23,* 524–530.

Rivera, F. G., & Erlich, J. L. (1981). Neo-Gemeinschaft minority communities: Implications for community organization in the United States. *Community Development Journal, 16,* 189–200.

Sarason, S. B. (1972). *The creation of settings and the future societies.* San Francisco: Jossey-Bass.

Siegel, D. I. (1984). Primary group supports in age homogeneous versus age heterogeneous areas for the elderly. Paper presented at the Council on Social Work Education Annual Program Meeting, Detroit.

Solomon, B. B. (1976). *Black empowerment: Social work in oppressed communities.* New York: Columbia University Press.

Solomon, B. B. (1983). Social work with Afro-Americans. In A. Morales & B. W. Sheafor, *Social work: A profession of many faces* (pp. 415–436). Boston: Allyn & Bacon.

Sue, S., & Morishima, J. K. (1982). The mental health of Asian Americans. San Francisco: Jossey-Bass.

Thurow, L. C. (1975). Poverty and discrimination: A brief overview. In T. F. Pettigrew (Ed.), *Racial discrimination in the United States* (pp. 240–247). New York: Harper & Row.

Turner, J. B. (1972). Forgotten: Mezzosystem intervention. In E. J. Mullen, J. R. Dumpson, & associates (Eds.), *Evaluation of social intervention* (pp. 129–145). San Francisco: Jossey-Bass.

Walters, R. W. (1982). Race, resources, conflict. *Social Work, 27,* 24–30.

Washington, R. O. (1982). Social development: A focus for practice and education. *Social Work, 27,* 104–109.

Webb, G. E. (1972). Rethinking macrosystem intervention. In E. J. Mullen, J. R. Dumpson, & associates (Eds.) *Evaluation of social intervention* (pp. 111–128). San Francisco: Jossey-Bass.

Weems, L. (1974). Awareness: The key to Black mental health. *Journal of Black Psychology, 1,* 30–37.

Weil, M. (1981). Southeast Asians and service delivery issues in service provision and institutional racism. In *Bridging cultures: Southeast Asian refugees in America* (pp. 136–163). Los Angeles: Asian American Community Mental Health Training Center.

8

Termination

In social work practice, termination refers to the ending stage of the social work process. Over the course of the process, a relationship has been built up that now must end. Ending a relationship is an emotional event. Both client and worker must work through the dynamics of the separation process (Strean, 1978). Investment of emotions and feelings in one person by another may entail grief. The client may go through the following reactions: denial of termination, return to earlier behavioral patterns or reintroduction of problem situations, explosive behavior at the worker's termination decision or break-up of the relationship by the client before the worker leaves the client (Compton & Galaway, 1979). Termination dynamics include separation and loss, clinging to therapy and the practitioner, recurrence of old problems, introducing new problems, and finding substitutes for the practitioner (Hepworth & Larsen, 1982).

Part of the client's reaction to termination is due to the client's dependency on the worker. A major aim of social work practice is to guide the client away from the worker, who must extricate himself or herself during the course of the process stages. Gambrill (1983) observes:

> Endings are often handled poorly because of the social worker's hangups about endings. It is thus important to explore your own beliefs and feelings about endings to make sure that these will not interfere with learning and using the skills necessary to bring about planned rather than unplanned endings. One of the requirements of planned endings is recognition of the limits of your own responsibilities for other people's lives. Some social workers have difficulty ending because they assume more responsibility than they should for the well-being and decisions of others [p. 357].

The termination phase should not be structured so that the emphasis is on separation and overdependency. Rather, there are positive change dimensions that can be built into termination (Gambrill, 1983).

From the standpoint of minority social work there are hardly any adequate treatments of termination. In fact, Strean (1978) believes that superficial attention is paid to termination because it conjures up rejection, abandonment, and loss for the social worker and the client. Moreover, unsuccessful intervention is often the reason a case is closed, and many social workers may wish to overlook the reasons for premature termination (Strean, 1978). However, the newness of the field of minority practice is reason enough for the lack of literature on termination. There are few frameworks for ethnic minority practice that adequately address the process stages of social work.

In view of the paucity of material, this chapter draws upon several minority practices analogies that allude to and are applicable to ethnic dimensions of termination. Elaborating on the core principles of termination in Chapter 3, we will speak about termination as destination, recital, and completion. In the course of the discussion, ethnic minority perspectives will be introduced at crucial points. Figure 8-1 illustrates the joint participation of client and worker in the termination process.

Client and Worker Systems Practice Issues

We have spoken of termination as an end point that signifies closure of the present relationship, noting that the manner and circumstances of termination have a bearing on future growth patterns of the client. The termination process can mean one of three things: resolution of the identified problem(s), major readjustments in interventional goals resulting in another series of sessions, or conclusion of the relationship due to barriers between the client and the worker. Of paramount importance in termination is the functioning of the person's social system during this concluding phase. To what extent have intervention goals been achieved and measured against the problem? Is there partial resolution or adequate closure on a problem situation at the time of termination? These are some of the crucial issues relating to the dynamics of termination.

Certain concepts associated with termination have implications for minority practice. Termination means end, conclusion, or finish. It comes from the Latin root *terminus*, which refers to an outcome, result, or goal. In the present context, termination connotes completion in the sense of accomplishment of a goal or achievement of some result. *Terminus* is the name of the ancient Roman deity who presided over boundaries and landmarks. The word thus implies the concept of destination in referring to arrival at a

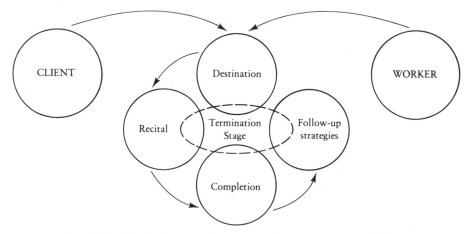

Figure 8-1.   Termination stage: client system and worker system practice issues.

predetermined point, boundary, or landmark. Recital is a part of the termination experience: the retelling of major events that brought the worker and client to the point of completion and destination. In this sense, recital is review and playing back of the whole practice process experience.

Termination as Destination

We have stated that the well-being of people of color is dependent on membership in an ethnic community that has natural and social service support systems. This corporate entity provides identity, support, and cultural resources. It is important to rediscover supportive elements in one's own ethnic family, community, and belief system of customs, rituals, and practices. We believe that this type of reunification with ethnic roots is a significant dimension in the process of termination. Ethnic identity, or a new sense of what it means to be Black, Latino, Asian, or Native American, is a powerful motivator for coping with the kind of living and problem situation confronting the client. Moreover, gaining a sense of ethnic selfhood creates an integrative source to draw upon personally. It involves establishing linkage with significant ethnic family and community persons who are able to play a meaningful part in the life of the client. This direction runs counter to an attempt on the part of the worker to alienate the client from his or her ethnicity. It recognizes instead the importance of ethnic bonding, which has a positive, sustaining influence on the client. The worker-client relationship in termination should not focus on separation and loss. It should be the passage to ethnic wholeness through the joining of the client with ethnic resources.

Termination has a destination. It is reunification with the ethnic community network rather than continuance of the single worker-client entity. Devore and Schlesinger (1981) highlight the importance of alternative sources of support in the termination phase. They particularly suggest kinship and neighborhood networks, the church, or a heightened sense of ethnic identity. They view these ethnic community resources as effective safeguards against the client's interpretation of termination as rejection or abandonment. Carrillo (1982) observes that the focus of Latino culture is harmony through cooperation with the ethnic community. The emphasis is on the development, maintenance, and enrichment of interpersonal relations through social gestures, friendliness, sentimentality, and an appreciation for light-heartedness and humor during conversation. This community bonding is linked to a deep respect for affiliation, affection, and the need to belong to a network of family and friends. It implies lifelong commitments, the cultivation of relationships, and presence in crisis.

Social casework trends on termination emphasize the importance of ongoing linkages to significant others, new activities, natural communities, and environmental resources. Gambrill (1983) discusses arranging for the maintenance of positive outcomes among a variety of community linkages. The involvement of significant others is important in light of their continuing role of influence on change. New behavior of significant others has a positive effect on the client for change and for maintaining change. Socializing agents who impart positive feedback, such as teachers and parents, sustain progress and stability of change. Gambrill (1983) suggests introducing clients to local centers where social and behavior skills are amply supported in interactional situations. These are naturally reinforcing communities where people are taught to seek out sources of feedback in order to maintain behavior. Praise for good work is an example of positively reinforcing feedback. Natural environments can be shaped to benefit clients along these lines. Identifying enriching programs, settings, and other community resources and encouraging clients to participate are ways to use environmental supports. Gradually the minority client is integrated into the group life of the ethnic community.

Termination as Recital

Termination as recital is an opportunity to review the worker-client relationship and to recount the major changes that have occurred from beginning to end. Recital involves review and playback. Like a piano student, the client has practiced the parts and the whole of the composition with the assistance and instruction of the worker. Through diligent effort he or she has mastered those procedural steps needed for functioning in life situations. Now comes the opportunity for retrospective recital. The client reflects on the work and plays it back to the worker. The worker listens, comments, and focuses on various aspects of the life situation. The worker and client play their respective parts so that both can hear, listen, and learn. Termination necessitates reciting back the growth process. It also previews the next steps of helping and future learning, much as a piano teacher previews the next lessons with the student, demonstrating crucial passages of a new selection, giving instructions on how to play, and teaching new techniques. The preview helps the student to practice effectively, having a knowledge of what is expected. Likewise, termination is an opportunity to anticipate problems and to design ways of coping through role playing situations. The client is helped to anticipate problems that may arise in the coming weeks and months.

The analogy of the piano recital is seen in the life-enhancement model of psychosocial counseling. Szapocznik, Santisteban, Kurtines, Hervis, and Spencer (1982) have applied life-enhancement counseling to their work with Cuban elderly. It builds on the elderly's strengths, reduces environmental sources of conflict and stress, and facilitates acceptance of past life experiences. The life-review approach focuses on the completion of unfinished business and identifies capabilities available to clients. Once strengths have been identified, the potential for mobilizing them in current conditions is assessed. Strategies of directive counseling and ecological intervention activate the past strengths of the elderly client. They emphasize psychosocial development of present strengths in the client's life. Reviewing past experiences of a client is a source of meaning, life acceptance, and ego integration. Meaningful transactions are fulfilled in the here-and-now. Fulfillment comes from acceptance of the past and current interactions between the client and the environment. The life-review aspect of the life-enhancement model of counseling enhances the recital dimension of termination.

Life-review procedure involves the recounting of life events and experiences. It encourages the client to reminisce. The worker probes uncovered areas and elicits memories of the client. The approach has a cathartic value because it allows for expression of feelings and organization of thoughts, which bring closure to those experiences. It identifies events, incidents, and relationships that are filled with meaning for the client. Directive reinterpretation provides the client with an alternative perspective on past events or experiences that helps to move the person toward a therapeutic goal. The primary aim is to identify themes that give meaning and purpose to life and that can be translated into the present. Throughout the life review, the worker listens for experiences reflecting the client's values and definition of meaning and reactivates them in the present. For example, a lifetime of work or dedication to raising a family provides a relevant and meaningful theme. Or there may be opportunities to develop areas that were secondary in the client's earlier life, such as interest in gardening, cooking, painting, fishing, or cultivating friends. These areas become a source of pride, hope, and meaning.

Recital at termination recalls the past events in the helping process. Unresolved feelings or decisions may emerge. There is an opportunity to learn about crucial junctures, strengths of the client, community resources, and effective coping. Recital of the past moves toward planning for the present and the future to maintain the patterns of change.

Termination as Completion

Termination as completion points to the theme of outcome. It addresses the pragmatic issue of accomplishment of goals based on the agreement in interventional planning. Goal outcome depends on problem identification and on resolution at the time of termination. A primary issue of termination is whether the interventional approach based on assessment has had an impact on the identified problem. A number of questions are crucial to practice process evaluation during termination:

Have there been significant changes with respect to the identified problem?
Can these changes be measured by conditions prevailing before and after implementation of the interventional plan?
What were the interventional tactics contributing to the changes: resources, organizations, significant others?
What time span did the process of change cover?
Did change occur as the result of actions of the client, the worker, the client and worker, or a third-party resource?

These issues stress the need to document specific, objective data that contributed to change and that can be verified by an impartial third party.

There are several criteria for evaluating results in these areas of concern. Firestein (1978) offers the following criteria of termination:

1. disappearance of symptoms: the problem that brought the client to the worker is eliminated, mitigated, or made tolerable;
2. change in client's personality: change for the better in the client's ability to deal with crisis and conflict;
3. social situational change: improvement in psychosocial functioning, capacity for planning, and relationships with significant others;
4. intuition: increased perception, particularly in observations and feelings;
5. change in the client's relationship with the worker: the client is able to deal with the worker as one mature adult with another.

Munoz (1982) identifies five factors that are relevant to effectiveness of termination with minority clients:

1. dropout rate, which can be evaluated by identifying the factors that increase the probability of continued treatment;
2. improvement rate by approach, which examines which therapies work most effectively with which problems for which clients;
3. time effectiveness, which shows which modality utilized fewer sessions with similar results than the other;
4. maintenance rates, which demonstrate continued improvement after termination versus the "revolving door" effect;
5. consumer satisfaction with the way minority clients were treated.

However, research data on these areas have yet to be reported on a large scale for termination with ethnic minority clients.

CASE STUDY

The Hernandez Family

After four weeks, it is apparent the interventional strategy plan is taking hold with the Hernandez family and the two immigrant families from Mexico. The two brothers-in-law are working steadily with the Mexican-American contractor, who has received several bids from a number of housing projects in the **barrio**. Mr. Hernandez is home nearly every night, spending time with the three children and particularly helping Ricardo with his homework. Mrs. Hernandez is enjoying her ESL class, and several of her friends are classmates. The family is helping her practice English words and sentences. Ricardo is adjusting to school. The latest report from his teacher says that Ricardo is doing his work at school and is more relaxed and happier than a month ago. The two other families seem to be adjusting to urban American life.

Mr. Platt, the social worker, is satisfied with the progress that the families have made. They have become linked to resources within their ethnic minority community. These community supports, located at Catholic Social Services in their neighborhood, have drawn them closer to the church and the Latino community. They have gained a sense of satisfaction and pride in knowing that assistance is available in the Latino community. Together, the church, school, and social services have forged a strategy to help these families-in-need.

At the next session, Mr. Platt encourages review of the major progress and change that have taken place. Most significant is the relief of stress on Mr. Hernandez and Ricardo. Before, the father was overburdened with the strain of two jobs and his son was a disciplinary problem in school due to the absence of his father during the evenings. Now there has been measurable progress in job finding, stability of home life, school tutoring, and English classes, which have brought a change to the family. Recounting the movement that has been made during the sessions helps the family to contact former negative affect and present feelings of happiness and contentment.

With respect to achievement of goals, the two families from Mexico have been assisted in obtaining full-time construction work leading to apprenticeship. Mr. Hernandez is therefore able to work at just his regular job and spend his evenings with his family. Ricardo's classroom tutoring with a high school aide and his father's help in the evenings are having a marked effect on his grades (B average) and his positive peer relations (no fights in the last three weeks). His teacher has noticed his happiness, contentment, and willingness to settle down and begin his work. Mrs. Hernandez is in the process of learning to speak, read, and write English through her classes. She is well on her way, learning how to ask and answer questions in English about daily living situations. Through the assistance of the Latino volunteer and their friends, the two families from Mexico are able to find their way around the city well enough to shop, pay the bills, and drive.

Task Recommendations

The principles of termination have been expressed in terms of destination, recital, and completion. Select a minority case that was completed successfully and review how termination as destination, recital, and completion might be applied to the case. The following questions point out uses of the three principles:

1. Was there an effort to connect the client with a positive element in the minority community for identity, support, and cultural resources? If so, elaborate on such use of kinship and neighborhood networks, the church, or community activities.

2. Was there an opportunity to review and play back the major changes that had occurred in the client's life during the social work helping process? Were certain areas explored further or events interpreted and integrated into the client's life?

3. Were criteria for goal outcomes established at the beginning of intervention and used as measures at termination? To what extent did the minority client complete the stated goals? What were the strategic changes, time framework for accomplishing the goals, and significant others who participated in the process of change?

Follow-Up Strategies

Termination is a crucial stage of practice process because it shapes future growth patterns of the client. In some instances, the worker-client relationship is dissolved because of such counterproductive factors as numerous absences of the client, the client's resistance, the worker's bias, and personality dissonance. The worker and client may renegotiate and schedule another series of sessions. It may be appropriate to define another problem area and to establish a contract for a different set of goal outcomes. However, when the client terminates the present helping relationship, there is a need for follow-up strategies to establish a transitional period of change and stability. Fischer (1978) views termination as the provision of procedures to enhance the transfer of positive change from the artificial situation to real life. Without this transfer and follow-up, gains witnessed in the office are limited to the client's learning to verbalize problems differently or please the worker with reports of success. Accomplishing the tasks of transfer and follow-up means the adaptation of behavioral change learned in the helping relationship to the client's life situation.

The social worker facilitates continuity of change through a number of procedures. There should be a gradual tapering off of sessions between the worker and client. They agree to meet every other week or once a month and evaluate the client's progress between extended sessions. What has happened to the client in the interval? Has the client been able to cope successfully when problem stress occurred? What lessons learned from the worker-client relationship have been applied in life situations during the interval? How has the support network of the ethnic community been used during this time? The gradual fading of contact offers an opportunity for reality testing.

During a one- to two-month trial period, telephone contact between the worker and client is helpful to monitor progress. From a close distance, the worker is available to offer support and to assess whether changes have been maintained with the client. Follow-up contacts by telephone impose minimal demands on the time and effort of the worker and client and are an efficient means of checking on carry-over effects. Hepworth and Larsen (1982) recommend a follow-up session at a point from two to six months following termination. They identify these advantages of follow-up: encouragement of clients to continue progress after termination, brief assistance for residual difficulties during a follow-up session, assessment of the durability of change, and continuance of the worker's interest in the client.

After formal termination, the worker should maintain an open-door policy. The worker should communicate the fact that the client is free to call for a return appointment. This offer does not mean that the client has failed in the process. Rather, it is a natural invitation based on friendship and concern. Gilbert, Miller, and Specht (1980) point out that former problems can recur and new problems do arise. Because some problems will not be solved in this helping relationship, the client should be assured that the worker is available to assist the client if the need arises. Should the client return, it is important to reassign the same worker to the client, if possible, for continuity of care. Much time is saved in relationship building and obtaining background information relevant to the case.

It may be necessary to terminate the present worker-client relationship if the changing needs of the client require referral to another resource. Every social worker has an individual personality and an orientation to practice that are imparted to the client. It may be helpful to refer certain clients to other community resources when the worker's capacity for helping them has been reached. Adequate referral is a three-way process involving the client, the worker, and the referral resource. The worker must prepare the client for the referral and discuss the need for, and importance of, the referral. The worker should discuss with the client any hesitations he or she might feel and any doubts and questions about the new agency. It is crucial for the client and worker to examine a range of referral resources. Usually the worker maintains a working relationship with colleagues in other community agencies. Developing an informal network of referrals facilitates the referral process when there are waiting lists at those agencies. It is important for the client and the worker to participate in the referral process. The client should make an appointment at the new agency after there has been clearance between the two workers. This groundwork involves discussing the needs of the client and advocating the new agency's acceptance of the client. The worker should make sure that the client accepts the referral, contacts the agency, and becomes involved with its services.

Premature termination also occurs when minority clients drop out of the helping relationship after the initial interview (Sue, 1981; Sue & Morishima, 1983). Strean (1978) points out that unsuccessful intervention is often the reason a case is closed. Beck (1962) reports in a family agency study that one-third of clients do not return for a second interview and that fifty percent of all applicants have one interview or less. Strean (1978) believes that in cases of premature termination the client has experienced some antagonism toward the worker and agency. He also suggests that many social workers wish to overlook the reasons why the client does not continue in the helping process.

Premature termination among minority clients is a crucial area of concern for study. Hepworth and Larsen (1982) propose that premature termination is the result of unresolved resistance. The worker should provide the client with an opportunity to express negative feelings and to work toward resolving them. However, direct confrontation of unresolved resistance may drive away the person of color. It is important to personalize the relationship and become acquainted with the minority client. Putting the minority client at ease, structuring the purpose of the helping process, and allowing the client to set the pace for disclosure of problems are effective ways of dealing with resistance. Another reason for premature termination is the client's claim that the problems have cleared up. Sudden and miraculous improvement may be symptomatic of denial of problems or wishful thinking. For minority clients an abrupt termination may be due to numerous reasons, such as mistrust of the worker, pressure from the worker to disclose the problem, difficulties with transportation, problems with child care, and inability to pay for the services. A minority client may be too embarrassed or polite to reveal the reason for termination. Gambrill (1983) offers some helpful suggestions about premature termination. Mistakes are inevitable and are opportunities for learning.

A social worker has professional and personal limits and will not be able to help all clients. However when a minority client terminates prematurely the agency needs to review its procedure, approach to casework, and techniques of practice to determine whether they address the needs of the minority client. This book has sought to distinguish characteristics of ethnic minorities that are pertinent to social work practice. Reviewing these principles of minority practice is a useful effort to ensure successful termination.

CASE STUDY

The Hernandez Family

At their termination session, Mr. Platt and the Hernandez family agree to begin the process of tapering off. Mr. Hernandez will call Mr. Platt on a weekly basis to brief him on the progress of the family. They will meet in a month to assess the extent of growth, to find out what has happened in the interim, and to evaluate the usefulness of the ethnic community's social service system. Mr. Hernandez reflects on his period of crisis as a major transitional adjustment triggered by the move of relatives during a time of particular economic strain. He feels that the family has been strengthened as a result and can now handle a similar situation, should one arise, since they know about the social services in the local Latino community.

Mr. Platt states that if the family is still functioning adequately at home and school after one month, there will be a final termination. However, the family should feel free to get in touch with him at the Family Service Association in case of future need.

Task Recommendations

We have mentioned strategies for follow-up beyond termination for successful and unsuccessful cases. The case study of the Hernandez family illustrates how a minority family moves through the process stages of clinical social work and responds to a number of ethnic-oriented practice principles. However, some cases are terminated prematurely when minority clients drop out after an initial interview.

Select a case of premature termination with a minority client and conduct a retrospective analysis of causal factors behind the drop-out.

1. Did the agency have an ethnically sensitive system of service delivery that was responsive to minority clients: tangible and practical services located near minority populations; bilingual/bicultural workers; extensive community outreach information and prevention programs; an agency setting that was congenial to people of color; and a culturally appropriate practice model? If some of these components were missing, how can they be introduced into your agency? Which ones would make a difference in retaining minority clients?

2. During the initial session with the minority client, was there an effort to convey a sense of understanding of the community, to practice relationship protocols, to share professional self-disclosure, and to communicate empathetic, open-ended responses?

3. Was there adequate time set aside to get acquainted with the

minority client's background and to permit the client to know who the social worker is as a person and as a professional?

Conclusion

This chapter on termination has emphasized new dimensions in the ending stage of the process of social work practice. Termination is explained as destination, recital, and completion. Destination underscores the importance of reunification with the ethnic community during the process of termination. Gaining a sense of ethnic selfhood is a powerful motivator for coping and integration. Striving to make this connection provides ethnic wholeness even after the dissolving of the worker-client relationship. Recital recalls the major changes that have taken place during the beginning, middle, and end of the practice process. It is a replay that has an analogy in the life-enhancement model of counseling. The life-review approach recounts major events and experiences that move toward achieving ego integrity. Directive reinterpretation and the identification of meaningful themes are involved in the process of review. Completion emphasizes the need for formulation and achievement of goals. There are criteria for measuring successful completion.

There are a number of follow-up strategies that aid the transition from practice process to the client's life situation. Among them are the gradual tapering off of sessions, periodic telephone contact during the interim, and the prevention of premature termination. These efforts result, we hope, in successful termination that meets the needs of the minority client and enhances the ethnic effectiveness of the social worker.

References

Beck, D. (1962). *Patterns in use of family agency service.* New York: Free Press.

Carrillo, C. (1982). Changing norms of Hispanic families: Implications for treatment. In E. E. Jones & S. J. Korchin (Eds.), *Minority mental health* (pp. 250–266). New York: Praeger.

Compton, B. R., & Galaway, B. (1979). *Social work processes.* Homewood, Ill.: Dorsey Press.

Devore, W., & Schlesinger, E. G. (1981). *Ethnic-sensitive social work practice.* St. Louis: C.V. Mosby.

Firestein, S. K. (1978). *Termination in psychoanalysis.* New York: International Universities Press.

Fischer, J. (1978). *Effective casework practice: An eclectic approach.* New York: McGraw-Hill.

Gambrill, E. (1983). *Casework: A competency-based approach.* Englewood Cliffs, N.J.: Prentice-Hall.

Gilbert, N., Miller, H., & Specht, H. (1980). *An introduction to social work practice.* Englewood Cliffs, N.J.: Prentice-Hall.

Hepworth, D. H., & Larsen, J. A. (1982). *Direct social work practice: Theory and skills.* Homewood, Ill.: Dorsey Press.

Munoz, R. F. (1982). The Spanish-speaking consumer and the community mental health center. In E. E. Jones & S. J. Korchin (Eds.), *Minority mental health* (pp. 362–398). New York: Praeger.

Strean, H. S. (1978). *Clinical social work: Theory and practice.* New York: Free Press.

Sue, D. W. (1981). *Counseling the culturally different: Theory and practice.* New York: Wiley.

Sue, S., & Morishima, J. K. (1983). *The mental health of Asian Americans.* San Francisco: Jossey-Bass.

Szapocznik, J., Santisteban, D., Kurtines, W. M., Hervis, O. E., & Spencer, F. (1982). Life enhancement counseling: A psychosocial model of services for Cuban elders. In E. E. Jones & S. J. Korchin (Eds.), *Minority mental health* (pp. 296–330). New York: Praeger.

Epilogue

Minority social work practice is a fertile ground for defining the unique knowledge and skills required to work with people of color. This epilogue is a closing interpretive commentary on a new field of social work practice that emphasizes the need for specialists in minority practice. In social work, competency-based practice is the current trademark of social work practitioners. Northen (1982) views competency in terms of values, purposes, and knowledge, which are translated into effective performance. The social worker uses judgment in the practice process, executing techniques of planning, assessment, and intervention and facilitating the achievement of tasks in each process stage. The practitioner keeps abreast of current practice theory and research in order to base actions on researched principles. Northen's competency base integrates social principles in practice and application and reflects sound performance based on knowledge, judgment, and currency in the field. Gambrill (1983) speaks about competency-based practice from an empirical perspective. Among its major characteristics are the pursuit of outcomes related to clients and significant others, cognitive and behavioral skills, empirical procedures of assessment and intervention, indicators for tracking progress, and personal assets and environmental resources. For Northen, competency stresses the performance of the social worker, who integrates and applies values, knowledge, purposes, techniques, and research to the process of social work practice. For Gambrill, it draws upon empirical information that governs selection of procedures and behavioral outcomes for the client.

Competency-based minority social work practice integrates minority-related service delivery structure, collective values, knowledge theory, and ethnic practice framework. Principles of minority social work have been related to practice process stages. The purpose of this epilogue is to reiterate the essential characteristics of competency-based minority social work practice and to point out new horizons and challenges for the minority practitioner-specialist. Toward this end, we hope to open a dialogue on distinctions between working with people of color and working with the majority society. It is our contention that social work practice has emphasized a generic systems framework and has not delineated factors of culture, ethnicity, and minority group status. We have sought to present an alternative framework for ethnic minority practice.

Competency-Based
Minority Social Work Practice

There are various principles of minority practice that are effective for an ethnically oriented social work practitioner. The following themes are essential characteristics of competency-based minority social work practice.

Minority Service Delivery

Competency-based minority social work structures the delivery of services on the basis of trends in usage by minority clients. Sources of tangible and practical services are located near areas of large minority population. Bilingual/bicultural social workers are employed for non–English-speaking clients. There are extensive outreach and educational programs for target community groups. The agency setting is conducive to the comfort of people of color. It features a bilingual receptionist, refreshments, and ethnic decor. The agency uses a cultural model of practice and participates in a clearinghouse for minority service organizations.

Minority Collective Values

Minority values involve corporate structures such as the family, kinship clan, and church. The individual wishes of a particular family member may be subordinate to the good of the family as a whole. The family is the vehicle for cultural values and traditions, child care, and decision making. The church plays the role of support in crisis, moral force, and provider of social services. A person's color and language reinforce his or her minority identity as a member of an ethnic community group.

Minority Knowledge Theory

A theoretical base of minority knowledge is essential for practicing with people of color. On the community level, conflict theory speaks to the dominimation of the "haves" who possess power and authority over the "have-nots." Racism, prejudice, and discrimination are the results. On the family level, systems theory offers an understanding of the individual in relation to a natural support system of family, friends, neighbors, and community. The network of care givers is available to a certain degree whenever the occasion arises. On the individual level, role theory focuses on individual role relationships within an ethnic family and community. Members of the family have assigned roles. Community spokespersons are in charge of speaking to public officials on behalf of an ethnic family or community.

Minority Practice Framework

A framework for minority practice focuses on process stages, client and worker systems practice issues, and task recommendations. The *contact* phase involves establishing a relationship between the social worker and the minority client. The worker gains a preliminary sense of the psychosocial functioning of the person-in-the-situation. Understanding of the minority community involves becoming acquainted with the geographic area, leaders, and residents comprising the ethnosystem. Relationship protocol acknowledges the authority of the father and the collective family. It is also necessary to practice professional self-disclosure, which personalizes the relationship and fosters rapport and trust. Worker-client tasks consist of nurturing and understanding the minority client.

The *problem identification* stage views a problem as an unmet need. It moves from a view of problems as pathology toward positive strivings to satisfy unfulfilled wants. Poor and minority people constantly cope with gaps in program services, crisis events, and survival needs. People of color are often hesitant about disclosing problems to helping professionals. A minority client may seek out the initial reactions of the worker by asking a series of questions about a hypothetical situation. Once the problem has been disclosed, it needs to be subdivided into observable, clear, and specific components. For minority people, racism, prejudice, and discrimination emerge as problem dynamics in the form of oppression, powerlessness, exploitation, acculturation, and stereotyping. Worker-client tasks of problem identification involve learning and focusing.

The purpose of *assessment* is to understand and analyze the dynamic interaction between the client and the situation. The worker must assess the impact of the problem on the client and the resources available for helping. Rather than focusing on the pathological effects of the problem, the assessment stage emphasizes identifying strengths, state of health, and support systems for coping with the problem. Assessment categories include socioeconomic survival, ethnic behavioral dimensions, cultural/psychological issues, and psychosomatic factors. Socioeconomic survival consists in meeting practical needs in order to sustain life functioning. Ethnic behavioral dimensions involve indigenous community support systems that are sources of nurturance. Cultural/psychological issues are related to ambivalence and resolution of conflict, tolerance of stress, and problem-solving skills. Physical-somatic factors include disharmony, emotional reaction, and other mind and body relationships. The worker-client tasks are those of interacting with psychosocial functioning and evaluating resource supports.

Intervention is a change strategy that alters the interaction of the client with the problem environment. Micro interventions apply relevant principles of psychodiagnostic, crisis-intervention, existential, problem-solving, and behavioral approaches to a minority client's particular situation. Meso intervention is based on the assumption that minority well-being involves membership in a positive and meaningful ethnic community. The family and church are essential components of natural community support systems. Macro intervention draws on social policy, planning, and administration as practice skills for working with complex social issues and target populations. Strategies using community network, political organizing, and legal advocacy are examples of interventional modalities. The worker-client tasks of the intervention stage are creating formulations to address present problems and changing the existing situation of the client to produce different consequences.

Termination is an end point at which closure is placed on the worker-client relationship. There are numerous reasons for termination: resolution of problems, redefinition of goals, or counterproductive factors. Termination takes the form of destination, recital, and completion. Destination focuses on restoring supportive linkages to family, significant others, and community. Recital reviews the major changes that have occurred during the previous stages of the worker-client relationship. Completion focuses on the accomplishment of specific goals that have dealt with the identified problems. Follow-up strategies associated with termination are gradual tapering off of sessions, periodic telephone contacts, an open-door policy, and the prevention of premature termination. Termination marks the mature growth, dynamic change, and intuitive learning that have taken place in the interaction between the client and the worker. The worker-client tasks reinforce the achievement of a desired aim and the resolution of a problem situation.

New Horizons and Challenges
for Minority Social Work Practice

Minority social work practice identifies distinct patterns of working with people of color. The social work profession is committed to ethnic minority clients. Minority practice principles have been delineated with the intent of refining specific approaches to minority practice. It is an opportune time to reach social work practitioners and students with information about minority practice. A program of dissemination should be launched to update and train agency staff and university students in the latest approaches to minority practice. Its effect would be the expansion of the minority knowledge and skills of social workers and the restructuring of minority service delivery.

In the midst of adjusting to this new emphasis, social work practitioners must chart new horizons and challenges for minority practice. The following sections identify several major trends of ethnic minorities.

Bridging the Gap Caused by
Growth in Minority Population

At the midpoint of the eighties, there has been increased population growth among minorities in the United States. Between 1970 and 1980, the minority population grew from 12.5% to 16.8%. They now represent approximately 17% of the total population of 226.5 million. That is 38.2 million people. All ethnic minority groups have experienced major increases. Among Latinos and Chicanos, there has been a 16% increase, from 9.1 million in 1970 to 14.6 million in 1980. Blacks have increased by 17%, from 22.6 million in 1970 to 26.5 million in 1980. Asian and Pacific Islanders have the largest proportional increase, from 1.5 million to 3.5 million (126%) between 1970 and 1980, as a result of mass immigration. Even Native Americans, Eskimos, and Aleutians have increased by 71%, from 800,000 to 1.4 million, in this ten-year period. In some states such as Hawaii, Alaska, New Mexico, and California, minority people compose or are approaching the point of composing the majority of the population.

The implications for social work practice are self-evident. It must reexamine its assumptions about its treatment values, knowledge, and skill in serving people of color. It is our contention that social work practice has concentrated on building generic theory and has not differentiated practice approaches that are effective with ethnic minorities. Smith, Burlew, Mosley, and Whitney (1978) describe five areas of deficiency in the relationship between ethnic minority client and White social worker:

1. the inability of the worker to comprehend the social, economic, and cultural customs of minorities;
2. the worker's lack of awareness of his or her own feelings regarding race and class;
3. minimal research on the particulars of minority behavior;
4. use of theoretical constructs designed by and for Whites to treat minority clients;
5. culturally deficient clinical training that does not communicate a minority helping perspective.

The assumptions of social work practice should be examined and redefined to include minority perspectives. There are at least three areas of concern: individualistic social work values versus collective minority values; emphasis on problem identification and assessment versus the primacy of relationship building; and the use of individual treatment versus social changes the minority community can affect in its psychosocial environment. The differentiation of approaches for minority clients and the enlargement of perspectives on social work practice are overdue.

Recognizing the Differences and Similarities among People of Color

In the United States there are major geographic, cultural, socioeconomic, political, and behavioral differences among the four principal minority groups. Black Americans originated in Africa and the Caribbean. Latino Americans are Mexicans, Puerto Ricans, Central and South Americans, Cubans, and Spaniards. Asian Americans include Chinese, Japanese, Pilipino, Korean, Vietnamese, Cambodian, Laotian, East Indian, and Pacific Islanders. Native Americans encompass numerous American Indian tribes, Eskimos, and Aleutian Islanders. In fact, a case could be made for further distinctions among the minority subgroups. The task of minority social work is to describe commonalities and to bridge distinctions within each group. Cultural pluralism tends to insulate each minority group from others. McAdoo (1982) recognizes each group's lifestyle, values, and individual adaptation to minority status. However, she identifies similarities among minority groups using such common themes as kinship involvement, extended family relationships, widespread economic poverty, family and societal conflicts, and social stereotyping. It is our hope that ethnic minority social work educators and practitioners will address unifying themes that bind Third World people together.

Meeting the Practical Needs of Minority Clients

Minority social work practice cannot remain micro-individualistic in its orientation to treatment. Critical, concrete needs are emerging that require a micro-meso-macro interventional strategy. McAdoo (1982) indicates that minority group trends show a future of increasing size, youth, and poverty among populations of color. Although the late eighties are projected as a period of affluence for two-earner families, people of color will not benefit from the increased income. Minority women are, by necessity, already in the labor force and will not represent an extra source of income. Social work practice must incorporate such areas of practical assistance as education, occupational training, preventive health care, and child day care. The implication is that minority practice cannot deal with the client apart from the client's life-sustaining needs. Program services, financial assistance, and upward economic mobility bring a sense of well-being to the minority client.

It is critical for social work practice to anticipate these future trends and be ready to meet them by the end of this decade. Not only must social work practitioners know how to work with minorities, but they must have expertise in relating to minority children, parents, and family lifestyle. Social work education necessarily must bring together methodology for working with distinctly different minority groups so that the two spheres become operational for the worker and client.

Becoming Oriented to the Importance of the Minority Family

Central to the existence and vitality of the minority client is affiliation with the family. Pinderhughes (1982) points out that the Afro-American ethnic identity system mediates individual and family interaction with environmental systems and influences the level of family coping and adaptation. Augmented and extended families strengthen the nuclear family and develop an interdependent kinship and mutual-aid system. From this structure, members acquire a sense of identity, emotional security, and access to resources. Ghali (1982) speaks of the Puerto Rican family in terms of an extended system encompassing companion parents, godparents, and friends. Delgado and Humm-Delgado (1982) underscore the importance of the extended family as a major component of the Latino natural support system. The Latino family is the primary social support for individuals in crisis. It consists of blood relatives and adopted friends who fulfill informal and formal functions within the extended family. Of particular importance is the ritual kinship process, *compadrazgo*, which involves *compadre* (godfather) and *comadre* (godmother) in baptism, first communion, confirmation, and marriage.

The importance of the family is emphasized because social services have separated family members in child-protective services, adoptions, and other family-related agency policies. Social work policy, program, and practice must be coordinated to maintain family members within the sphere of the extended family. It must utilize positive significant others within the broader family to assist with restoring family equilibrium. These caring and supportive persons are potential surrogate and foster parents. Moreover, ethnic minority families possess strengths such as values and beliefs, positive authority, and collective decision making.

Contributing to the Building of Minority Theory

Minority practice theory is in an early stage of development. Montiel and Wong (1983) have identified at least eleven areas for significant research. Among the crucial issues for inquiry are these:

- the relationship between the social work profession and minorities

- historical or comparative analysis within or between minorities
- systematic definition and research application of such concepts as racism, cultural sensitivity, ethnocentricity, ethnic aspirations, acculturation, assimilation, change agents, and minority communities
- the tendency to write about minorities as victims
- failure to distinguish between the differing aspirations of minority communities and minority social work professionals
- the need for a theoretical framework analyzing the consequences of acculturation and assimilation and the goals of minorities in a neoconservative society
- the need for intensive critical evaluation of scholarship in the area of minority studies and knowledge of ethnic communities

The goals, objectives, and purposes of minority communities, minority social work professionals, and the social work profession must be differentiated in minority social work research. Vigorous work on empirically based definitions is required to build case effectiveness in minority social work practice. At this juncture we have constructed a framework for practice theory that relates the various elements of needs and resources of the minority community, minority social work knowledge and skills, and social work practice process. However, further research efforts are required to take minority social work practice beyond the conceptual stage.

Conclusion

Beginning in 1986, the United States observes the third Monday of January as a national holiday remembering Martin Luther King, the first member of an American ethnic minority group to be so honored. The designation of this holiday marks a milestone in the recognition of people of color and their contribution to our life. In a small measure, this book also represents a milestone. It is the first treatment of minority social work with a practice process-stage approach. It emphasizes the importance of service delivery relevant to people of color, collective minority values, a framework for ethnic minority practice, and major process-stage principles.

It is my hope that this book brings a minority-conscious dimension to the practice and teaching of social work. The integration of traditional and minority social work practice is essential to an understanding of the nature of the profession, its values and knowledge base, its framework for practice, and its process stages. It is particularly crucial with an increasing minority clientele. I trust that social work practitioners will find these minority-related insights and practice principles useful in enhancing their knowledge and skills. Above all, I hope that ethnic minority social work scholar/educators and clinician/practitioners will use this text as a point of departure for further creative work in the field of social work practice with people of color.

References

Delgado, M., & Humm-Delgado, D. (1982). Natural support systems: Source of strength in Hispanic communities. *Social Work, 27,* 83–90.

Gambrill, E. (1983). *Casework: A competency-based approach*. Englewood Cliffs, N.J.: Prentice-Hall.

Ghali, S. B. (1982). Understanding Puerto Rican traditions. *Social Work, 27,* 98–103.

McAdoo, H. D. (1982). Demographic trends for people of color. *Social Work, 27,* 15–23.

Montiel, M., & Wong, P. (1983). A theoretical critique of the minority perspective. *Social Casework, 64,* 112–117.

Northen, H. (1982). *Clinical social work*. New York: Columbia University Press.

Pinderhughes, E. B. (1982). Family functioning of Afro-Americans. *Social Work, 27,* 91–97.

Smith, W. D., Burlew, A. K., Mosley, M. H., & Whitney, W. M. (1978). *Minority issues in mental health*. Reading, Mass.: Addison-Wesley.

Index

Acculturation, 134–135
Addams, J., 26–27
Amir, Y., 130
Aragon de Valdez, T., 65
Arroyo, R., 91, 92, 93–94, 95
Asian Americans:
  apprehension about helpers, 104
  family structure, 32, 64
  health and illness, 156
  history, 7, 8, 10, 11–12, 13–14, 63, 64
  religious values, 33
  silence, 157
Assessment, 72–75, 145–148, 155–162
Atkinson, D. R., 149

Bates, F. L., 48
Beck, D., 205
Bell, C. C., 180–181
Bilmes, J., 47, 48
Biopsychosocial, definition of term, 4
Black Americans:
  church, 184–185
  distrust of social workers, 104
  extended family and kinship network, 30, 31,
    63, 158–159
  history, 6, 7, 9, 11, 12, 14
  religious values, 32–33
  silence, 157
  social class types, 54
Blackwell, J. F., 178
Bland, I. J., 180–181
Bloom, M., 76, 139–140
Bochner, S., 50–51, 82, 177
Boggs, S. T., 47, 48
Bonacich, E., 131
Boulette, T. R., 85
Boyd, N., 141, 158–159
Bradshaw, C., 119
Brislin, R. W., 66, 85, 130, 131
Brown, G., 140
Burlew, A. K., 213

Cantor, M. H., 185
Caplan, G., 158
Carrillo, C., 184, 199
Cheetham, J., 59, 161–162
Cheng, A., 169
Chestang, L., 32, 35, 49–50
Chicanos:
  behavioral characteristics, 65
  families, 32
  history, 8, 10, 11, 12–13
Church, 184–185
Communication:
  meaning of, 84–86
  minority dimensions, 85
  style of, 105–108
Compton, B. R., 197
Contact, worker-client:
  definition, 81
  diagram, 82
  overview, 68–71
  relationship deficiencies as barrier, 213
Cook, K. O., 140
Council on Social Work Education:
  minority concerns as priority, 15–16, 21
Cox, F. M., 7, 9
Cuellar, B., 48
Cultural assimilation, 53
Cultural pluralism, 46–47
Culture:
  definition, 46
  functions, 4
  theoretical models, 48–52

David, K. H., 126
Davis, F. J., 129–130
Delgado, M., 190, 214
Devore, W., 3, 60–62, 84, 118, 199
DeVos, G., 36, 43
Dieppa, I., 14–15, 20–21, 145
Discrimination:
  dynamics of, 131–132